Destiny and Race

Destiny and Race

Selected Writings, 1840–1898

Alexander Crummell

Edited with an Introduction by

Wilson Jeremiah Moses

AMHERST

The University of Massachusetts Press

Printed in the United States of America

LC 91–44849

ISBN 0–87023–788–8 (cloth); 789–6 (pbk.)

Designed by David Ford

Set in Galliard

Printed and bound by Thomson-Shore

Library of Congress Cataloging-in-Publication Data
Crummell, Alexander, 1819–1898.
    Destiny and race : selected writings, 1840–1898 /
Alexander Crummell ; edited with an introduction by
Wilson Jeremiah Moses.
        p.   cm.
    Includes bibliographical references and index.
    ISBN 0–87023–788–8 (alk. paper) — ISBN 0–87023–
789–6 (pbk. : alk. paper)
    1. Afro-Americans.   2. Afro-Americans—
Colonization—Liberia.   3. Afro-Americans—Religion.
4. Liberia—Church history—19th century.   I. Moses,
Wilson Jeremiah, 1942–   .   II. Title.
E185.97.C87A25   1992
973'.0496073—dc20   91–44849
                                                                              CIP

British Library Cataloguing in Publication data are available.

This book is published with the support and cooperation
of the University of Massachusetts at Boston.

This publication has been supported by the National Endowment
for the Humanities, an independent federal agency.

For William and Jeremiah

Contents

Acknowledgments

People often ask me why I have spent so much time studying the writings of Alexander Crummell. They ask what elements of his philosophy might be useful to those of us living in this closing decade of the twentieth century. My first response is to say that Crummell and his generation had no specific message for us, because they could not have known our concerns. We can be certain that past generations did not live out their lives in hopeless longing for the clarity of vision that we have finally realized in our day of wisdom and enlightenment. They knew much that we do not know, just as we know much that they did not know. If the sermons of Alexander Crummell have anything to teach us, it is a lesson of humility. We should look upon them as windows into different worlds, ideological universes that seem at times to resemble our own, but that are based on strikingly different premises about truth, beauty, and wisdom.

The appearance of this volume would have been impossible without the encouragement of Paul Wright, my editor at the University of Massachusetts Press, who urged me to complete the project. Pam Wilkinson was very patient in dealing with my authorial temperament. The staffs of the Schomburg Library and the Library of Congress were in every way helpful and cooperative. My wife, Maureen Connor Moses, gave me invaluable assistance with the index. In addition to giving her technical assistance and wise counsel, she helped me believe in myself and the project during times of under confidence, depression, and self doubt. This book is dedicated to our sons, William and Jeremiah.

Destiny and Race

Introduction

Wilson Jeremiah Moses

Alexander Crummell (3 March, 1819–10 September 1898) was born in New York City. His parents, Boston Crummell and Charity [Hicks] Crummell, were members of a population then referred to as "Free Africans." Boston Crummell, according to at least one account, had been converted to Christianity as a child in Africa, but was, nonetheless, captured and enslaved at around the age of thirteen and brought to New York. On reaching maturity he refused to serve his master any longer, and went into business as an oyster vendor. Little is known of Charity Crummell, except that her people had lived on Long Island for several generations and had some association with the famous Hicks family of Quakers. Charity Crummell was, however, an Episcopalian (as was her husband), and the Crummells brought up their children in that religion. During the 1820s the family was fairly prosperous and able to provide Alexander with a basic classical education in the New York African Free School and through private tutors.[1]

The problems encountered by black children seeking education were considerable and Crummell described some of these difficulties in his eulogy on the life of his friend Henry Highland Garnet. He tells of his travels with Garnet and Thomas Sipkins Sidney into the state of New Hampshire in an attempt to attend the Noyes Academy, and he also

---

[1]The best sources for details of Crummell's life are Otey M. Scruggs, *We the Children of Africa in This Land* (Washington, D.C.: Howard University Department of History, 1972); Luckson Ejofodomi, *The Missionary Career of Alexander Crummell in Liberia, 1853–1873* (Ann Arbor, Mich.: University Microfilms, 1974); M. B. Akpan, "Alexander Crummell and His African Race Work," *Historical Magazine of the Protestant Episcopal Church*, June 1976, pp. 177–99; Gregory Rigsby, *Alexander Crummell: Pioneer in Nineteenth-Century Pan-African Thought* (Westport, Conn.: Greenwood Press, 1987); Wilson J. Moses, *Alexander Crummell: A Study of Civilization and Discontent* (New York: Oxford University Press, 1989); John Oldfield, *Alexander Crummell and the Creation of an African-American Church in Liberia* (Lewiston, N.Y.: Edwin Mellen Press, 1990). The story of Boston Crummell's conversion is in the unpublished short biography of Crummell by George W. Forbes in the George W. Forbes Papers, Rare Books Room of the Boston Public Library, p. 1.

describes his years at the Oneida Institute in upstate New York. Refused admission on purely racial grounds by the General Theological Seminary [Episcopal] in New York, he was ordained by Bishop Lee of Delaware in 1844, after receiving private instruction from sympathetic clergymen. In the meantime, Crummell conceived the idea of studying in one of the ancient English universities, Oxford or Cambridge. During several years that he spent in England, lecturing on the abolitionist circuit and raising funds for his church, the Church of the Messiah in New York, he was enrolled in Queens' College of Cambridge University. He passed the so-called additional examination for the bachelor's degree in 1853 and was graduated from Cambridge that spring.[2]

He sailed, almost immediately, for Liberia, West Africa, where, between 1853 and 1872, he spent sixteen years, working as a farmer, educator, small businessman, and Episcopal missionary. He made two trips to the United States during that time and was able to maintain ties to the abolitionist movement and to the cause of the newly emancipated "freedmen." Crummell returned to the United States for good in 1872, although he usually rounded off the period of his Liberian residency at twenty years.[3] After some initial uncertainties, he settled in Washington, D.C., where he established St. Luke's Episcopal Church in 1879. He served as its pastor until 1894. He spent his final years writing and lecturing, and in 1897 he founded the American Negro Academy as a challenge to the increasing power of Booker T. Washington.

Crummell's seventy-nine years were filled with colorful travel and adventure. His interests touched on European and American letters and politics, African missionary work, and the broad range of social and moral issues that constitute the work of an educated minister. He influenced the young W. E. B. Du Bois and a number of other young men, including John W. Cromwell and Francis J. Grimké. Two of his protégés, John E. Bruce and William H. Ferris, became senior officials in the movement led by Marcus Garvey in the 1920s. Crummell, a man of large intellect and

---

[2]Crummell had difficulties with the mathematics sections of the first round of examinations, and failed to pass it; he thus had to take the "additional examination" which was administered to students who had been "bumped" on the first round. The additional examination was administered to thirty-seven persons and Crummell was one of eleven who passed. A description of the examination appears in Moses, *Alexander Crummell*, p. 71.

[3]Compare his claims in *Jubilate* to Moses, *Alexander Crummell*, pp. 194 and 334. The journal *Spirit of Missions* 37 (1872):486 reports his arrival in the United States in May 1872. A letter from Rev. John W. Lewis to Bishop W. R. Whittingham, dated 12 June 1872, speaks of a meeting with Crummell.

volatile temperament, was a prolific writer on a wide variety of subjects, not always related to race relations. Those papers of his that have survived, most of which are in the Schomburg Collection of the New York Public Library, contain over four hundred sermons and political essays and an often vitriolic correspondence.

In my recent biography, *Alexander Crummell: A Study of Civilization and Discontent,* I have summarized what is currently known of Crummell's life and personality. He was a passionate man with a keen, acerbic wit, but he was also a dark, brooding, Miltonic figure. He was optimistic concerning the future of black people in America and what he called "the destined superiority of the Negro." But he was also pessimistic about human nature and spoke repeatedly of human degradation and depravity. Crummell was a complex figure, whose significance cannot be understood so long as we cling to the standard clichés about African American culture or stereotypes concerning the black preacher. Crummell absolutely rejected the "get-happy" philosophy of "feel-good religion." His writings illustrate the existence of a strenuous black "protestant" ethic that was later to be manifested in the puritanical discipline of the Nation of Islam under Elijah Muhammad and Malcolm X.

Crummell's writings provide a mechanism for expanding (not necessarily for expelling) the conventional interpretations that have become solidified with the black studies movement.[4] His work is capable of sustaining the interest of mature scholars who seek knotty problems and who welcome the challenge of defining the subtler contours of black American literary and intellectual history. Although Crummell's life and writings tell us much about black people in the nineteenth century, they illustrate matters that have by no means disappeared from American or world politics during the twentieth century. The questions of religious authority and national culture that were of interest to him have not vanished. The concerns dealt with in his writings usually extend beyond the boundaries of the black protest tradition.

[4]Sterling Brown in criticizing this convention speaks of "grafting primitivism on decadence." See Brown, "The New Negro in Literature (1925–1955)" in *The New Negro Thirty Years Afterward,* ed. Rayford W. Logan, Eugene C. Holmes, and G. Franklin Edwards (Washington, D.C., 1955), p. 59. Also see Alain Locke's interesting statement, "too many of our younger writers . . . are pot-plants seeking a forced growth according to the exotic tastes of a pampered and decadent public" ("Art or Propaganda?" *Harlem, A Forum of Negro Life* 1 (November 1928):12. Locke's metaphor was probably borrowed from Crummell's essay "Common Sense in Common Schooling" (1886), which was republished in *Africa and America.*

The purpose of this collection is to present a body of erudite writing by a black American literary figure in a form that may be useful to research scholars, as well as to college undergraduates. The present texts have been selected with two objectives in mind—to give a chronological view of Crummell's development as a thinker and a writer and to represent the broad variety of his concerns—religious, historical, and literary.

Note on Methods

Because of limitations on my time, energies, and finances, I have not been able to offer a complete scholarly edition of the works of Alexander Crummell. Instead I have had to be content with providing a concise, albeit representative, selection of Crummell's published and unpublished writings.[5] Some of the pieces in this volume are printed for the first time. They are published here with the kind permission of the Schomburg Research Center of the New York Public Library, from whose collections they are taken. Several of the sermons and all six of the letters are among those items that have never been published before. The letters are taken from the John E. Bruce Collection of the Schomburg Center, but they are collected with the microfilm edition of the Alexander Crummell Papers, as compiled from the collections of the Schomburg Center by the Kraus Thompson Organization and by the 3M International Microfilm Press. In other words, although properly speaking the letters are from the Bruce Collection, they are included in the standard microfilm editions of Crummell's works.

The *Calendar of Manuscripts in the Schomburg Collection of Negro Literature Located at 135 Street Branch New York Public Library Compiled by the Historical Records Survey Works Progress Administration New York City 1942* (New York: Andronicus Publishing Company, Inc., n.d.) provides a cumbersome, though useful, guide to Crummell's sermons and addresses. A note from the publisher indicates that the volume "was printed by photo offset lithography directly from page proofs and the manuscript

[5]Three books by Crummell were published during his lifetime: *The Future of Africa* (New York: Charles Scribner, 1862); *The Greatness of Christ and Other Sermons* (New York: Thomas Whittaker, 1882); and *Africa and America* (Springfield, Mass.: Willey and Co., 1891). His unpublished sermons have been preserved in the collections of the Schomburg Research Center of the New York Public Library, The Library of Congress, the Archives of the Episcopal Church in Austin, Texas, the Massachusetts Historical Society, and the Columbia University Library. The Schomburg and Library of Congress collections are readily available on microfilm. There is no definitive bibliography of Crummell's works, but partial listings are to be found in the biographies by Ejofodomi, Moses, and Oldfield, listed above in note 1.

prepared and marked for correction in 1943 by research librarians under the auspices of the WPA. Production of this volume was interrupted in 1943. We have entered corrections (where possible) or retained them in their original and hand written form. Certain passages marked for deletion were retained to provide helpful information to present day users."

One should also consult the hand-written guide "Manuscripts of Dr. Alexander Crummell," which was microfilmed along with the manuscripts in the collection. Unlike the hand-written guide, the *Calendar* does not arrange the items according to the MS.C. numbers that are hand-lettered at the bottom of each of the original documents, although the entries do include the MS.C. numbers. The *Calendar* utilizes a numbering system based on dates of the manuscripts, but unfortunately, over a third of Crummell's unpublished sermons and addresses are undated. An even greater number are untitled, although various catalogers have assigned arbitrary titles to some of them. Apparently this process of assigning titles occurred both before and after their acquisition by the Schomburg. Some of the assigned titles are inaccurate, and in some cases a title assigned by one cataloger may contradict that assigned by another. There are numerous hand-written cross-outs and emendations in the Schomburg's *Calendar* of manuscripts. Furthermore, Crummell sometimes gave the same title to more than one sermon, or drafted altered versions of the same sermon under more than one title. In cases where Crummell did not assign a title, or where the title assigned by one of the catalogers is inaccurate or nondescriptive, I have provided new titles suggestive of the contents. The following list indicates the MS.C. catalog numbers by which the microfilm edition is arranged, followed by the title that I have used for this edition. I have also included all information concerning the variant titles that have been assigned to each sermon or address.

MS.C. 392 [Extract from] "Eulogium on the Life and Character of Thomas Sipkins Sidney." Crummell provided the title and date for "Eulogium on the Life and Character of Thomas Sipkins Sidney," delivered 4 July 1840.

MS.C. 23. "Africa and Her People." Crummell provided no title and no date for these lecture notes, listed in the Schomburg *Calendar* as "Africa and Her People."

MS.C. 26. "Keep Your Hand on the Plough." Crummell provided no title and no date for this sermon on Luke 9:62. The Schomburg *Calendar* incorrectly identifies it as "African Civilization."

MS.C. 234. "The Day of Doom." Crummell provided no title for this sermon on Matthew 24:30, delivered first on 17 December 1854. The Schomburg *Calendar* lists it as "The Second Coming."

MS.C. 340. "The Work of the Black Priest." This is an extract from an untitled undated sermon on Psalms 51:5; Job 15:15; and Romans 7:24. The Schomburg *Calendar* lists it as "Human Nature" but in the handwritten list, "Manuscripts of Dr. Alexander Crummell" that accompanies the microfilm edition, it is called, "The Wreck and Ruin of Human Nature; Hence the Need for Man's Restoration."

MS.C. 111. "Piety, Moralism, and Enthusiasm." This is an extract from an untitled sermon on Ephesians 4:20–21, dated 12 October 1890. The Schomburg *Calendar* lists it as "The Religion of Jesus as Thoroughly Practical."

MS.C. 310. "No Man Cared for My soul." Crummell delivered this sermon in England, on 31 May 1848, giving it a title after its text, "No Man Cared for My Soul" (Psalms 142:4). The Schomburg *Calendar* lists it with that title as MS.C. 310. It should not be confused with either of two other manuscripts, numbered MS.C. 244 and MS.C. 311, which have the same title but differ dramatically in content.

MS.C. 315. "The Negro as a Source of Conservative Power." Crummell entitled this document simply "Address." Internal reference to twenty-five years of freedom suggests a date around 1888. The Schomburg *Calendar* lists it as "The Negro as an American Citizen Must Make a Contribution to Its Life and Character."

MS.C. 16. "The Discipline of Freedom." Crummell provided the title but no date for this essay on 1 Corinthians 16.13: "Quit you like men, be strong." In manuscript the verse is incorrectly identified as 1 Corinthians 16.14.

In this introduction, I have tried to present Crummell's writings in terms that my researches indicate would have been at least understandable, if not always acceptable, to their author. There has been much sophisticated discussion of the question of authorial intent by literary theorists in recent decades, as well as a tendency to debunk all attempts at historical contextualizing. I have sought to avoid passing judgment on Crummell in terms of present-day academic trends. My awareness of current theoretical controversies has forced a degree of humility upon me with respect to fully understanding another writer's mind, but it has not discouraged me from the attempt. Thus, while I recognize the impossibility of realizing any ideal in this world of shadows, I have endeavored to approach Crummell's ideas and to justify his ways to an audience that may find much of what he says unfamiliar or occasionally offensive. My goal has been to elucidate, not to criticize, and I have found it far more fascinating to evaluate contemporary ideologies in Crummell's terms than to measure Crummell's ideology according to the standards of current academic discourse.

I have made few editorial decisions in compiling this anthology. Those materials that have been transcribed from Crummell's handwriting have undergone little alteration. Obvious misspellings resulting from haste have been corrected. Abbreviations have usually been written out in full. Words that were undecipherable in the original handwriting have been so identified in the present text.

W. E. B. Du Bois on Alexander Crummell

Du Bois's famous eulogy on Crummell was delivered at a Tuskegee conference in 1899 with the title "Strivings of a Negro for the Higher Life." The narrative is poignant and sincere, but it amounts to a sentimental treatment of Crummell, who simply was not the frail, neurasthenic martyr who emerges from Du Bois's portrait. Crummell was a combative, irascible person who needlessly made enemies with his sarcastic tongue and pen and who was accused of an icily contemptuous manner. William Wells Brown described him as "somewhat punctilious" and even friends like Francis J. Grimké and Henry L. Phillips knew him as "a perfect Tsar," who "could not brook opposition." Crummell's response to the charge of rigidity was to say, "I am proud of this criticism. It is in evidence that I tolerated no iniquity, and that I rebuked depravity."[6]

Documents Containing Biographical Information

Jubilate: The Shades and the Lights of a Fifty Years' Ministry.

This brief piece, published in 1894, is the closest Crummell ever came to publishing an autobiography. It is a guarded piece and tells us very little about its author's professional life as a minister. It reveals even less about

[6]William Wells Brown, *The Rising Son or the Antecedents and Advancement of the Colored Race* (Boston: A. G. Brown and Company, 1874), pp. 455–56. Francis J. Grimké, *Works of Francis James Grimké*, 4 vols. (Washington, D.C.: Associated Publishers, 1942), 1:31. Henry L. Phillips, *In Memoriam of the late Rev. Alex. Crummell, D.D.* (Philadelphia: The Coleman Printery, 1899). Alexander Crummell, *Jubilate: The Shades and the Lights of a Fifty Years' Ministry* (Washington, D.C.: R. L. Pendleton Printer, 1894), p. 20 (reprinted in this volume).

his family life or political involvements. As a source of insight into Crummell's theological, literary, aesthetic, and intellectual opinions it is disappointing. On the other hand, its qualities of opacity and defensiveness make it interesting as an illustration of Crummell's maddening lack of ability to seize opportunities for diplomatic self-presentation. The very reticence and taciturnity of its author, usually so highly opinionated and voluble, could be the subject of a scholarly treatise, and the discreet silences and omissions are in a sense revelatory of Crummell's idiosyncratic and quirky character. It is an unspeakable tragedy that Crummell apparently did not see the importance of leaving a true *apologia pro vita sua* to posterity.

Letter to Elizur Wright; extracts from "Eulogium on the Life and Character of Thomas Sipkins Sidney" and from "Eulogium on Henry Highland Garnet, D.D."

These three documents, written in 1837, 1840 and 1882 respectively, provide insight into the early character formation of Alexander Crummell. The letter to Wright is reproduced from the original in the Elizur Wright Papers, Library of Congress. Crummell wrote it when he was eighteen to apologize for an incident that had occurred when he was around fourteen. The eulogy on Sidney was composed and delivered when the author was twenty-one. It was delivered before an audience of friends and relatives of the deceased and, in addition to showing the development of Crummell's youthful style, reveals something of his early development as an intellectual. Since Crummell never wrote a full autobiography, we are greatly dependent on these eulogies for what little we know of his early life. Limitations on space prohibited publication of the complete eulogies for Sidney and Garnet in this volume, but both bear reading in their entirety. The eulogium on Garnet is a particularly important source on one of the principal black nationalists of the antebellum period.

"Africa And Her People": Lecture Notes; "Report from Buchanan, Liberia, . . ."; "Report from Caldwell, Liberia, . . ."; and "Letter on Ethnology."

Crummell's descriptive powers were unevenly developed, as the undated fragment on Africa and her peoples reveals. Crummell was much more comfortable when writing about personalities and ideas than when describing visual objects and images. As he says in the course of his narrative, the splendid qualities of the country exceed his powers of description, and this he proceeds to demonstrate with tedious prolixity. The fragmentary statement is important, nonetheless, for the glimpse it provides of Crummell's sense of closeness to his father and grandfather. Unfortunately this glimpse is all too fleeting and superficial. His characterizations of the various African peoples provide some insight into his prejudices and his race chauvinism, but offer little information on the customs and values of the peoples he describes. Crummell's published reports from Buchanan and Caldwell in *Spirit of Missions* provide us with better insights and show something of the quality of his life during the later part of his African years. Letter on Ethnology, published in *The Southern Workman,* reveals Crummell's continuing interest in the peoples of Africa after his return to the United States and his desire to link that interest to cultural and political concerns in the black communities of the United States.

Statement to the Congregation of St. Luke's Church and Letters Concerning T. Thomas Fortune, Booker T. Washington, and Others.

Crummell's statement to his congregation was privately published in 1893. It reveals its author's ability to make a mountain of a molehill and to engage in the most vituperative attacks on the character of those who opposed him. The six letters to his friends John E. Bruce and John W. Cromwell require little explanation. Like the *Statement to the Congregation of St. Luke's Church,* they reveal the volatility of Crummell's temperament. They are also significant for what they reveal of his hostility to mulattoes. There were a number of men of mixed ancestry for whom Crummell had the utmost respect, including Francis J. Grimké and W. E. B. Du Bois, but in general, it is certainly no overstatement to say that he tended to view mulattoes with suspicion. The letter to Bruce written from England in August 1897 is unreadable on microfilm. I was able to decipher it by reproducing on a photocopy machine the original in the Schomburg Center. The reader is no doubt aware that the various models of copiers possess varying attributes. The particular virtue of the machine I happened to use was that it *did not* reproduce gray tones, but brought out contrasts. The result is that the copy I have is more readable than the original. Other technologies may eventually reveal the few remaining mystery words, but I believe I have captured the sum of the document's contents.

Sermons Revealing the Theological Basis of Social Theories

"Keep Your Hand on the Plough."

I have invented the title for this unnamed and undated sermon, basing it on its opening line and remembering the refrain of an old "Negro Spiritual." It is interesting for its systematic organization and for its attack on enthusiastic evangelical religion. Crummell's theological leanings were in the direction of moralism and Arminianism rather than pietism and antinomianism.[7] Crummell's religiosity was complex and eclectic. On the one hand, he was contemptuous of the enthusiastic, revivalistic tradition, which emphasized an emotion-laden conversion experience, but he had nonetheless made a somewhat dramatic "profession of religion," as his letter to Elizur Wright reveals. As an Episcopalian, he faithfully supported the doctrine that sinners were saved by grace, not through their own worthy efforts. Nonetheless, in most of his sermons, Crummell stressed the doctrine of works and upright living. He believed in human depravity and insisted that no one could be saved without the grace of God or the vicarious atonement of Jesus Christ, but he constantly emphasized the Pauline injunction, "work out your own salvation." He was thus caught up in a paradox that is not peculiar to Christians—the attempt to reconcile the logic of determinism with that of free will. In this essay, as in the other essays represented in this anthology, Crummell seems fully committed to the idea that Christians are saved by their deeds, rather than by a passive reliance on grace.

"The Day of Doom."

Delivered on 17 December 1854, this untitled sermon, like that which precedes it, emphasizes the importance of good works in the life of the

[7]The following terms are defined variously by divers sects of Christianity. In brief, Arminianism refers to the teachings of the Dutch theologian Jacobus Arminius (1560–1609), which modified the doctrine of predestination, emphasized human freedom, and stressed the importance of free will in attaining salvation. Nineteenth-century Roman Catholicism supported the doctrine that constant striving to perform good works was necessary to attain salvation. Evangelical Protestantism emphasized the doctrine that good works were purely the result of grace, and thus viewed the writings of Arminius as heretical. The pietistic tradition often tends toward antinomianism, from the medieval Latin *antinomus* (against the law). It is based on the belief that salvation is effortlessly attainable if the convert has truly experienced conversion through the grace derived from Christ's sacrifice and the faith that true conversion irresistibly imparts. *God Struck Me Dead*, ed. Clifton Johnson, is a compilation of slave narratives emphasizing the conversion experience.

Christian. From the standpoint of evangelical Protestantism, Crummell seems to be dangerously skirting the edges of Arminianism, or even popery, with his insistence that "there is no safety this side of heaven." The sermon demonstrates his only moderately successful attempt to appeal to his less-educated parishioners with descriptions of the coming of the Lord. The verse quotation toward the end is translated from the Roman Catholic Mass for the dead, a poem written in the twelfth century by Thomas of Celano.

"The Episcopal Church in Liberia: On Laying the Corner Stone at St. Andrew's."

This is interesting for reasons other than the place and circumstances of its delivery. Crummell felt that the Episcopal church, which stressed the law of Moses as well as reliance on the grace of God, was particularly suited to the needs of black people. Religion should meet a people's material needs as well as their spiritual ones, and the Episcopal church, by its stress on the ten commandments as a "rule of life," would help black people to take control of their own destinies in this world.

"The Greatness of Christ."

Based on Matthew 2:11, this sermon was delivered on 25 December 1879, and is published here as it appears in *The Greatness of Christ and Other Sermons* (1882). It is a statement of Crummell's Christian progressive theory of history. The terms B.C. and A.D. had more than traditional significance for Crummell, because it was clear to him that most human progress had taken place since the birth of Christ. Thus all moral, material, and intellectual growth in the modern world was the result of the historical appearance of Jesus Christ. In this sermon, Crummell asserts his strong belief in the doctrine of vicarious atonement. The evangelical impulse seems here to have won out over the doctrine of works, which he usually stressed.

Excerpt from an untitled sermon, here called "The Work of the Black Priest."

This extract provides an additional illustration of Crummell's hostility to extreme evangelical enthusiasm and reveals his belief that true religion must inform a doctrine of social responsibility. Leading in the direction of a social gospel, these lines give evidence of Crummell's affinity to a reform or "revolutionary" philosophy and to the American Christian doctrine of social perfectionism.

Excerpt from the untitled sermon, "Piety, Moralism, and Enthusiasm."

This essay, which the Schomburg Catalog dates at 1890, is a specific example of Crummell's engagement in the piety versus moralism controversy. It represents Crummell's hostility to the heresy of antinomianism, or, as others would put it, the essay represents his gravitation to the heresy of Arminianism. Crummell's commitment to the doctrine that the Christian is saved not only by faith or by the redeeming power of grace but also by deeds placed him outside the mainstream of grass-roots evangelical Protestantism in America. It also placed him in opposition to the majority of black American preachers, who appealed to converts with frenzied "ring shouts" and ecstatic experiences in which the convert was first "struck dead" by the power of God and then "born again" during an intense experience of seeing Jesus.

Statements of Social and Political Ideology

"No Man Cared for My Soul."

This sermon went through several versions, as can be seen by comparing Schomburg manuscripts nos. 244 and 311 with this (310). The version printed in this volume was delivered in England in 1848. Despite its lengthy, abstract, and pietistic beginning, it is soon revealed as a document of considerable social interest because of its author's discussion of the problems of the free African population in the northern states. Three versions of this sermon, in which the opening paragraphs are very similar in wording and content, are listed in the Schomburg Manuscripts Catalog. All are undated, but the quality of the handwriting marks two of them (MS.C. 244 and MS.C. 310) as products of the 1840s, and the third (MS.C. 311) as having been drafted years later. MS.C. 244, probably the earliest version, is almost exclusively religious in content. Its almost incidental appeals to British munificence and the problem of slavery are neither sustained nor specific, and it provides the audience with little information on the condition of either the slave or the free population. MS.C. 310 was apparently revised for delivery to a non-British congregation. The version of the text reproduced here, with its detailed descriptions of American racial problems and its appeal to British philanthropy, is probably the speech described in the following report from *The Bath & Cheltenham Gazette,* 5 July 1848:

> A Negro Clergyman
> On Wednesday evening a numerous congregation assembled at St. Michael's Church to hear a sermon from the Rev. Alexander Crummell, an Episcopal clergyman of African descent on behalf of a Negro Church, which it is proposed to erect in New York for the accommodation of a colored congregation to which Mr. Crummell ministers. The preacher took for his text, Psalms cxvii. 4, "No Man Cared For My Soul."

"Address to the British and Foreign Anti-Slavery Society."

This was published in *The Antislavery Reporter* of 2 June 1851 and was delivered on 19 May 1851. Crummell argued that the roots of slavery were not to be found in legal frameworks so much as in the "weakness, the benightedness, and the degradation of that particular class brought into slavery." He argued that the solutions to the problems of slavery and discrimination in the United States could only be found through the education and uplift of the masses of the African American people. It is interesting to note that in this address Crummell strongly denied the responsibility of black Americans to uplift or evangelize the continent of Africa. Within two years he would be fully committed to Liberian missionary work and within a decade he would be writing "The Relations and Duty of Free Colored Men in America to Africa."

"The Progress and Prospects of the Republic of Liberia" and "Our National Mistakes and the Remedy for Them."

The first of these sermons was delivered at the annual meeting of the New York State Colonization Society in 1861. It was an optimistic speech in which Crummell described Liberian commercial and cultural development and called on black Americans to accept "the obligations which Divine Providence has brought upon us." The sermon was reprinted in Crummell's first book, *The Future of Africa,* the entirety of which amounts to an extended treatment of this theme. The second sermon, originally published in 1869, is much less optimistic and offers an authoritarian approach to African regeneration. It is published here in its 1871 form as reprinted in *Africa and America,* 1891.

"The Destined Superiority of the Negro."

This essay is reprinted in its 1877 form, which is as it appeared in *The Greatness of Christ and Other Sermons*. It bears comparison to the title sermon of that volume because the two sermons taken together provide some of the elements of Crummell's theory of history. The temporary retardation of the progress of the Negro was to be seen as part of the divine plan in which the black race was being prepared for a role in modern history, comparable to that of the Jews in the ancient world.

"Industrial Education: How to Apply the Unclaimed Bounty."

This article from 1880 is reproduced here from a text in *The People's Advocate,* a newspaper published in Washington, D.C. by Crummell's close friend John W. Cromwell. In this piece Crummell appeared as a strong advocate of education in the trades, a position that he had supported since his days as principal in an agricultural school in Cape Palmas, Liberia. Although Crummell never opposed classical or literary education, he often commented on the irony of the fact that those who pursued the highest educational goals were often confined to menial occupations. Crummell's position was assailed by his respected friend and colleague Rev. Francis J. Grimké, who insisted that prejudice would never be overcome by industrial education.[8]

"The Black Woman of the South: Her Neglects and Her Needs" (1883).

This is an extremely important essay that informed Du Bois's later discussion of the black woman in *Darkwater*.[9] It bears some kinship to and probably, through Du Bois, had some influence on E. Franklin Frazier's *The Negro Family*. Numerous other writers, including Frazier and Daniel Patrick Moynihan, followed in the tradition of asserting that African family institutions had been destroyed by slavery and that the elevation of

[8]The theme of education in Crummell's philosophy is treated more fully in Moses, *Alexander Crummell,* pp. 232–36, 246–47, and 261–62.

[9]W. E. B. Du Bois, *Darkwater: Voices from within the Veil* (New York: Harcourt, Brace, and Howe, 1920). See discussion in Moses, *Alexander Crummell,* pp. 217–20, 299.

the black masses could be effected only if the traditional, patriarchal, middle-class American family ideal could be replicated in black American social structure. It is interesting to note, however, that whereas Moynihan's approach was to focus on reconstructing the black male role in society, Crummell's centered on the needs of the black woman.[10]

"The Assassination of President Garfield" (1881); the untitled sermon "The Negro as a Source of Conservative Power" (undated); the untitled sermon "The Discipline of Freedom" (undated); and "The Social Principle among a People" (1875).

These four addresses outline the conservative, collectivist, and authoritarian bases of Crummell's political philosophy. By the time these pieces were published, Crummell had abandoned the emigrationist position of his middle years and had come to believe that the future of the American Negro was in America. He viewed the future contribution of black Americans to the United States in ethnological terms. Black Americans were not genetically or culturally predisposed to violence as were the Irish and the Germans; on the contrary, they were an essentially conservative people who, if given a chance, would contribute a law-abiding element to the national mixture. "The Social Principle among a People," which is an early statement of the black power philosophy, argues that black Americans must develop their own institutions in the United States. Only by self-development would black Americans eventually be able to make their way in America. Neither white folks' charity nor moral suasion would be sufficient to meet the challenges of the future. The position was a direct assault on the assimilationist preachments of Frederick Douglass.

"Civilization as a Collateral and Indispensable Instrumentality in Planting the Christian Church in Africa" and "The Absolute Need of an Indigenous Missionary Agency for Evangelization of Africa."

These two addresses delivered at the Atlanta Exposition of 1895 symbolize Crummell's complete break from the colonization movement, despite his continuing Pan-Africanism. As in the speech delivered before the British and Foreign Anti-Slavery Society in 1851, he argued that those black

[10]See text of the Moynihan Report in Rainwater and Yancy, *The Moynihan Report and the Politics of Controversy*, pp. 39–124. Also see E. Franklin Frazier, *The Negro Family in the United States* (Chicago: University of Chicago Press, 1939).

people who were indigenous to Africa would be best suited to carry the Gospel into their home lands. As he had in "The Greatness of Christ" and elsewhere, he continued to argue that Christianity always went hand-in-hand with civilization.

"Civilization, the Primal Need of the Race" and "The Attitude of the American Mind Toward the Negro Intellect."

Crummell's two addresses at the first meeting of the American Negro Academy in 1897 represent his opposition to the materialism of Booker T. Washington. Crummell believed that industrial education was necessary in order to develop a technocratic elite, but he also believed that liberal arts education was necessary for the creation of cultural and intellectual leadership. In this essay one may readily discern the roots of the "Talented Tenth" philosophy later developed in the writings of W. E. B. Du Bois.[11]

Subjective Reflections

I hope that publication of these texts will serve to make a generation of scholars aware of a maverick intellectual whose variety of thought is unfamiliar to many casual students of African-American literature. Crummell's life and writings illustrate a paradox to which I have alluded elsewhere—that black nationalism has been a principal conduit for the transmission of assimilationist values into black American subcultural communities.[12] Crummell was at home with the traditions of literate European Christianity and attempted to fashion a black nationalism based on what he considered their unquestionable value. Like a black Prometheus, he hoped to steal fire from the usurping gods of Europe and with it forge a mighty tradition among black leaders and intellectuals. He never faltered in his belief that people of African ancestry would assume leadership and "superiority" in the coming Kingdom of Heaven.

Aside from their importance to the history of black American thought, these documents may serve to focus attention on some other aspects of literary and intellectual history that have recently fallen into neglect. The

---

[11]The comparison to the "Talented Tenth" philosophy was made in John R. Bracey, Jr., August Meier, and Elliott Rudwick, eds., *Black Nationalism in America* (Indianapolis: Bobbs-Merrill, 1970), p. 124.

[12]See Wilson Jeremiah Moses, *The Golden Age of Black Nationalism* (Hamden, Conn.: Archon Books, 1978; reprint, New York: Oxford University Press, 1988).

rediscovery of Crummell and his tough view of the universe will perhaps lead some of my contemporaries to reconsider a truth that Crummell and the nineteenth century knew so well. The world will never be shaped to suit the fancies of even the most righteous souls. "Constant anxieties" and "agonized strain" are the inescapable and eternal fate of all thinking creatures.[13]

Rumford, Rhode Island
October 21, 1991

---

[13]Alexander Crummell, *The Solution of Problems: The Duty and Destiny of Man* (Philadelphia: Recorder Press, n.d.). Reprinted from *A.M.E. Church Review*, April 1898.

"Of Alexander Crummell"

W. E. B. Du Bois

Then from the Dawn it seemed there came, but faint
As from beyond the limit of the world,
Like the last echo born of a great cry,
Sounds, as if some fair city were one voice
Around a king returning from his wars.

—Tennyson.

This is the history of a human heart,—the tale of a black boy who many long years ago began to struggle with life that he might know the world and know himself. Three temptations he met on those dark dunes that lay gray and dismal before the wonder-eyes of the child: the temptation of Hate, that stood out against the red dawn; the temptation of Despair, that darkened noonday; and the temptation of Doubt, that ever steals along with twilight. Above all, you must hear of the vales he crossed,—the Valley of Humiliation and the Valley of the Shadow of Death.

I saw Alexander Crummell first at a Wilberforce commencement season, amid its bustle and crush. Tall, frail, and black he stood, with simple dignity and an unmistakable air of good breeding. I talked with him apart, where the storming of the lusty young orators could not harm us. I spoke

From W. E. Burghardt Du Bois, *The Souls of Black Folk: Essays and Sketches* (Chicago: A. C. McClurg, 1903), chapter 12, pp. 215–27.

to him politely, then curiously, then eagerly, as I began to feel the fineness of his character,—his calm courtesy, the sweetness of his strength, and his fair blending of the hope and truth of life. Instinctively I bowed before this man, as one bows before the prophets of the world. Some seer he seemed, that came not from the crimson Past or the gray To-come, but from the pulsing Now,—that mocking world which seemed to me at once so light and dark, so splendid and sordid. Four-score years had he wandered in this same world of mine, within the Veil.

He was born with the Missouri Compromise and lay a-dying amid the echoes of Manila and El Caney: stirring times for living, times dark to look back upon, darker to look forward to. The black-faced lad that paused over his mud and marbles seventy years ago saw puzzling vistas as he looked down the world. The slave-ship still groaned across the Atlantic, faint cries burdened the Southern breeze, and the great black father whispered mad tales of cruelty into those young ears. From the low doorway the mother silently watched her boy at play, and at nightfall sought him eagerly lest the shadows bear him away to the land of slaves.

So his young mind worked and winced and shaped curiously a vision of Life; and in the midst of that vision ever stood one dark figure alone,—ever with the hard, thick countenance of that bitter father, and a form that fell in vast and shapeless folds. Thus the temptation of Hate grew and shadowed the growing child,—gliding stealthily into his laughter, fading into his play, and seizing his dreams by day and night with rough, rude turbulence. So the black boy asked of sky and sun and flower the never-answered Why? and loved, as he grew, neither the world nor the world's rough ways.

Strange temptation for a child, you may think; and yet in this wide land to-day a thousand thousand dark children brood before this same temptation, and feel its cold and shuddering arms. For them, perhaps, some one will some day lift the Veil,—will come tenderly and cheerily into those sad little lives and brush the brooding hate away, just as Beriah Green strode in upon the life of Alexander Crummell. And before the bluff, kind-hearted man the shadow seemed less dark. Beriah Green had a school in Oneida County, New York, with a score of mischievous boys. "I'm going to bring a black boy here to educate," said Beriah Green, as only a crank and an abolitionist would have dared to say. "Oho!" laughed the boys. "Ye-es," said his wife; and Alexander came. Once before, the black boy had sought a school, had travelled, cold and hungry, four hundred miles up into free New Hampshire, to Canaan. But the godly farmers hitched ninety yoke of oxen to the abolition schoolhouse and dragged it into the middle of the swamp. The black boy trudged away.

The nineteenth was the first century of human sympathy,—the age when half wonderingly we began to descry in others that transfigured spark of divinity which we call Myself; when clodhoppers and peasants, and tramps and thieves, and millionaires and—sometimes—Negroes, became throbbing souls whose warm pulsing life touched us so nearly that we half gasped with surprise, crying, "Thou too! Hast Thou seen Sorrow and the dull waters of Hopelessness? Hast Thou known Life?" And then all helplessly we peered into those Other-worlds, and wailed, "O World of Worlds, how shall man make you one?"

So in that little Oneida school there came to those schoolboys a revelation of thought and longing beneath one black skin, of which they had not dreamed before. And to the lonely boy came a new dawn of sympathy and inspiration. The shadowy, formless thing—the temptation of Hate, that hovered between him and the world—grew fainter and less sinister. It did not wholly fade away, but diffused itself and lingered thick at the edges. Through it the child now first saw the blue and gold of life,—the sunswept road that ran 'twixt heaven and earth until in one far-off wan wavering line they met and kissed. A vision of life came to the growing boy,—mystic, wonderful. He raised his head, stretched himself, breathed deep of the fresh new air. Yonder, behind the forests, he heard strange sounds; then glinting through the trees he saw, far, far away, the bronzed hosts of a nation calling,—calling faintly, calling loudly. He heard the hateful clank of their chains, he felt them cringe and grovel, and there rose within him a protest and a prophecy. And he girded himself to walk down the world.

A voice and vision called him to be a priest,—a seer to lead the uncalled out of the house of bondage. He saw the headless host turn toward him like the whirling of mad waters,—he stretched forth his hands eagerly, and then, even as he stretched them, suddenly there swept across the vision the temptation of Despair.

They were not wicked men,—the problem of life is not the problem of the wicked,—they were calm, good men, Bishops of the Apostolic Church of God, and strove toward righteousness. They said slowly, "It is all very natural—it is even commendable; but the General Theological Seminary of the Episcopal Church cannot admit a Negro." And when that thin, half-grotesque figure still haunted their doors, they put their hands kindly, half sorrowfully, on his shoulders, and said, "Now,—of course, we—we know how *you* feel about it; but you see it is impossible,—that is—well—it is premature. Sometime, we trust—sincerely trust—all such distinctions will fade away; but now the world is as it is."

This was the temptation of Despair; and the young man fought it doggedly. Like some grave shadow he flitted by those halls, pleading, arguing, half angrily demanding admittance, until there came the final *No;* until men hustled the disturber away, marked him as foolish, unreasonable, and injudicious, a vain rebel against God's law. And then from that Vision Splendid all the glory faded slowly away, and left an earth gray and stern rolling on beneath a dark despair. Even the kind hands that stretched themselves toward him from out the depths of that dull morning seemed but parts of the purple shadows. He saw them coldly, and asked, "Why should I strive by special grace when the way of the world is closed to me?" All gently yet, the hands urged him on,—the hands of young John Jay, that daring father's daring son; the hands of the good folk of Boston, that free city. And yet, with a way to the priesthood of the Church open at last before him, the cloud lingered there; and even when in old St. Paul's the venerable Bishop raised his white arms above the Negro deacon— even then the burden had not lifted from that heart, for there had passed a glory from the earth.

And yet the fire through which Alexander Crummell went did not burn in vain. Slowly and more soberly he took up again his plan of life. More critically he studied the situation. Deep down below the slavery and servitude of the Negro people he saw their fatal weaknesses, which long years of mistreatment had emphasized. The dearth of strong moral character, of unbending righteousness, he felt, was their great shortcoming, and here he would begin. He would gather the best of his people into some little Episcopal chapel and there lead, teach, and inspire them, till the leaven spread, till the children grew, till the world hearkened, till—till— and then across his dream gleamed some faint after-glow of that first fair vision of youth—only an after-glow, for there had passed a glory from the earth.

One day—it was in 1842, and the springtide was struggling merrily with the May winds of New England—he stood at last in his own chapel in Providence, a priest of the Church. The days sped by, and the dark young clergyman labored; he wrote his sermons carefully; he intoned his prayers with a soft, earnest voice; he haunted the streets and accosted the wayfarers; he visited the sick, and knelt beside the dying. He worked and toiled, week by week, day by day, month by month. And yet month by month the congregation dwindled, week by week the hollow walls echoed more sharply, day by day the calls came fewer and fewer, and day by day the third temptation sat clearer and still more clearly within the Veil; a temptation, as it were, bland and smiling, with just a shade of mockery in its smooth tones. First it came casually, in the cadence of a voice: "Oh, colored folks? Yes." Or perhaps more definitely: "What do you *expect?*" In voice and gesture lay the doubt—the temptation of Doubt. How he hated it, and stormed at it furiously! "Of course they are capable," he cried; "of course they can learn and strive and achieve—" and "Of course," added the temptation softly, "they do nothing of the sort." Of all the three temptations, this one struck the deepest. Hate? He had outgrown so childish a thing. Despair? He had steeled his right arm against it, and fought it with the vigor of determination. But to doubt the worth of his life-work,—to doubt the destiny and capability of the race his soul loved because it was his; to find listless squalor instead of eager endeavor; to hear his own lips whispering, "They do not care; they cannot know; they are dumb driven cattle,—why cast your pearls before swine?"—this, this seemed more than man could bear; and he closed the door, and sank upon the steps of the chancel, and cast his robe upon the floor and writhed.

The evening sunbeams had set the dust to dancing in the gloomy chapel when he arose. He folded his vestments, put away the hymn-books, and closed the great Bible. He stepped out into the twilight, looked back upon the narrow little pulpit with a weary smile, and locked the door. Then he walked briskly to the Bishop, and told the Bishop what the Bishop already knew. "I have failed," he said simply. And gaining courage by the confession, he added: "What I need is a larger constituency. There are comparatively few Negroes here, and perhaps they are not of the best. I must go where the field is wider, and try again." So the Bishop sent him to Philadelphia, with a letter to Bishop Onderdonk.

Bishop Onderdonk lived at the head of six white steps,—corpulent, red-faced, and the author of several thrilling tracts on Apostolic Succession. It was after dinner, and the Bishop had settled himself for a pleasant season of contemplation, when the bell must needs ring, and there must burst in upon the Bishop a letter and a thin, ungainly Negro. Bishop Onderdonk read the letter hastily and frowned. Fortunately, his mind was already clear on this point; and he cleared his brow and looked at Crummell. Then he said, slowly and impressively: "I will receive you into this diocese on one condition: no Negro priest can sit in my church convention, and no Negro church must ask for representation there."

I sometimes fancy I can see that tableau: the frail black figure, nervously twitching his hat before the massive abdomen of Bishop Onderdonk; his threadbare coat thrown against the dark woodwork of the book-cases, where Fox's "Lives of the Martyrs" nestled happily beside "The Whole Duty of Man." I seem to see the wide eyes of the Negro wander past the Bishop's broadcloth to where the swinging glass doors of the cabinet glow in the sunlight. A little blue fly is trying to cross the yawning keyhole. He marches briskly up to it, peers into the chasm in a surprised sort of way, and rubs his feelers reflectively; then he essays its depths, and, finding it bottomless, draws back again. The dark-faced priest finds himself wondering if the fly too has faced its Valley of Humiliation, and if it will plunge into it,—when lo! it spreads its tiny wings and buzzes merrily across, leaving the watcher wingless and alone.

Then the full weight of his burden fell upon him. The rich walls wheeled away, and before him lay the cold rough moor winding on through life, cut in twain by one thick granite ridge,—here, the Valley of Humiliation; yonder, the Valley of the Shadow of Death. And I know not which be darker,—no, not I. But this I know: in yonder Vale of the Humble stand to-day a million swarthy men, who willingly would

> " . . . bear the whips and scorns of time,
> The oppressor's wrong, the proud man's contumely,
> The pangs of despised love, the law's delay,
> The insolence of office, and the spurns
> That patient merit of the unworthy takes,"

all this and more would they bear did they but know that this were sacrifice and not a meaner thing. So surged the thought within that lone black breast. The Bishop cleared his throat suggestively; then, recollecting that there was really nothing to say, considerately said nothing, only sat tapping his foot impatiently. But Alexander Crummell said, slowly and heavily: "I will never enter your diocese on such terms." And saying this, he turned and passed into the Valley of the Shadow of Death. You might have noted only the physical dying, the shattered frame and hacking cough; but in that soul lay deeper death than that. He found a chapel in New York,—the church of his father; he labored for it in poverty and starvation, scorned by his fellow priests. Half in despair, he wandered across the sea, a beggar with outstretched hands. Englishmen clasped them,—Wilberforce and Stanley, Thirwell and Ingles, and even Froude and Macaulay; Sir Benjamin Brodie bade him rest awhile at Queen's College in Cambridge, and there he lingered, struggling for health of body and mind, until he took his degree in '53. Restless still and unsatisfied, he turned toward Africa, and for long years, amid the spawn of the slave-smugglers, sought a new heaven and a new earth.

So the man groped for light; all this was not Life,—it was the world-wandering of a soul in search of itself, the striving of one who vainly sought his place in the world, ever haunted by the shadow of a death that is more than death,—the passing of a soul that has missed its duty. Twenty years he wandered,—twenty years and more; and yet the hard rasping question kept gnawing within him, "What, in God's name, am I on earth for?" In the narrow New York parish his soul seemed cramped and smothered. In the fine old air of the English University he heard the millions wailing over the sea. In the wild fever-cursed swamps of West Africa he stood helpless and alone.

You will not wonder at his weird pilgrimage,—you who in the swift whirl of living, amid its cold paradox and marvellous vision, have fronted life and asked its riddle face to face. And if you find that riddle hard to read, remember that yonder black boy finds it just a little harder; if it is difficult for you to find and face your duty, it is a shade more difficult for him; if your heart sickens in the blood and dust of battle, remember that to him the dust is thicker and the battle fiercer. No wonder the wanderers fall! No wonder we point to thief and murderer, and haunting prostitute, and the never-ending throng of unhearsed dead! The Valley of the Shadow of Death gives few of its pilgrims back to the world.

But Alexander Crummell it gave back. Out of the temptation of Hate, and burned by the fire of Despair, triumphant over Doubt, and steeled by Sacrifice against Humiliation, he turned at last home across the waters, humble and strong, gentle and determined. He bent to all the gibes and prejudices, to all hatred and discrimination, with that rare courtesy which is the armor of pure souls. He fought among his own, the low, the grasping, and the wicked, with that unbending righteousness which is the sword of the just. He never faltered, he seldom complained; he simply worked, inspiring the young, rebuking the old, helping the weak, guiding the strong.

So he grew, and brought within his wide influence all that was best of those who walk within the Veil. They who live without knew not nor dreamed of that full power within, that mighty inspiration which the dull gauze of caste decreed that most men should not know. And now that he is gone, I sweep the Veil away and cry, Lo! the soul to whose dear memory I bring this little tribute. I can see his face still, dark and heavy-lined beneath his snowy hair; lighting and shading, now with inspiration for the future, now in innocent pain at some human wickedness, now with sorrow at some hard memory from the past. The more I met Alexander Crummell, the more I felt how much that world was losing which knew so little of him. In another age he might have sat among the elders of the land in purple-bordered toga; in another country mothers might have sung him to the cradles.

He did his work,—he did it nobly and well; and yet I sorrow that here he worked alone, with so little human sympathy. His name to-day, in this broad land, means little, and comes to fifty million ears laden with no incense of memory or emulation. And herein lies the tragedy of the age: not that men are poor,—all men know something of poverty; not that men are wicked,—who is good? not that men are ignorant,—what is Truth? Nay, but that men know so little of men.

He sat one morning gazing toward the sea. He smiled and said, "The gate is rusty on the hinges." That night at star-rise a wind came moaning out of the west to blow the gate ajar, and then the soul I loved fled like a flame across the Seas, and in its seat sat Death.

I wonder where he is to-day? I wonder if in that dim world beyond, as he came gliding in, there rose on some wan throne a King,—a dark and pierced Jew, who knows the writhings of the earthly damned, saying, as he laid those heart-wrung talents down, "Well done!" while round about the morning stars sat singing.

Materials of Biographical Interest

Jubilate: The Shades and the Lights of a Fifty Years' Ministry

And ye shall hallow the fiftieth year and it shall be a
jubilee unto you.—Leviticus 25:10

Notwithstanding the countless ills which befall us during our mortal life,
the conviction is almost universal that life is a great gift to man, and that it
has exceeding value. It is true that we hear now and then the moody
question, "Is life worth living?" True, that occasionally, the despairing
exclamation falls upon our ears, "I would that I had never been born!" But
you will notice that it is only one man out of thousands who makes these
doleful utterances. For, on the whole, men love life. Men study more or
less the uses of life. Men rejoice in life; because life, with all its adversities,
guarantees substance and affords a measure of reality.

Hence, everywhere in the societies of men we find the Anniversaries,
the Commemorations, the "Red Letter" days, the Annual Festivals, the
Centennials, and as of old, among the Jews—the JUBILEES, of persons
and families and nations. And these testify to man's conviction of the
excellence and worth of the life which God has given us.

I have fallen in, Friends and Brethren, with this common sentiment of
mankind; and this day, in accordance with a desire which comes from
many quarters, I stand here to celebrate, with your generous assistance,
the *Fiftieth Anniversary* of my ordination to the Priesthood.

I beg that you will put aside any thought or suggestion of personal
importance or merit in this observance. Its significance lies entirely in
three or four simple facts of a general nature: (1) That my term of service is
the longest of any man of my race, in this Church; (2) That I have

From Alex. Crummell, *Jubilate: 1844–1894, The Shades and the Lights of a Fifty Years'
Ministry, A Sermon at St. Luke's Church, Washington, D.C., December 9th, 1894* (Washington,
D.C.: R. L. Pendleton, Printer, 1894), pp. 5–25.

ministered in three different quarters of the globe; (3) That twenty years of this service was in the African field; and (4) That the termination of my pastoral life, comes, with the close of my Rectorship, at the end of this year; and that the whole story of this ministry has had intermingled with it a signal Providence and much human favor.

These several aspects of ministerial service suggest as a topic of thought this day, "The Shades and the Lights of a fifty years' ministry."

At an early period of my boyhood, stimulated by the catechising of my pastor, Rev. Peter Williams, then Rector of St. Philip's Church, New York, and kindled, as I well remember, by a sermon by Doctor (afterwards the Right Rev. Bishop) Whittingham, I determined to prepare for holy orders. There was not then a single college or seminary in the United States which would receive a black youth. It was a day of deep darkness and tribulation for the Negro race in this land. The pro-slavery and caste spirit dominated the country. Chief Justice Taney's statement, for which he was most unjustly criticised, was true to the letter; namely, that in "the common sentiment of the Nation the Negro had no rights which white men were bound to respect." This virulent Negro hatred was well nigh as strong in the Church as in the State.

The case of the three colored Rectors who preceded me in the ministry will illustrate this fact. These men were Absolom Jones, Peter Williams and William Levington; and each, respectively, in Pennsylvania, New York and Maryland, received orders under the shameful condition imposed upon them, namely: "That they would never apply for admission to the Conventions, in the Dioceses in which they lived." They suffered other gross indignities. My own pastor, Rev. Peter Williams, was always called "Peter" by the clergy of New York. It would have broken their hearts to have entitled him "Mr. Williams."

I was then, in 1839, but a youth; but I had determined that I would never submit to such degrading conditions; and that I would endeavor to get the fullest training for the ministry. I became a Candidate for Orders in 1839, and at once, under my Rector's direction, applied for admission to the General Theological Seminary in New York. Dr. Whittingham was then Dean of the faculty. Nothing could have been more gracious than his bearing towards me. A colored young man, Mr. Isaiah De Grasse, had made a similar application two or three years before; and Dr. Whittingham told me—"You have just as much right of admission here as any other man. If it were left to me you should have immediate admission to this Seminary; but the matter has been taken out of my hands in De

Grasse's case; and I am very sorry to say that I cannot admit you."[1] Under the advice of my Rector I drew up a petition to the Trustees of the Seminary. My petition was presented by the Rev. Dr. Milnor, then Rector of St. George's Chapel, New York. It is impossible to tell the exasperation caused in this august body. After a fierce and angry debate, in which that lion-hearted prelate, the Right Rev. George W. Doane, of New Jersey, stood alone in my behalf, the petition was rejected. Immediately, that is during the session of the Trustees, Bishop Onderdonk sent for me; and then and there, in his study, set upon me with a violence and grossness that I have never since encountered, save in one instance, in Africa.

What, you ask me, was the kernel of this difficulty? It was chiefly this: South Carolina had endowed a Professor's chair in the Seminary to the amount of several thousands of dollars; and the Bishop was determined that South Carolina should not be offended by the presence of a Negro in that Seminary. The upshot of the case was that, by a pitiful device, my name was stricken from his list of candidates.

I was, as you may judge, completely at sea; and the ministry seemed to me a hopeless thing. My application to the Seminary made me a marked man. Hardly a churchman, clerical or lay, would touch such a presumptuous Negro, such a disturber of the peace as myself. The anger against me on every side was almost universal and intense.

There were, however, with a few others, four noble exceptions. There were three laymen in New York, illustrious by name and distinguished by position, who protested against the action of the Trustees and the conduct of the Bishop. These were the Hon. William Jay and John Jay, Esq., the son and the grandson of the illustrious John Jay, the first Chief Justice of the United States; and Charles King, Esq., then editor of the "New York American," and a son of the eminent Senator of a former day, the great Rufus King. One eminent clergyman is to be added to these, the Rev. Manton Eastburn, D.D., Rector of the "Church of the Ascenscion." At the instance of these gentlemen, with their assistance and letters, I went to Boston. There I became a Candidate for Orders; and two years after-

[1]How genuine and abiding this high, tender, delicate, gentlemanly sentiment was in Bishop Whittingham, may be seen by a single incident. "Age could not wither it, nor Custom"—the pagan CASTE-CUSTOM of America.—"stale it!"

On a visit to the United States, in 1861, I called on the Bishop, at his residence in Baltimore. At the close of a long conversation, he paused, of a sudden, his face coloured up, and he remarked to me—"Mr. Crummell, I feel ashamed and mortified that I haven't a pulpit to offer you on the morrow! But you know the state of things in this city." This was amid the hurly-burly of the incipient Civil War; and only the night before my life was in peril, from the ruffians of the city.

wards, May 1842, was ordained to the Diaconate, in St. Paul's Church, in that city.

My first charge was at Providence, R.I.; but there I could not get support. From Providence I went to Philadelphia. When I went to Philadelphia, the Bishop of the diocese, Rt. Rev. H. U. Onderdonk, made this demand on me: "I cannot receive you into this Diocese unless you will promise, that you will never apply for a seat in my Convention, for yourself or for any church you may raise in this city." My reply was an immediate one: "That, sir, I shall never do." That ended the interview; but, as I was leaving his study, he called me and said: "You may wait a few days, and I will communicate with you."

The Pennsylvania Convention met, at its annual session, a few days after this interview. The Bishop in his address suggested that possibly some other African Church might spring up in the diocese; and advised, that in such an event, it would be well to prepare a Canon that "no such church, or its minister, should be admitted to the Convention."

The Convention was all in the dark concerning my application; but the horror of a black face in their midst was enough! The Canon was passed quickly, without question or debate; as though a calamity or pestilence was to be avoided. Within forty-eight hours afterwards the Bishop sent me word that my "Letter Dimissory" had been accepted.

But, as in Providence, so in Philadelphia, the clergy, save in rarest instances, would not sustain me: I had been a disturber of the peace, and I must be punished by neglect. Not seldom, reverend divines were rude and insulting: and the result was poverty, want, and in the end sickness. On one occasion I was in a state of starvation. I gave up my work in Philadelphia, and went to New York. It would be useless as well as tiresome to enter into the particulars concerning my work in New York. It was, for the most part, a repetition of the misfortunes of Providence and Philadelphia. The clergy stood aloof from my work. One grand exception, however, was that hero, orator, and philanthropist, Dr. S. H. Tyng, the then Rector of St. George's Church. His whole soul rose up in holy hatred of both slavery and caste. If it had not been for him, and the constant and unfailing generosity of my great patron, Hon. John Jay, I think I must have died; for poverty, want, and sickness had well nigh broken me up.

It was at this juncture that the suggestion arose that I should go to England, and appeal for funds to build a church. It came, I think, from Rev. Evan M. Johnson, Rector of St. Mary's Church, Brooklyn. Mr. Johnson was one of the most singular characters I ever met with. I am incapable of speaking of his intellectual calibre; but his positiveness, his dogmatism, his singular eccentricities, his unique and original utterances, mingled with his high Christian character and real nobility of bearing, often made me think of Boswell's portraiture of old Samuel Johnson. He utterly despised and trod upon the pro-slavery and caste usages of the day. In the face of popular prejudice he maintained his right to invite me into his pulpit, and to entertain me as a guest at his table. His own work was largely self-sustained; and thus he was unable to take upon himself any responsibilities of my missionary endeavors. He suggested an appeal abroad, as a solution of the difficulty.

I close, just here, the chapter of distress and calamity to turn to a brighter page. My life, up to this point, had been, for the most part, one of clouds. But it was not all shades and darkness. For how can I pass over the gracious sympathies and the large generosity of eminent Priests, Bishops, and distinguished Laymen, who rose above the spirit of the age, and spurned, with indignation, the common inhuman despite against the Negro.

But how shall I speak of these exalted characters? How can I set forth their calm disdain of the ignoble Negro hate of their country? How set forth the gracious condescension with which they received, succored and encouraged an obscure Negro youth? I am perplexed at the task which lies before me. The simplest statement, however, will, I think, help me out of it.

You will remember, just here, that my application to the New York Seminary caused the loss of my candidateship, and barred my way to the ministry. Distinguished friends gave me letters to Boston. One of these letters introduced me to the Rev. William Croswell, then Rector of the "Church of the Advent," and, not only a Divine, but one of the sweetest poets of our church. Mr. Croswell was deeply interested in the Negro race, and in the evangelization of Africa. Let me pause here but a moment, to read to you a Sonnet of his, which seems to me fully equal to the glowing verse of Montgomery, on Africa, or the fine Sonnet of Wordsworth to the Negro Lady fleeing from France:—

> "Joy to thy savage realms, O, Africa;
> A sign is on thee, that the Great I Am
> Shall work new wonders in the land of Ham;
> And while He tarries for the glorious day
> To bring again His people, there shall be
> A remnant left from Cushan to the sea.

And though the Ethiop cannot change his skin,
Or bleach the outward stain, he yet shall roll
The darkness off that overshades the soul,
And wash away the deeper dyes of sin.
Princes submissive to the gospel sway,
Shall come from Egypt; and the Morian's land,
In holy transport, stretch to God its hand:
Joy to thy savage realms, O, Africa."[2]

Mr. Croswell was one of the foremost of the then rising "Tractarian Party," in the American Church. He was a man of evident sanctity, and a character of peculiar excellence and purity. Never can I forget that more than earthly countenance, nor the gentle brotherly reception he gave me. He was well aware of the Seminary incident, and was pronounced, in his expression of personal sympathy, and of dissent from the action of Bishop Onderdonk and the Seminary Trustees. "Mr. Crummell," was his remark, "I will do all that I can for you. It happens, however, that I do not belong to that school, in the Church, which has the most influence here. Go to Dr. Vinton and to Rev. Mr. Clark. They will help you; and I will use all my influence with them and the Bishop, and you may rely upon me."

The Rev. Thomas M. Clark (now Bishop of Rhode Island) was then Rector of Christ Church. At the mention of his name, I am oblivious, for the moment, of the lapse of time since 1842. He was then a young priest in the full flush of a brilliant and most successful ministry. He stands out before me a splendid spiritual Knight-Errant, glowing with Godly ardor; "valiant for the truth;" with all the impulses of the Christian hero; swaying by his inspiring eloquence and his crystal character, the crowds of worshipers who flocked to the old church in Temple street, to drink in his teachings, and to be guided by his instructions.

Dr. Alexander H. Vinton was in most respects, a contrast to Mr. Clark. Somewhat phlegmatic in temperament, quiet in demeanor and utterance, seemingly emancipate from impulse or passion, full of masterful control in every section of his grand being, and regulated by massive intellect; he impressed me with the idea of a grand Christian philosopher, standing on the very apex of intellectual and Christian life. Dr. William Ellery Channing, the eminent Unitarian Divine and Thinker, had but a little while before passed away; and not a few of *his* disciples thought that the light of New England was, for the time, extinguished! But Daniel Webster and

---

[2]This poem was written on the occasion of the Ordination of the Rev'd. Mr. Olsten, a colored man, sent as a Missionary to Africa.

Francis Wayland, the one in the political, the other in the religious world, seemed the great magnates, the intellectual giants of the day; and I thought, at the time, that Dr. Vinton was worthy, with them, to form a grand Triumvirate.

Dr. Vinton, Mr. Clark and Mr. Croswell became my friends and patrons; and through their influence I was introduced to the venerable Bishop Griswold.

The Bishop received me with fatherly interest and cordiality; and he concluded his conversation with me with this generous remark: "Mr. Crummell, I wish there were twenty men of your race applying for orders. I should be more than glad to receive them as candidates for the ministry in this Diocese."

My removal from New York to Boston seemed to me a transition from the darkness of midnight to the golden light of a summer morning; and it filled me with transport and aspiration. Never before, I judge, had a Negro youth, in this land, had such a golden experience.

Just think of a simple black boy in 1840 being received, in the very Mecca of American culture, refinement and piety, with courtesy, with manly recognition, with Christian fraternalism!

All honor to New England! Land, indeed, of sterile soil and bleak mountains! Land of chilling winds and wintry frosts; yet, notwithstanding these physical drawbacks, the land of noble hearts, of Christian brotherhood, of generous sympathy, and of large philanthropy!

I have already referred to my removal, first, from Providence to Philadelphia; and as I am now referring to the brighter incidents of my ministry, there can be no more fitting place to set before you a notable occurrence connected with the name of the Right Rev. Bishop Doane, of New Jersey.

Bishop Henry U. Onderdonk refused to receive me into his Diocese, save under degrading conditions and an ignoble promise. Pending his decision I went down to Burlington, New Jersey, for counsel and advice from Bishop Doane. I did not know the Bishop; but I had heard of his energetic protest against my non-admission to the General Theological Seminary. I can never forget that interview; never forget the grand man who received me. He was standing, with some parting friends, on the banks of the Delaware, on the beautiful sward before his Episcopal Residence. His two boys, one, now, Bishop of Albany, were with him.

At a moment of leisure I approached and introduced myself. I then told him the demands of Bishop Onderdonk, and stated my deep perplexities.

Those who remember him, will remember his strong, stalwart voice and utterance; and at once he thundered forth these words:—"Don't you do it! Don't you give him any such promise! Bishop Onderdonk is a strong personal friend of mine, but he has no right to demand any such promise from you. You have the same rights in the Church of God as any other man, and don't you give way to any such demands."

Here again was not only light, but strength and encouragement. I left Burlington not only with a lighter heart, but with a more fixed purpose never to submit to the ungracious and degrading conditions which ever before had been imposed upon colored clergymen. Subsequent to these occurrences, I went to New York; and there, after severe trials, was advised to seek English aid for the erection of my church. And thus, in the providence of God, I was ushered into a further scene of light.

I reached England on the 26th of January, 1847. I was much broken in health; but at the same time full of earnest purpose and bright hopes. My letters from Rev. Mr. Johnson and others brought me into relation with eminent personages in both the political and ecclesiastical world. Everywhere I went I was received with favor and courtesy. My appeal for funds was kindly responded to. I was permitted to preach in London, Liverpool, Birmingham, Manchester, Bath, Gloucester and many other towns. My work, however, was interrupted by fits of illness. Once it was so extreme that through the kindness and influence of a clerical friend, I fell into the hands of the eminent Sir Benjamin Brodie. Meanwhile unsolicited, nay, unthought of by myself, a personal interest sprung up in my behalf; and the request came to me that I should retire for a season from over-work, and become a student in the University of Cambridge. And so it came to pass that I was entered at Queen's College, Cambridge, in 1851. During my Terms, however, I was often in the hands of doctors. Not seldom I fell into a state of discouragement and despair, on account of my health. Now and then my studies were interrupted. At length came the earnest counsel of my medical advisor that I must seek a warm climate.

It was this advice which led me to Africa. It was perfectly natural that abandonment of my work in New York, gave offence to my old school friends, who had rallied about me; and also to several of my white friends. But I knew that, with my broken health and with the inevitable penury that was before me in New York, I could not stand, and would surely succumb.[3]

---

[3]The FUND collected in England amounted to $8,300. It was remitted to New York; and now forms a part of the ENDOWMENT of St. Philip's [Colored] Church, in that city, yielding annually the sum of $373.50.

My five years' residence in England was, save the interruptions of sickness, a period of grand opportunities, of the richest privileges, of cherished remembrances and of golden light.

Now what shall I say with regard to these associations? Shall I reckon with the fear of misrepresentation? Shall I take counsel of possible misconception of my motives? I confess to much embarrassment in this matter. But I remember the words of a great poet,

"Our fears mislead, our timid likings kill."

Do I not owe as much gratitude, and the expression of it, to the great people across the waters, as to their kindred great people in New England? I hardly think ı shall be justified, in shutting out from sight the recognition and the hospitality of my English hosts, any more than those of a former day in Boston.

I have spoken of the *"Lights"* of my ministerial life. They came, first, in New England. That was a grand prelude. It took a wider sphere of illumination in grand Old England.

The insular and commercial position of the English makes them curious concerning the character and condition of other peoples. Joined to this is their great love of liberty. Curiosity, however, is the key which opens the door to foreigners. In nine cases out of ten the condition, and the facts of the condition, abide; the individual is lost sight of.

My letters carried me, first of all, to the hospitable board of one of England's most majestic characters, Sir Robert Harry Inglis—great as statesman, philanthropist and a pillar of the Church. Soon one, and then another, and then another of the prelates of the Church of England, gave me cordial recognition. Among these were Wilberforce, the great Bishop of Oxford; Bishop Blomfield of London; Dr. Stanley, the Lord Bishop of Norwich; Bishop Hinds, who, at a later day, licensed me, for six months, to a Curacy in Ipswich. Once I had the privilege of spending a morning with the Dean of St. Paul's, Dr. Thirwell, Bishop of Landaff; the most learned Bishop of the English Church; and was charmed and left wondering at the great simplicity of his character, married as it was to his marvelous weight of learning.

Now and then I had the privilege of entrance into the circle of noted families—the Froudes, the Thackerays, the Patmores, the Caswells and others of *literary* note; the Sturges, the Croppers, the Kinnairds, the Laboucheres, the Noels and the Thorntons of the *philanthropic* world. It was at the latter place I listened, for two or three hours, to that brilliant avalanche of history and biography, of poetry and criticism which rushed from the brain and lips of Thomas Babington Macaulay. Numbers of the clergy gave me hospitality, in some cases lasting friendship, which abides to the present, save where death has interposed. I cannot do otherwise than mention the names of the great Biblical writer—Rev. Thomas Hartwell Horne; Rev. Henry Venn, the great Secretary of the Church Missionary Society; Rev. Henry Caswell; Dean Close, and Rev. Daniel Wilson. Two of my greatest friends, must receive special mention, Wm. T. Blair, Esq., once Mayor of Bath; and Mrs. Clarkson, widow of the great Thomas Clarkson, the ABOLITIONIST.

Pleasant and flattering as were the incidents of my sojourn in England, I never thought of permanent residence there, notwithstanding generous suggestions, and kind offers. My heart, from youth, was consecrated to my race and its interests; and as I was ordered to a tropical clime, I chose the land of my forefathers, and went to West Africa.

I landed in Liberia in 1853, and at once threw myself into the work of that young, so-called nation. It was not, in a true sense, a nation. It has never risen above crude and simple Colonial life; for it was, at first, driven, by untoward circumstances, and these not of its own creation, to assume, and before due time, exaggerated and almost crushing national functions. I found there great crudities, and sad anomalies. How could it have been otherwise? Was not Liberia the fruit, the product of slavery? Did not its illiteracy and its immorality spring directly from the plantation?

And yet, notwithstanding its many disabilities, I saw at once noble ambitions, earnest, zealous, if not definite, aspirations; and I felt proud to ally myself with those qualities, far distant, as I saw their realization must certainly be.

I can say but little of my missionary life, because it was hedged up and crushed out by the malignant and spiteful caste spirit, in Bishop and many of the missionaries, which they brought from America, and which marred their own labours. But I can say, in all simplicity, that, so far as the Liberian communities were concerned, I strove with all my might to build up my race.

I spent nigh twenty years in Africa. The predictions of Doctors in England proved correct. After my acclimation, I entered into health, such as I had never had before, and such as I have never had since. Under a tropical sun I became vigorous, elastic, life-enjoying. If I had not gone to Africa, I am quite sure I should have died years ago.

I threw myself vigorously into all my work. It was beset, everywhere, with supreme difficulties—the mistrust and ignorance of the colonists, and the prejudices of the white missionaries. I have, however, the assurance that it was healthful and elevating. During my residence in Africa I was Pastor; Master of the High School; Professor in Liberia College; School Farmer; Missionary.

I kept myself abstinent entirely from politics; but I felt myself forced, by the condition of the country and the demands of the people, to take my place as a public Teacher. I do not shrink the egoism which is implied in this statement. The people wanted my opinions concerning national life, and, as a devoted Negro, I was glad to advise and give counsel by public speech. And thus, on divers occasions, I was called upon to deliver public addresses. One of their leading officials, then a pupil of mine, but now Secretary of State, visited this country last year; and he told some friends, in my presence, that while in Liberia I "was a little too rigid." I am proud of this criticism. It is in evidence that I tolerated no iniquity, and that I rebuked depravity. I told the people of Liberia the naked truth, on all occasions, without flattery, and as a censor of great faults. All peoples, on their first passage from slavery to freedom, need moral rigidity. Restraint, moral and political restraint, is, and will be, for a long time to come, the great need of such a democratic system as that of the Republic of Liberia. Having experienced the galling discipline of slavery, they need, as a corrective to license, the sober "discipline of freedom."

The criticism, albeit an exaggeration, gratifies me, inasmuch as it emphasizes the anxious solicitude of my life in Liberia, as a teacher; namely, to aid in training a class of young men rightly to fulfill the higher duties of Church and State. I am glad and proud, too, to say that not a few of these youth have become noted and prominent men on the West Coast of Africa; in Sierra Leone; in Liberia; and at Lagos. Some are wealthy merchants; some are teachers; some are Ministers of the Gospel; one, for years, was a Professor in Liberia College; one is now Secretary of State in Liberia; another is editor of the "Lagos Weekly Recorder," and one is the Bishop of Cape Palmas. That they appreciate my miscalled "rigidity," is manifest by the grateful letters which come to me, year by year; by the visits they make to my house, in this city, when they visit the United States; and by the superior life and character which they show in the sight of men, in their several communities.

After nigh twenty years' residence in Africa I returned to the United States in 1873, and soon after took up my residence in this city. I have now been Rector of St. Luke's Church well nigh twenty-two years. On the last day of this month I shall retire from Pastoral care and Rectorial responsibility. I need not dwell upon the nature of my service here. It must speak for itself.

I am conscious of the weariness of my words, this morning, and equally so of their personal quality. But, my friends, some of the facts I have related should not, I think, lose their record. But no one, save myself, could set forth the noble generosities of the Bishops, Priests and eminent Laymen whose courage and philanthropy I have brought before you. I, myself, shall be forgotten; but God forbid that their goodness and mercifulness should be left unremembered!

And now you may ask me—What is the conception of life which my experiences have wrought within me?

My answer is, first of all, that no age, no Church, no people are ever left, by the Almighty, destitute of grand prophets, devoted priests, and glorious reformers. The great benefactors to whom I have referred lived, in what has been called, the "Martyr Age" of American history, the times when it was a reproach for any man to show devoted interest in the Negro race.

I have given you the acts of not a few of the greatest names in the annals of our Church. I have chronicled the large benevolences of historic characters in our Communion. They were not obscure personages. Most of them were Dignitaries. Go back fifty years in the life of this Church, and where will you find greater names than these I have mentioned? Who were more distinguished than Whittingham and Doane and Eastburn, than Vinton, Croswell and Clark? These were the men who faced the deadly caste spirit of the age with lofty scorn, and bent, with the largest magnanimity, to the most despised people in the land. Theirs, too, was no tardy and reluctant philanthropy. It was prompt, gracious and spontaneous. No such case as mine had ever come before them. It required but the touch of circumstance, and the spring of generous brotherhood started, as though awaiting elastic and gracious movement. In a "day of trouble and rebuke and blasphemy" they championed, with zeal and alacrity, the cause of a Negro! My friends, Burke's elegiac utterance was not true! "The age of chivalry is not gone! The unbought grace of life has not passed away." It lives perennial and undying in all the grand sacrifices, the noble self-abnegation, the saintly condescensions of the Church of Christ, of which I have given you grand examples.

The most conspicuous of these, however, was that illustrious philanthropist who but recently joined the number of the elect, and whose life and character have elicited encomiums the rarest and most lustrous for a generation or more. The Hon. John Jay was the very first of my benefactors. I was sitting in a garret room, in Church street, New York, utterly bewildered on Bishop Onderdonk's rejection of me. All of a sudden I was told that a young gentleman wished to see me. It was Mr. Jay. He climbed the narrow stairway, and entered my little cabin. I myself had not then reached my majority, and he could not have been more than a year or two older then myself, a recent graduate from college. I was charmed with the grace and elegance of his manners, and that mingled beauty and manliness of person that he carried with him through life, but then, in its early youthful glow. He had heard of the rude and unjust treatment I had received, and came to tender his sympathy and succor.

Here was a young man, fully equipped by ancestry and name, culture and wealth and position for the highest prizes in life; yet, seemingly oblivious of them all, and looking about him for a career. And then with the spirit of a martyr deliberately devoting his life to philanthropy, by vindicating the cause of the down-trodden Negro.

"The age of chivalry is not gone!" Never in all the history of the world has the Almighty been wanting of the gallant spirits, ready, at any sacrifice, to vindicate the cause of the poor and needy, and to "wax valiant in fight" for the downtrodden and oppressed. "The glorious company of the Apostles," "the goodly fellowship of the Prophets," "the noble army of Martyrs," have never yet come short, in finality. Their ranks are unbroken, unceasing, and immortal! "When the enemy shall come in like a flood, the Spirit of the Lord shall lift up a standard against him."

One other large truth I wish to put before you, namely, that standing now more than three score years and ten, in age; the scars of bitter caste still abiding, I am, nevertheless, a most positive OPTIMIST. All along the lines of my own personal life I have seen the gracious intrusions of a most merciful providence. Every disaster has been surmounted and eclipsed by some saving and inspiring interposition. It is not merely a personal experience. It is a wider truth. It is a fact and a principle which pertains to the large and struggling race to which we belong. There is a Divine, an infinite, an all-powerful hand which moves in all our history; and it moves for good! Incidentally it allows severity and anguish; but its primary trend is redemptive and saving. The Lord Jesus came into this world to save men. Not seldom the perversity of man puts the *nill* of depravity, in the place of the enlightened *will* of Conscience and Reason. But the all gracious love of God comes even to unwilling souls, and puts a divine purpose into their lives and history. And thus it is that the crazy rush of the "madding crowd" is kept constantly under His searching eye; and it is restrained by His almighty hand; and by His merciful will is turned not seldom into channels of good and blessedness. "Even the wrath of man shall praise Him, and the remainder of wrath does he restrain."

> "In the unreasoning progress of the world,
> A wiser spirit is at work for us."

ᵛ   It may be distant; it may not come in a day; nay, it may take generations for its grand fulfilment; but surely it will come, that wrong, and error, and injustice, and craft, and outrage shall utterly be destroyed! Some day the precious hopes of the righteous shall be realized, and the gracious promises of God shall be fulfilled! I am just as sure it thus shall be, as I am that I am standing here, this morning!

> "I know the truth shall crush the lie;
> Somehow, sometime, the end will be."

And so, and then, all the perturbations of earth shall subside; all the distractions of men and societies shall cease; all the darkness of sin and Satan shall be scattered; all the clouds and gloom, all the shadows and mist which obscure our vision shall vanish away, and fade, at the last,

> "Into the light of coming day."

Letter to Elizur Wright, 22 June 1837

Oneida Institute Whitesboro June 22, 1837

Mr. Elizur Wright
 Sir

Between three and four years since, when I was at your office in Nassau Street, you sent me to your house in Grant St with a rocking chair, which I broke by driving fast. When enquired of by you I told you something different—a palpable falsehood; which, when you afterward doubted, I still held to.

Since I have been a member of Oneida Institute I have made a profession of Religion—about two years ago. Perhaps you may think I have held on to this sin; —afraid to confess it. Not at all. I never thought of it till a few evenings since. And it was under these circumstances.

A few evenings since in 'Bible Class' in the chapel—Prest. Green was endeavoring to inculcate the principle, that, 'the man who would not submit to evidence, had the elements of *lying* in him,' and to enforce this he related an occurrence that took place in W. R. College. What it was I am not now able, to distinctly tell. But he told us that a young man thought much of both by the Faculty, and Students, for his Christian activity and enterprise; —upon some moral question which had divided the opinions of the College, he took a wrong side; and although light and evidence were poured in upon him, still he clung to his opinion. 'With all his conduct,' Mr. Green said, 'he had connected a lie which Prof Wright undertook to find out:' —when Mr. G. got here the thought immediately occurred to me— 'I have done the same thing'. I immediately made up my mind to inform you of. Since that time it has caused me some distress. I

Transcribed from A.L.S., Library of Congress, Elizur Wright Papers, printed with permission.

deeply regret, and am extremely sorry that after having done wrong I had not courage enough to confess it then to you. I then had no principle, as I am disposed to think very few, if any, have who love not God. Such things as these have learned me a lesson, which I think I will never forget I have earnestly entreated the forgiveness of God, for this; and am ~~almost~~ quite certain of receiving yours.

Henceforth my aim and endeavor shall be, to be a man of *Principle;* convinced that nothing but principle and honesty in every department of life, will make a man,—a man of usefulness.

With great regard and Esteem.
Very respectfully yours

Alex^r Crummell

PS This letter has been written ever since June and I have not had a chance to send till this time.

A.C.

From "Eulogium on the Life and Character of Thomas Sipkins Sidney"

A great spirit has passed from among us. Our chief, in the spring tide of his years, the dews of age yet fresh upon him, has been taken from our midst. Sidney! the great, the magnanimous, the pure minded, the self sacrificing. Thomas S Sidney has been transferred from the ranks of the living; his name is enrolled upon the memorials that commemorate the great and distinguished dead.

Bear with my agitated feelings and the deep and sore anguish I feel on this occasion; while I attempt a feeble delineation of a character, which, by its singular blending of great peculiar traits and talents; baffles all successful description.—

Here in the midst of us—here where he was gathered unto his Sires—was he born. In his immediate ancestry he was greatly blessed. His Father was Thomas York Sidney, much distinguished in the counsels of his brethren, and who manifested no little interest in the welfare of the People. His mother was the daughter of the late Thomas Sipkins, a man who by his worth and industry contributed much to the respectability of our people in this City.

From childhood our Friend gave marks of Talent and Wisdom. In his infantile days he was thoughtful and observing. As he emerged from childhood into youth, these propensities more fully developed themselves. His aim and object at all times, was to gain information, treasure up thought, and study character. So greatly was this last trait developed in

Transcribed from MS. C. 392. "Eulogium on the Life and Character of Thomas Sipkins Sidney, who Died in the City of New York, June 17th 1840, Age 23. Delivered Before the Phoenixonian Literary Society of the City of New York, July 4th 1840." Schomburg Collection, New York Public Library, and printed with permission.

him, that, as he has frequently told me, being brought in connection with individuals while with his Grand Father in business he then formed opinions of the character of various personages, which subsequent acquaintance and observation fully established and confirmed.

His youth augured his manly strength and vigor of mind and purity of conduct. Free, open, and generous in his deportment; strong and decisive in his opinions; fixed and unalterable in his determinations; he was the object both of strong regard and respect on the part of his school mates, and of marked dislike on that, of an unprincipled School Master.

He was much distinguished for his good scholarship, keeping pace with many who were far in advance of him in age and advantage. Plain and republican in his principles and associations—he was a great favorite. His talents and manners secured him general popularity; and he was looked upon as a leader. With all this he was free from ostentatious pride or vanity. He would suffer no one to tread upon him, and at the same time he considered himself no better than common humanity. Even at this time, with all the glow and warmth of genial youth, and the effervescence of a boyish heart—even then great thoughts were stirring within him; and noble objects and purposes were working in his soul. It is full ten years ago while standing one Sunday by a group of boys wasting their time and dishonoring the day by foolish and wicked jesting—the question was put to him why he was so silent? Promptly, yet not presumptuously did the boy of thirteen reply—"A fool has his tongue in continual motion, but a wise man keeps his silence." "Then you consider yourself a wise man," was the quick and angry retort. "No, I am trying to be," was his strong and decided answer.

My own boyishness then kept me from saying anything; but I noticed his keen eye, his manly looks—the earnest of his future goodness, and I felt my soul grow toward him. He was trying to be—"trying to be" did he say? He was wise even then. . . .

It was in the year 1831 that he began to look round, and stir himself. He was then in his fourteenth year. It was at that period when the passions begin to assert unwonted control, on the one hand; and on the other, the great purposes of existence, begin gradually to unfold themselves to youthful observation. With barely a pause for choice and reflection, he pursued the road of Public Service and Patriotism. . . .

At this early age upon his suggestion a few of us met every day after school hours and debated serious questions upon the rights of man and the liberties of our People. Here while in intellectual combat, we became more aware of that strength of thought, and that winning and powerful eloquence, which, while it dealt destruction to the shallow hindrances of Error, completely unfolded Truth, and carried the mind along to gentle acquiescence in its high commands.

During the Winter of the ensuing year, three or four lads might have been seen every Saturday evening bending their course to the hall of the Philomathean Society in Duane Street. It was a cold winter, that. The fierce winds often drove the drifted snow against us, and dashed the rain like a flood around us. Yet he was always present. In that Hall by a pale light not unfrequently without fire, did we meet, consult and weigh various opinions and divers suggestions. The result of these deliberations was the adoption of a Constitution, which bears with its amendments and alterations the impress of his reflective mind; —and the formation of this Society which I have the honor of addressing of which he was a chief pillar, and whatever brightness of Talent or Character it may have gained, all his fellow-members, will, I am confident, readily grant, that it was derived very considerably from the light of his intellect. Here for a few minutes let us pause! Around this green spot let us linger. It is full of grateful recollections and fond remembrances—a bright Oasis in the barren waste. What a crowd of thoughts throng and gather around this event! —thoughts destined to an eternal existence among the treasures of memory and invested with all the mellowing hues that cluster around early sympathies and associations!—

Immediately after the formation of our Society he proved himself more active than ever; his assiduity and effort were remarkable. In debate, in Recitations as a Lecturer, in preparation for Public exercises—he was always active and energetic, throwing out important suggestions, and as if entirely unaware of it, scattering rich and valuable information upon all subjects.

At the Annual and Semi-Annual meetings he always had something fresh weighty and original to present. His speeches on such occasions we may say and not in the least disparage others—were the chief points of attraction. Many present will remember how on one of these our Anniversaries, by clear arguments, by historical research, by erudition beyond his years, he ably and successfully vindicated African Talent, and adorned with new brilliancy the ancient glory and magnificence of our ill-fated Father-land.

His efforts and exertions at this time, his increasing acquaintance with the world, and knowledge of the superior advantages of the Oppressor by means of Literature and Science impressed him with a sense of deficiency, and determined him to seek some means of improving those talents his Maker had so abundantly bestowed upon him. In the Spring of 1835, a school under the superintendence of some distinguished friends of man in New England was opened at Canaan, New Hampshire for the instruction of youth aside from arbitrary distinctions. A few of us in the city with like views and feelings, gladly welcomed the offer and anxiously set about appropriating its advantages to ourselves.

Sidney was then in the strength of his youth. Eager and anxious for intellectual improvement he had long been seeking such an institution, and so soon as he saw the opportunity he eagerly seized upon it.

In company with our worthy and talented companion and Brother, Henry H. Garnet, we bade adieu to our Parents and Friends for this Canaan—as we hoped a land of Literary Promise. I cannot tell the thrilling tide of emotion which coursed through our frames, as we started upon this novel expedition; nor how young hope fluttered in our breasts till we reached the end of our journey. I remember well with what a special favor our Friend was regarded there by all. His manly bearing, his correct demeanor, his finished and powerful eloquence, and exact scholarship placed him in the front ranks among his mates.

We had not been members of the Academy a long time before we were kindly invited to address the friends of Human Freedom at Plymouth in the same state on the 4th of July. The invitation was accepted and we immediately commenced preparation.

On the 4th of July 1835, while you fellow members as you were used, were assembled at your annual Literary feast, training and preparing for manly efforts—our dear deceased Friend in a distant state, as he was accustomed, was endeavoring to effect something of honor and credit for his brethren in a new field and manner. On that occasion he was brilliant and impressive in an unusual degree. He gave universal delight. While descanting upon the oppressions and wrongs of his people, his soul became fired with patriotic ardor. In severe and pointed terms did he dissect the hypocrisy of American Christianity and Republicanism. As he progressed warmly and eloquently did he vindicate the character of his Brethren.

Winning, graceful, and felicitous in his style and manner, he stole upon the feelings of his hearers and carried them along with him.

At the close of his speech a spontaneous burst of applause expressed the delighted feelings of his listening auditory.

My time will not allow, nor does necessity require that I should enter into an account of the outrages that forced us to abandon all idea of remaining at Canaan and continuing our studies there. With sad and sorrowful feelings we left our friends there, and started for home. It was the latter part of August. The weather was delightful—and the prospect engaging and attractive: —but we saw it not. The beautiful scenery and the pleasant landscapes along the valley of the Connecticut through which we passed and the rich fields and abundant harvests in the hither part of Western New York arrested not his attention. The moving song of the tuneful warblers, the gentle breathings of summer breezes among the leaves, and the sweet music of rippling rills, fell unheeded upon his ears. Yet he was a great lover of nature, and delighted in her numerous and varied beauties.

But now his soul was stung with the sense of deep injury; and as we rode many a long mile, —in deep and silent meditation he sat, reflecting not upon his own wrongs, but those of his people—the infliction of which upon himself in this instance symbolized to his mind those immemorable and monstrous oppressions which have well nigh shrivelled our humanity.

After eight days from our return, I left him here in the city and went to Oneida Institute. In two months he joined me there, and we took rooms immediately opposite each other for mutual aid, counsel, and friendship. His continuance there was not long owing to the death of his Grand Mother, whose affairs demanded his presence at home.

While a member of the Oneida Institute his manners, habits, and abilities attracted much attention and gained him great respect from his fellow students. I recollect well the first time he debated. It was in a Society which he had joined during the vacation. Several had spoken on either side of the question and the Debate was drawing to a close, —when Sidney rose without preparation without notes, and enchanted the audience by his earnestness of manner and persuasiveness of eloquence. On few occasions have I heard him acquit himself better. All eyes were turned upon him. It was his maiden speech in the Institute and as a Speaker, established his character. Coming from the Debating room a Friend remarked "I had no idea he was going to speak, especially in that manner."

He left the Oneida Institute and returned home and here devoted himself to study and reading. He became acquainted with Grecian and Roman History at a very early age. With the chief occurrences of English History—and with History in general, he was long familiarized. Poetry he read and studied with delight and ardor. There is scarcely an English Poet of note, but whose writings he possessed, and whose chief and choice passages he had committed to memory. Especially was the case with Shakespeare and Milton and Coleridge and Wordsworth.

His attainments in Science were by no means inconsiderable. In the Latin, Greek and Hebrew languages, he had made much proficiency, and he commenced not long since the study of German and French in such a manner, as promised before long with the blessing of good health, large results.

But it was in metaphysical investigation he chiefly delighted. In one so young, who had spent but eighteen months in schools of a high character, and who was almost entirely his own teacher in the higher branches, an intimate acquaintance with the minutia of speculative science could not be expected. There are hidden reaches where the eye of philosophy has never pierced, there are depths and profundities which have never been fathomed, and there is a shoreless ocean of divine Truth, whose borders the vessel of the hardy navigator in thought has never passed, and whose virgin waves her keel has never parted. Much less then from our Friend could a great deal be anticipated. . . .

A few days before I left the city, we were talking together about the theme that ever occupied his mind—"Our people," when he made the following observation—"I tell you confidentially and you will not mention it, what my intentions are as far as it respects our political enfranchisement. From the property that has been left me, he remarks, I derive all the benefits—rents etc.—but it will not be entirely mine until I reach my twenty-fifth year. I think, strictly speaking, I have no right to vote. I have been to my physician, who says I am unable to stand any great exposure or strong excitement at this time. I believe the Law that deprives us of the right of voting, while we pay taxes and help support the burdens of the State—to be unconstitutional. But if God spares my life, I am determined to test this matter; and spend every cent of my money, and sacrifice every particle of my property, but what decision upon decision as high up in the Judications as it can go—are given; and some effort, successful or unsuccessful is put forth, to make us something more than political serfs and slaves!". . . .

It is befitting here that I should speak of the religious character of our Friend, for be it known to you he was a religious man. He never joined any Christian denomination. "He preferred," to use his own language, "to be a Christian like Milton and his namesake the great Sidney a Christian after his own manner."

It was in the year 1835 we went to the Oneida Institute. Though not entirely indifferent to the claims of God our Father upon us, we were nevertheless in a state of sinful rebellion—without God and without hope in the world. Our situation was made the subject of special prayer by faithful men; the exceeding love of God in the Savior was held up to us, and earnestly and kindly were we entreated for a long while to renounce sin and the world, and become the followers of Christ. These efforts and prayers excited the hearts' natural opposition, strongly and wickedly for some time were they striven with. I noticed being in continual association with him, the change that came over our Friend. He became remarkably thoughtful and serious.

Long—long in the imperishable colors of [illegible] will remain the recollection of the evening he knocked at my door, and coming in sat down and with a beaming countenance spoke of the change that had taken place in his feelings, and his determinations for the future. His whole life and habits underwent a remarkable transformation. Sabbath after Sabbath in mid summer did he go four miles to Sunday School, and teaching and explaining the Holy Scriptures, and by powerful and pungent remark and eloquent entreaty, labor for the best and highest interests of man.

At the Institute, I have said, we roomed immediately opposite each other. We were accustomed to rise before daybreak and aid each other in our lessons, and we had agreed whoever rose first should enter the other's room and awake him. Several times for this purpose, I entered his room, but instead of being in bed asleep I found him in the dark, not unfrequently undressed, sometimes the room cold—in deep and fervent prayer! . . .

Up to the time I left the City, we met almost daily; and much of the time we spent with each other, was appropriated to the perusal of the sacred oracles in the original and translation, or discussing at times some scriptural doctrine.

I recollect once that we were conversing on one occasion upon Truth, and that its triumph was certain from the life eternal in its nature—which [blank space in original MS]

I can never forget with what animation his countenance now lit up, and how his entire heart was given to the subject, while he kept pouring forth rich and weighty remarks upon the topic. In the course of conversation I directed his attention to the words of St. Paul, "he can do nothing against the truth, but for the truth." The text attracted his attention and he inquired where it might be found. By mistake, however, I gave the wrong direction. A day or two afterward we met, and after his usual kind and friendly salutations, his first remark was where he might find that text. We had been pondering the great truth uttered by the Apostle, and he was intent upon turning it to practical account. . . .

The race not infrequently has been blessed with a superior class of men, whose intense desire has been to be controlled by principle as the habit of soul—to go through the world unmindful of the inclinations of sense and passion, with cheerful godliness, submitting to the dictates of Reason working continually for the glory of God and the spiritualization of man. Such a Spirit was our Friend. He loved the truth for its truthfulness. He could see more beauty in her than in all the gay scenes and splendid objects of created nature. The stern mandates—the imperative call of duty was far more musical to him than all the melody of streams and fountains, or, the gentle sighing of summer winds. He was decidedly the most conscientious man of my acquaintance. Unlike the most of us, he had few struggles with selfish inclinations with regard to duty. With him the perception of Truth was intuitive; and when he saw where it led there he immediately took his position. It mattered not whether he was accompanied, or whether he stood alone; whether he was assailed in his course, or whether he had to remove hollow hearted and unprincipled encumbrances from the way—in the paths of duty *he would* go. Alas! how often alone. Our dear Friend would have gone to the stake or gibbet, rather than yield one jot or tittle of those eternal truths which constituted his beings might.

From "Eulogium on Henry Highland Garnet, D.D."

Before the Union Literary and Historical Association;
Washington, D.C., May 4th, 1882.

In 1825 the Garnet family came to New York city, and soon after took apartments at 137 Leonard street, the very next door to my father's house. And here, as little boys, Garnet and myself became school-mates and life-long friends.

I remember his father well. A grander, nobler, more stately man, both in stature and character than George Garnet, I have rarely met. He was as tall as his more celebrated son; a perfect Apollo, in form and figure; with beautifully moulded limbs and fine and delicate features; just like hundreds of the grand Mandingoes I have seen in Africa; whose full blood he carried in his veins.

Unlike his son, he was grave and sober in his demeanor, but solid and weighty in his words; not given to talk, and reminding one of the higher Quaker character; deeply religious; and carrying in his every movement strength and dignity. I remember well the self-restraint his appearance always evoked among my playmates, and a certain sense of awe which his majestic presence always impressed us with.

His mother was as notable a person as his father, both in personal presence and traits of character; a most comely and beautiful woman; tall and finely moulded with a bright, intellectual face, lit up with lustrous, twinkling, laughing eyes—which she gave as an inheritance, to her son; and the very soul of fun, wit, frolic and laughter.

From this brief description you can see whence our late friend got that

---

From Alex Crummell, *Africa and America: Addresses and Discourses* (Springfield, Mass.: Willey and Co., 1891), pp. 272–305.

readiness, humor, intellectual fire, steadiness of character and strong native thought, which were his grand characteristics. They came from both parents; but like most great men they were especially the gift of that grand mother. Blessings for ever upon all good and noble mothers!

From such a stock, with both physical and mental greatness in both lines of his ancestry, Henry Garnet inherited that fine physique, that burning vitality, that large intellectual power, that fiery flame of liberty, and those high moral and spiritual instincts, which are generally characteristic of the great.

Coming to New York he entered at an early day the African Free School, in Mulberry street, and became the schoolmate and friend of those distinguished colored men, then boys, whose names have become celebrated in the history of our race in this land: —Patrick Reason, Prof. Charles L. Reason, Geo. T. Downing, Ira Aldridge, the great tragedian; Isaiah De Grass, James McCune Smith, M.D., and Samuel Ringgold Ward.

Owing to the necessities of the family he spent two years at sea as a cabin boy. During his absence, in 1829, an event took place which is impressed very vividly upon my memory, and which can not be omitted from this narrative. I saw the occurrence with my own eyes, playing, after sunset, before my father's door. One evening, in the month of July or August, a white man, a kinsman of the late Colonel Spencer, the old master, walked up to Mr. Garnet's hired rooms, on the second floor of the dwelling. He knocked at the door, and Mr. Garnet himself opened it. "Does a man by the name of George Garnet live here?" was the question put. "Yes," was Mr. Garnet's reply; and immediately, as by a flash, though years had passed away, he recognized one of his old master's relatives. The slave-hunter, however, did not recognize George Garnet. "Is he at home?" was the next question, to which, with quiet self-possession, Mr. Garnet replied: "I will go and see." Leaving the open door Mr. Garnet, without saying a word to his wife, daughter, and a friend in the room, passed into a side bed-room. The opened window was about twenty feet from the ground; between the two houses was an alley at least four feet wide; the only way of escape was to leap from the side window of the bed-room into my father's yard. How Mr. Garnet made this fearful leap, how he escaped breaking both neck and legs, is a mystery to me to this day; but he made the leap and escaped. In my father's yard was a large ill-tempered dog, the terror of the neighborhood. The dog, by a wondrous providence, remained quiet in his early evening slumbers. After jumping several fences

Mr. Garnet escaped through Orange street, and the slave-hunter's game was thus effectually spoiled.

On his return from one of his trips to Washington, Henry Garnet found his father's family scattered by this raid of Maryland slaveholders.

The news almost crazed him; and having purchased a clasp-knife he walked Broadway, expecting and prepared for an attack from the slave-hunters. His friends, however, hurried him out of the city, and for a time he was concealed on Long Island.

Just after these occurrences, by an accident, he contracted white-swelling in his right leg, and thus became a cripple for life. These startling occurrences, above narrated, proved the pivotal event of Henry Garnet's life. From that time forward he was a man. The breeze of nature began to stir within him. Large and glowing ideas circled his brain. The mystery of life had sprung upon him! There are certain plants which carry latent in their folds, special virtues, odors, medicinal qualities, electric power, which to ordinary sight are unrecognized and unknown; but step upon them, crush them with the slightest tread, and immediately all their latent qualities spring to the surface, and marvelous powers startle the touch, or exhalations fill the air! So the anguish of this family calamity gave birth to a giant soul! From this terrible ordeal Henry Garnet came forth like gold thoroughly refined from the fire! The soberness which comes from trial, the seriousness which is the fruit of affliction, the melancholy and the reflection which spring from pain and suffering, for he was now a cripple, soon brought Garnet to the foot of the Cross. He had attached himself about this time, to the Sunday-school of the First Presbyterian church, under the care of the celebrated Rev. Theodore S. Wright.

His wonderful aptness, great cleverness, immediately attracted the attention of his pastor and teachers, and he at once took there, as wherever else he went, the foremost place in the school. Parson Wright baptized him, and at once became his patron and friend. And when soon afterward he decided to enter the ministry, he looked upon Garnet as his own "son in the gospel;" and always, to the day of his death, cared and provided for him in all his efforts to secure a liberal education and to reach the ministry.

In 1831 the leading colored men in New York city established a High School for classical studies, for colored youth. Garnet, with Sidney, Downing, George Lawrence, (now of Texas,) and several others of our school-mates were, its first pupils. This school only whet our youthful appetite for larger facilities of training and culture. But, alas! in those days the doors of all academies and colleges were closed to colored youth. Our parents looked one way and another; but not a ray of hope was discoverable on the intellectual horizon of the country.

Fortunately, however, just at this time, it was in the year 1835, the abolitionists of New Hampshire, disgusted with the negro-hatred of the schools, and mortified at the intellectual disabilities of the black race, opened a school at Canaan, N.H. Youth of any and all races, and of both sexes, were to be received in it. I cannot tell the delight its announcement gave our little band in the Canal Street High School. Three of us New York boys, Henry Highland Garnet, Thomas S. Sidney* and myself, at once took advantage of this opportunity, and off at once we started for Canaan.

I cannot pause to relate the incidents of this journey from New York to New Hampshire. You will remember that Garnet was a cripple, weak, sickly, feeble; but he had a wonderful spirit and marvelous energy and perseverance. The difficulties of the journey you can hardly imagine. On the steamboat from New York to Providence no cabin passage was allowed colored people, and so, poor fellow, he was exposed all night, bedless and foodless, to the cold and storm. Coaches then were in use, and there were no railroads; and all the way from Providence to Boston, from Boston to Concord, from Concord to Hanover, and from Hanover to Canaan, the poor invalid had to ride night and day on the top of the coach. It was a long and wearisome journey, of some four hundred and more miles; and rarely would an inn or a hotel give us food, and nowhere could we get shelter.

Sidney and myself were his companions during the whole journey; and I can never forget his sufferings—sufferings from pain, sufferings from cold and exposure, sufferings from thirst and hunger, sufferings from taunt and insult at every village and town, and ofttimes at every farm-house, as we rode, mounted upon the top of the coach, through all this long journey. It seems hardly conceivable that Christian people could thus treat human beings traveling through a land of ministers and churches! The sight of three black youths, in gentlemanly garb, traveling through New England was, in *those days, a most unusual sight;* started not only

---

*It is difficult for the author to speak in moderate terms of the genius, talent and character of this great young man Thomas S. Sidney, his and Dr. Garnet's school-mate, companion and friend. Dr. McCune Smith, thus describes him:— "The wit, the pure patriot, the almost self-taught scholar, cut off, alas! in the very bloom of his promising youth." He died at the early age of 23. And it was *then* (in 1841) the author's melancholy duty, as now in the case of his friend Garnet, to deliver before the people of New York the eulogy upon his life and character.

surprise, but brought out universal sneers and ridicule. We met a most cordial reception at Canaan from two score white students, and began, with the highest hopes, our studies. But our stay was the briefest. The Democracy of the State could not endure what they called a "Nigger School" on the soil of New Hampshire; and so the word went forth, especially from the politicians of Concord, that the school must be broken up. Fourteen black boys with books in their hands set the entire Granite State crazy! On the 4th of July, with wonderful taste and felicity, the farmers, from a wide region around, assembled at Canaan and resolved to remove the academy as a public nuisance! On the 10th of August they gathered together from the neighboring towns, seized the building, and with ninety yoke of oxen carried it off into a swamp about a half mile from its site. They were two days in accomplishing their miserable work.

Meanwhile, under Garnet, as our leader, the boys in our boarding-house were moulding bullets, expecting an attack upon our dwelling. About eleven o'clock at night the tramp of horses was heard approaching, and as one rapid rider passed the house and fired at it, Garnet quickly replied by a discharge from a double-barrelled shotgun which blazed away through the window. At once the hills, for many a mile around, reverberated with the sound. Lights were seen in scores of houses on every side, and the towns and villages far and near were in a state of great excitement. But that musket shot by Garnet doubtless saved our lives. The cowardly ruffians dared not to attack us. Notice, however, was sent us to quit the State within a fortnight. When we left Canaan the mob assembled on the outskirts of the village and fired a field piece, charged with powder, at our wagon.

We returned home over the Green Mountains of Vermont, along the valley of the Connecticut, through Troy, down the Hudson to New York. All through the route Garnet was a great sufferer; at Troy we had misgivings for his life, and on the river we had to bed him with our coats and shade him with our umbrellas.

We sojourned at our home a few months, when information was received that Oneida Institute, at Whitesboro, a Manual Labor Seminary, had opened its doors to colored boys.

Thither we three New York boys at once repaired, and spent three years under the instruction of that master-thinker and teacher, Rev. Beriah Green. Garnet graduated in 1839, and immediately afterward entered upon public life.

Settling at Troy, he taught the colored school in that town, studying theology at the same time under the celebrated Dr. Beman, and acting as secretary to the colored Presbyterian Church. He was licensed to preach in 1842, and was ordained and installed the first pastor of the Liberty-Street Presbyterian Church, in that city; and there he remained ten years, publishing, part of the time, a paper called the *Clarion*.

"Africa and Her People": Lecture Notes

From my early childhood my mind was filled with facts and thoughts about Africa and my imagination literally glowed with visions of its people, its scenery, and its native life. In my boyhood I read the "Arabian Nights Tales," and all you who have read them know how they stimulate the youthful mind. It was just thus with me with regard to Africa. I will tell you how all this came about:—

My father was born in the Kingdom of Timanee. He was stolen thence at about twelve or thirteen years. His burning love of home, his vivid remembrance of scenes and travels with his father into the interior, and his wide acquaintance with divers tribes and customs, constantly turned his thoughts backward to his native land. And thus it was by listening to his tales of African life, I became deeply interested in the land of our fathers; and early in my life resolved, at some future day, to go to Africa.

The opportunity came in 1853. I had just graduated from college in England, and an appointment came to me as missionary of my church in Liberia, West Africa. I left England in May 1853, on the *first* of the line of steamers which now run constantly from Liverpool to the West Coast. If I had time I should like to pause and tell you of the singularly attractive route from Southampton to the Coast. The voyage is a grand panorama of sights and incidents; bringing to the traveller's sight the Channel with its several isles, the Bay of Biscay, the peak of Teneriffe, Madeira, with its varied and cosmopolitan life, and its beautiful scenery; and its aristocratic society.

After about ten days voyage from England, we reached the coast. We sailed out from Madeira about sunset, and in the afternoon of the following day we had our first view of the continent of Africa. Right before us

Transcribed from MS. C. 23. Untitled Manuscript. Schomburg Collection, New York Public Library, and printed with permission.

there rose up a bright bare rocky projection, jutting out into the sea, some 100 feet in height; crowned at the top by a small fort. So bright and glistening was it in the burning sun that it pained the eye. Nothing else was visible, as we approached nearer land; but at length we saw that we were nigh a most desolate region. Goree stands at the outer Southwest limits of the desert of Sahara. Not a blade of grass could be seen. A sandy plain stretches out on every side. At the back of the hill we after landing saw a small trading town with a few inhabitants. As we crossed the bar and entered a small creek, and turning, of a sudden, a sharp point of land, we saw, just a short distance out of the village, a group of men and women sitting on the ground. They were all wrapped in large striped cotton clothes; their heads bent toward their knees and talking in deep low gutteral tones. As we stept on shore the whole company sprang to their feet; and I saw a group of the tallest human beings that I had ever met with. They were Jolloffs, of the Senegambia region of Africa. Their average height was about 6 feet 3 or 4, but with their remarkable slenderness, they appeared two or three inches taller. I was much struck with both the depth and the brilliancy of their complexions. Such utter blackness of colour I had never seen in our race; not either the copper or the ashy blackness which is common to the Negro of America; but black like Satin; with a smoothness and thinness of skin so that you could easily see the blood mantling in their cheeks.

Goree was the first stopping place on the coast, and a more sterile desolate spot I had never seen. Nothing but sand, sand, sand, as far as the eye could stretch glistening in the intense sunlight. This you may judge was rather a discouraging introduction to Africa. Let me assure you that Goree was not to be taken as an indication of the true aspects of African scenery. I cannot pause here to describe each of the settlements we stopped at sailing down the West Coast to Liberia. But I wish to say here in general that people in the higher latitudes can hardly form a true idea of the variety, richness, grandeur and even sublimity of African scenery. After leaving Goree our next stopping place was Gambia; and here we had our first glimpse of the glories of the continent. Two days after we reached the [illegible] stead of Freetown, the capital of Sierra Leone.

European travellers are often heard to say "See Naples and die." One is led almost to a like exclamation on approaching the peninsula of Sierra Leone. As we drew nigh to the land we saw, right before us, rising up majestically some 2500 feet, peak after peak of mountains, until the highest were lost in the white fleecy clouds. As we entered the Bay, we were met on every side with every variety of herbage and color. The waters were crowded with canoes and boats of the native fishermen; and craft of various size were lying in the harbour, loading or unloading their cargoes. And all around us were the mansions of the rich, and the hamlets of the natives everywhere interspersed with fruit trees, garden plots, and the brilliant large-sized flowers of the tropics.

I leave a description of Sierra Leone for later notice; and right here, amid the Eden like spot of beauty and magnificence I use my opportunity to say a few words upon African scenery. I attempt no description; for the luxuriance and the grandeur of the country far exceed all attempts which I might possibly make. The land possesses every variety and form of beauty. It abounds with the picturesque. Flowery landscapes constantly greet the eye of the traveller; beautiful dales; lovely valleys; grand and majestic mountains, clothed to their highest tops with charming verdure; with the land everywhere intersected with brooks and streamlets singing on their way; —all these make up the glories of African scenery.

Once I ascended the Cavalla river 100 miles, and I have no hesitation in saying that in beauty and majesty it is not only the rival of the glorious Hudson, but far surpassing it in richness of tropical colouring; and exhuberance of verdure. On one occasion I travelled three days through the Vey country and the whole journey; through beautiful valleys, by gentle streams, over high reaching mountains, through deep and lofty forests; was a constant succession, hour by hour, of the most enchanting surprizes of bright and beautiful aspects of nature. The trees give Africa one [of] the most conspicuous features of its majestic scenery. It is quite beyond my capacity to describe the variety, the usefulness, the prodigious size, or the beauty of the African forest. In sailing along the coast, one of the first things which attracts the stranger's attention is some of these trees, grand giants of the forest, seen far off at sea, which serve as land-marks, for the mariners, to identify certain local points. The cotton tree is the special tree which serves this purpose. It is often found on the sea board 200 feet in height with a girth of nine to twelve feet.

The natives use this tree for making the largest canoes and I have seen them at sea with over one hundred men in it. These great canoes are the *naval* vessels of the natives, but used likewise for carrying to the shore the cargoes of the merchant vessels, trading along the coast. I say they are the *naval vessels;* and I will tell you what I mean by that

(1) The coast men act as sailors for the trading vessels.
(2) Kroos and Fishmen.
(3) New tribes often have difficulties.
(4) Challenge each other to fights on the sea

Perhaps the most important tree in West Africa is the palm tree. It is not so large as most of the other trees of the African forest. Judged by mere sight, a stranger would regard it as of but little importance. It is a tall slender tree, soaring up without any branches, some sixty or seventy feet, crowned at the top by spreading, out-stretching branches, somewhat like a fan.

The palm tree furnishes the most important article of African commerce. The *gums*, the *hides*, the *ivory*, the *cotton cloths*, the *woods*, the *oils* of Africa, and the common exports from the whole line of the coast. *Gold* too, for centuries, has been a great demand; and you all know the celebrity, for centuries, of what was called [blank space in the manuscript]

Interesting as all this is, it must give way to what transcends all the splendours of the skies, all the beauty of tropical fields and forests, all grandeur of mountain heights.

"The proper study of mankind is man," says Pope; and the people of Africa beyond any other primitive people I know of [possess] traits, points of interest and superiority which command our attention. While living in West Africa I have seen people of not less than sixty different tribes. In Sierra Leone, alone, a little spot not much larger than Manhattan Island, there were gathered together, from the recaptured slave vessels, men and women from tribes. It is impossible for [one] in the brief space of a lecture, to refer to *all* of these different peoples. I shall select a few of them for notice: tribes somewhat distinguished either for physical power or national greatness or personal beauty, or for mercantile shrewdness, or intellectual ability. Two or three general facts may first be mentioned.

The first of these is that the native African is physically one of the finest men on the face of the earth. One of the first things which attracted my attention on reaching the coast of Africa was the general manly strength, symmetry and bodily beauty of the natives. I had not only been taught, at school, in the geographies I had studied, the personal inferiority of the Negro, that he was a creature almost approaching the brute, in appearance, that he had a retracting forehead, flat nose, a long projecting heel; but I had also seen, in many places in [the] U.S.A. much physical inferiority, at times repulsiveness of the race. Hence it is that I was not only unprepared, but I was greatly surprised to find the native man in tribe after tribe, an erect, finely proportioned, well developed, symmetrical and a noble being. The same variety of type which prevails in Europe, as seen in the differences of physique, of English, Germans, Swedes, French, and Italian, prevails among the African tribes—differences of height, of bulkiness, of sharpness or heaviness of visage, and strange as it may seem, even differences of complexion. But so far as completeness and beauty of form is concerned, the native African is the equal of any and of every nation in Europe; can furnish as fine specimens of manly [physique]. He is *not* and I say it with emphatic utterance—he is not, so far as *natural proportions* are concerned, an inferior being. In *this* respect he is the equal of any other race of men on the globe. *Admiral Rogers testimony.*

With reference to stature I may say that there is a very great difference between the tribes. Some, like the Bassas, are short and slender; some again, as for instance the Akoos, Passas, Cingoes, are bulky and large. Others like the Mandingoes, the Veys are tall and slender. While the Kroos and the Fishmen, are both tall and immense in size. Their complexions vary. The Congoes are deep black. The Veys are yellow. The Bassas, Deys are the colour of a Havana cigar; and *this* is the general color of native Africans everywhere.

My time is too limited for a wide survey of the African tribes. I confine my remarks to six different tribes on the West Coast who, for various reasons deserve special notice. These tribes are

1 Greboes	4 Mandingo
2 Dahomans	5 Veys
3 Timmanee	6 Egbas

I have chosen these six Peoples from over sixty different tribes of West Africa which I have seen, for the simple reason that they have traits and peculiarities, mental and physical, which put them far in advance of all the other peoples I have met on the West Coast. Each and all, are distinguished for great physical proportions and manly beauty. There is one exception and that is the Egbas, who physically are inferior, and yet, on the other hand are characterized by qualities which make them at the present one of the most advanced among the peoples of Africa.

1. The GREBOES. When the traveller approaches the coast of Africa, say off the coast, near Sierra Leone, Monrovia; or, Cape Palmas; long,-sometimes before he spots land; he will see a little canoe, with perhaps two men paddling in it far out at sea; looking out for a vessel.

The Krooman! His occupation *sailor* etc.

[1]Location of tribe. [2]Breed of men. [3]Prodigious *size,* girth—breadth of shoulders. Physical power, eg. lift bbl flour!

Spirit—free men! *Marks of freemen.*

No slavery

No participation in S trade

Sturdy, independent

2. The finest, I say divinest set of men—for they looked like demi gods, were about sixty DAHOMANS I once saw at *Sinou*

Recaptives: from American Naval vessel

Their country

History: Warlike character, Cruel customs. Cannibals!

3. Right opposite Sierra Leone, in Bootrium country, a race of people called Timmanees. I may be excused for speaking of them, notwithstanding my own race. My father etc. *Characteristics.* First met in Sierra Leone. saw them passing through the street and inquired *who these people.* Great nobility of character. Indomitable spirit! Unconquerable! British subdued all others around them. Never them! Physique!

4. MANDINGOES. The most celebrated tribe in West Africa, i.e., more known of them, and have a more general and superior reputation than most other tribes (a) physical characteristics—six feet 2. (b) proportion; (c) character; (d) intelligence; (e) pursuits—*traders*—the caravans; (f) religion—

5. VEYS. There is a tribe on West coast in immediate neighborhood to Liberia—Veys. Not very large. Not equal to other Dahomans, or Mandingoes or Timmanees, in manly vigor, personal impress, or warlike power; but still greatly distinguished (a) one peculiarity—beauty of women. (b) Industrial activity in farming and manufacturing—e.g. weaving.

(c) My chief reason for mentioning them is their mental activity and real genius. e.g. Invention of Alphabet and Literary spirit.

6 EGBA TRIBE.

From what I have said this evening you can gather a few conclusions concerning character, capability and the destiny of the people of West Africa.

1st You have seen first of all that there is a physical basis, at the base of this peoples life. Strong, healthy—vigorous, long lived e.g. healthy:—no deformed people: disease seldom found. Longevity.

2 *Industrious* e.g. Farm life; plenteousness of food; *interior* markets of 10,000 people, mechanical ingenuity. e.g.

1. *Cotton cloths* 100,000 Looms in Bombas town
2. Iron—blacksmithing in Cavalla
3. Gold manufacturing in Freetown

Moral character: Pagans, and paganism [illegible] degradation of women; darkness of mind; cruelty in war.

But take the normal characteristics:

1 *Social purity of women*

2 *Honesty*

3 *Hospitality* to strangers: Experience (a) in Cavalla (b) in Vey country.

The stranger cared for; and if he die mourned for

Secret Societies

Future prospects of civilization

Sierra Leone

"Report from Buchanan, Liberia, on a Journey to St. Andrew's Church"

BUCHANAN, BASSA COUNTY, LIBERIA, W.A., 2d March, 1870.

At the request of the rector, wardens, and vestry of St. Andrew's Church, I have come down here to lay the corner stone of their church. The ceremony took place last Thursday, the 24th.

Failing to secure a direct conveyance by sea, I took the overland route; and thus have seen for the first time a few things, and met with some incidents which, perhaps, may interest you.

Spiritual Destitution

I left Monrovia on the 29th, and paddled up the Messurado river, some eighteen miles to its head. For nearly half its length it is quite a wide river, but gradually narrows its channel, until it becomes a tiny creek, with hardly sufficient room for another canoe to pass. We reached Reubensville, a small trading town, about 11 o'clock at night. Late as it was, and although everybody was aroused from sleep, yet the very first question after customary salutations was, "Ah, Mr. Crummell, what is the reason our Church don't send missionaries to preach to us traders in the country?" The young man who thus addressed me, acted as sexton when I organized Trinity Church, Monrovia, in 1853; and has ever since been connected with the Episcopal Church.

He represented to me that Liberian traders were residing in factories, all around him; and that natives of various tribes, and Congoes in large numbers, and villages, clustered about these factories; but that, month

From *Spirit of Missions* 35 (1870):414–19.

after month passed away and nobody came to preach to them. "Every Sunday," he added, "we can gather a good Sunday-school of Liberians and natives, and give you a good congregation. Send us a missionary; let him live here, or at some other town; and give us one Sunday, and take another factory another Sunday; and in this way keep us from living like heathens, and let us feel that we are yet Christians!"

We rose, Sunday morning before sunlight, and crossed the "Old Field," a level plain of four miles, which separates the Messurada from the Junk river. Here we came to a country, intersected on every side by little tiny creeks, natural canals, if I may so term them, running for miles in every direction. I have never seen such a country in America. The only thing anyway, resembling it, that I now remember, are the meadow lands of Wiltshire, England, with their numerous rivulets and water courses: only this land is a low, marshy country, abounding in standing pools, with the rankest vegetation, passing beyond the lowest banks, and shooting up in the most luxuriant forms even in the middle of these streams; the bamboo, the palm, and other tropical trees, overshadowing the streams, giving indeed continuous shade, but shutting out every particle of air, and intensifying the mephitic odors, and the deadly malaria of the swamp land.

Religious Service

After a few hours' ride in our canoe we stopped at the house of Mr. G——, who has taken up his residence in this almost desolate region for the purpose of trading. After our toilet duties, and a most welcome breakfast, I asked permission to hold Divine Service, which was most gladly given. I found here two married couples, Liberians, and four single men, and children; two native chiefs and their dependants and boys: but all speaking English. Both of the women were members of churches. One elderly man was an elder in the Baptist communion. My host had been a disciple, but had fallen; and alas, how low! The women thanked me with tearful gratitude for offering to preach to them. They had not heard a sermon for a year! I used the Sentences, Exhortation, Confession, and Morning Prayer. We then sang a hymn—"Come yet that love the LORD," &c., and preached to my mixed congregation of Americans and natives— sixteen of us, from 1 Timothy, 1–15: "This is a faithful saying," &c. I have every reason to believe that my exhortations had due effect; for, soon after service, all the men came to me in the yard, for conversation. *One* of them, the Baptist elder, and he the only person in the household, had absented himself from Service—he came to me and thanked me for my address; but on my remarking that he had been absent, he excused himself on account of his clothes, but he had heard every word I spoke. I used my opportunity to remonstrate with him for his absence on such a flimsy excuse, and to reprove him for living with these people for months, without assembling them, Sunday by Sunday, for prayer and Bible reading. He acknowledged his error, and promised that in the future, he would do his best on the LORD's day. Another one of the company, a young man, came voluntarily, confessing his sins, and inquiring what was his duty. He told me he had been utterly indifferent to religion, but recently he had felt his sins, and was desirous of serving his GOD. I strove to press upon him *immediate* self-consecration to CHRIST.

Native Tribes Desire Schools

I found the *native* men interesting persons. They come from the Gibbi country, a people kindred in blood and language to the Bassa people. They live in the hill country, two days walk from the coast; and my host informs me that they are a most enterprising, thrifty, and industrious people. On a recent trading visit to them, the king of the country begged him to get an American teacher for his people, and offered to build a house for the teacher and the school-room. This fact is now getting to be a common one in all our neighborhoods. I know of some four native kings who are ready to build school-houses, and dwellings for teachers, if teachers are sent to them. So constant has been our intercourse with native tribes, and so strong the influence we have exerted among these people, that they have become saturated, if I may use such an expression, with our civilized habits, customs, ideas and feelings: and there is an indefinable and pervasive desire extending through many tribes, quickening the pulsations of divers kings and headmen; not indeed for the Gospel, but for something elevating; and first of all it expresses itself in the earnest call for schools and teachers.

We spent the afternoon and evening in singing psalms and hymns. At bedtime I read GOD's Word, gave an exposition and prayed, and then retired for a few hours' rest.

A little after midnight I was called up, and we resumed our journey to Junk; for a few miles the scenery seen by moonlight was exceedingly wild, and the banks of the river in many places high and thickly covered with trees of a large growth. The wild animals were stirring, and noisy with clamors. This is the region of the alligator, the baboon, and the rhinoceros. The river is famous for fish, and contains the largest oyster banks in Liberia.

Treachery of a Headman

We reached Junk between 9 and 10 o'clock. At about 2 I started again up a third river, the Farmasetta, and travelled until 10 o'clock at night, without seeing a single civilized man or habitation, and meeting with but one canoe. This river, like the others, although at first broad, soon runs down to a single watercourse from 15 to 26 feet wide; exceedingly disagreeable from the lack of air, the unsightly banks of mud, and the deadly odors. Our journey ended at a rude country town, where I met a hospitable headman, who gave me a little house about 9 feet wide to sleep in, and a very hard bed to lie upon. Before I retired, however, his people brought me boiled rice, two boiled eggs, and a chicken, *fried* in palm oil, which tasted to me better than any fowl I ever ate before in my life. After a good night's rest I rose early to start for Bassa. But my *hospitable* host of the last night proved a rogue in the morning. Although paid beforehand to carry me in a hammock, he deceived me, and left me, carrying off the four hammock bearers.

Although quite lame, nothing was left for me to do but to pursue my journey on foot. At a short distance from the town I came upon factories of Liberians, some of whom I knew. Two miles further on I reached a mission of station and chapel, and remained a brief time to see the opening of the school. From this place I had six miles of hard travel on the beach, in the burning sun, to Little Bassa. And here, tired, faint, almost exhausted, I reached somewhat of an oasis.

A Christian Chief at Little Bassa

Little Bassa is the centre of a large section of the Bassa tribe. Its towns cluster in this neighborhood to a distance of ten or fifteen miles, with a population of from 10 to 12,000 people. Right here on the seaboard, perched upon a striking elevation, is the residence of L. K. Crocker, the son of the former king. Mr. C. is a civilized gentleman, residing in a commodious frame dwelling, with his people in their native huts and towns, dwelling on every side around him. I was exceedingly wearied when I reached this station, and staggered up the hill with no little difficulty. The first person I met was Mrs. Crocker, an active stirring little woman, with the brightest eyes and the cheeriest looks. On enquiring for Mr. Crocker, she directed me to the next buildings, his blacksmith's shop, where I was met by a short but rather stout man, who addressed me in a most courteous manner, in the plainest English, and invited me to his house.

An Early Pupil of Rev. Dr. Savage

"Cast thy bread upon the waters, for thou shalt find it after many days."

Mr. Crocker was a pupil of the Rev. Dr. Savage, when many years ago he was a missionary at Mount Vaughan. He speaks of his old master with warm affection and grateful respect. Mrs. Crocker is a Massachusetts woman. They have three children.

After leaving Mount Vaughan, Mr. Crocker became a Baptist, and was employed until the commencement of the late civil war as a Missionary Teacher. Being the son of the late king, and himself the chief personage in the neighborhood, his word is law among all the great chiefs, and his authority undisputed. His influence for Christianity has been great, and numbers of his people have been converted. At an Evening Service I held here, several of the native Christians were present, and listened with attention to the remarks I addressed to them. Mr. C. preaches to his people every Sunday, and has a congregation of from 50 to 60 persons—natives.

It is a matter of the greatest importance that this important post should be at once occupied again; and Mr. Crocker says that if the Baptists do not send a missionary, he will make arrangements for an Episcopal Missionary to occupy the field, and carry on the work of Missions among his people. At the same time he says there is plenty of room in the neighborhood for an Episcopal Mission, and he will give his sanction to any persons who will proclaim the Gospel of CHRIST.

Grand Bassa

Mr. C. very kindly procured me four hammock-bearers; and we started an hour or two after midnight for Grand Bassa. The bearers were fine, strapping fellows, who ran all the distance down—say twenty-seven miles—in six hours. Passing through Edina, I got a boat from that devoted layman, who is a pillar in the Episcopal church in Liberia, Mr. John Crusoe, and reached Rev. Mr. Wilcox's house Wednesday morning about nine o'clock. Half an hour before my arrival, he had written to Mr. Crusoe, giving me up, and had commenced the preparation of an address.

Laying the Corner-Stone—The Site Once a Battle-Ground

On the following morning, about noon, the people of Buchanan assembled on the ground, kindly given by a liberal and wealthy layman of our Church—Mr. S. Horace. The site is the sport where a most decisive battle was once fought between the Liberian settlers and the Bassa natives; and the corner-stone was laid in the very identical place where, in that same battle, Taplin's head, the man who led the heathen hosts, was cut off, during the fight, by an American settler. A daughter of that valorous American was present at our exercises. How strange are the ways of GOD!

General Interest Manifested

Great honor was shown us by the people of Buchanan and the neighboring villages. All the merchants, both Liberian and foreign, closed their stores, and gave us their presence. Seats were provided for the large assemblage, and we were canopied over in two beautiful aisles, by the graceful, long-stretching leaves of the palm. The Services were held at a desk placed near the corner-stone, where we were surrounded by the leading ministers of the various denominations, who rejoiced with our joy; and by the chief men, judges and magistrates of the country. The singing was unusually good, and sounded finely in the open air, aided by the deep bass of the neighboring ocean. At Mr. Wilcox's request, I laid the corner-stone, and then I delivered an address to the large assembly.

On Sunday, I preached for St. Andrew's congregation, and I was glad to see the presence of many leading persons in the community at this church—merchants, judges, and foreign residents. At noon, I visited, on request, the Methodist church, and addressed the Sunday-school, and afterward the Episcopal Sunday-school.

Wednesday, March 2d, I preached again for St. Andrew's people. The rest of the week I spent in visiting the river settlements, and looking after some of my former Mount Vaughan students. One I found here district attorney; another a merchant.

Favorable Impressions of Bassa County

I have been exceedingly pleased with my visit to Bassa County. The people are all alive with thrift and energetic activity. I noticed that although much wealth has been accumulated here, the people retain great simplicity of manners. But few servants are employed in the leading families, and mothers and daughters are content to do their own work. The wife of one of the leading merchants has herself opened a coffee farm on the Benson River, and, unassisted by any one, built her own house, where she spends most of her time coffee-planting. I found some of the most prominent citizens in the Sunday-schools, superintending or teaching. The chief patrons of GOD's work are rich men here—*not* patrons, but stewards of GOD, and, when called upon, they willingly give four and five hundred dollars for a good work and GOD's glory.

Great evils do abound; but with the zeal and devotedness of holy men and women in the community, their influence is greatly lessened.

Church and Schools

The schools are in a good state. Mr. Wilcox's parish school is well attended—nay, overcrowded—in a small school-room; and Mr. Blyden, his school-master, is both intelligent and painstaking. I was glad to hear Mr. Wilcox well spoken of by the good and holy.

I have found in Bassa County not a few civilized natives, living Christian lives: *two* men of standing and influence, and quite a number gathered in, with our Liberia children, in day and Sunday schools. Several are members of churches; a few are married to Liberian women; *one* I found a teacher in a Sunday-school. There are several native boys in Bassa, learning trades—cabinet making, carpentering, tinner's trade, and blacksmithing.

"Report from Caldwell, Liberia, on a Journey through the Dey and Vai Countries"

CALDWELL, NEAR MONROVIA, LIBERIA, W.A., *3rd April,* 1871.

Rev. and Dear Sir:—During the quarter which has just closed, the work at this station has been carried on as usual. Our Services, both at Caldwell and Virginia, have been quite regular, and, at Caldwell, well attended. Our Bible classes have met the same as usual, and at times a few strangers have swelled our number.

There has been a falling off in attendance at our Parish School incident to the season. From January to May, the farming population give themselves up to coffee picking, and the same sight meets one here that is seen in grape-gathering France, or hop-picking England, namely the assemblage of numbers of adults and children in the fields, gathering fruit from the trees. This has kept nearly half of our children from school for well nigh two months. A few years ago no such disturbing fact interfered with our school duties; for there were no coffee plantations to yield a revenue to families. Now this fact will serve to show the friends of Missions and this Republic some signs of

Material Progress

among this population. I regard it as one of the most hopeful incidents in Liberian life; for, as the people plant coffee and increase their means more comfort will prevail, and higher social and domestic ambitions will arise; civilization will advance, churches will become self-supporting, and new Missions will be originated in our religious bodies. This year many thou-

From *Spirit of Missions* 36 (1871):485–89.

sands of coffee scions will be planted in Caldwell, thus increasing the industry of the people, and raising their hopes for the future.

But our chief concern is

Christian Progress;

and I am happy to say we have evidence of a deeper spiritual life in the little company which attends St. Peters Church.

1st. The Holy Communion is better attended this year than it was last; and there is a more devout demeanor on the part of communicants. I find too that our Communion Sundays are sought after by Christian friends in other settlements, who are pleased to meet with us at the Table of the same blessed LORD.

2nd. At the commencement of the year, the communicants of our Church resolved to provide a supper and social meeting for communicants, previous to Holy Communion. At this gathering, we talk after supper on religious subjects, sing hymns, read extracts from Church papers on topics pertaining to personal religion and Christian duty. The meeting is closed with remarks from the wardens, and by a brief address by the Rector upon the next ensuing Communion. Anything social is so rare a thing in this country that we all look forward with pleasure to the recurrence of our Christian supper.

3rd. One other event deserves notice here. Last year the Church had several generous gifts bestowed upon it, and the communicants determined that, as a thank-offering for the same, they would attempt the erection of a small frame building, to be used as a hospital for destitute natives and Congoes, who every now and then are found, naked, diseased, and dying on the roads. Too poor to purchase, several offered to *give,* pieces of lumber for this purpose. It will probably take us a long time to complete the project; but a few pieces have already been given, and we hope to frame the building sometime within this coming quarter. We intend to put a thatched roof upon it, and close it in with thick mats. When thus completed, it will be fit for occupancy, and will enable us to save the lives or alleviate the sufferings, of many of these benighted heathen, as also of not a few of our own immigrant population.

I must not fail to mention that I have opened a new school in this district among the Congoes. Seventeen children have been offered by their parents, and a school building will soon be erected. The funds are provided by the New York State Colonization Society.

At the commencement of this quarter—i.e., in the middle of January—

I undertook a journey through the Dey and Vey countries preaching from village to village. I had been sent for by two chiefs, or kings, to talk with them about schools and missions. I started from the settlement of Virginia, and went throughout the Dey country first. I found the towns numerous, the people active with energetic labour, cutting their farms, willing everywhere to listen to the Word, some knowledge of which they have gained trading in our towns, or through resident traders in their homes, or through youth living in our Liberian families. But the truth has not penetrated deep: it has mainly suggested *intellectual* desire; for everywhere the demand was for schools and school-masters. At the second town which I visited, an old man followed me a long distance from town importuning me in the most serious, solemn manner to send him a teacher. The man's earnestness startled me. "But my friend," I said, "I have no teacher to leave here. I am only traveling through the country." "But," was the reply, in very clear English, "but your people promised me a school. I want my children taught; and you ought to send a man here." And for a half-hour he kept beside me step by step, urging his suit.

At Pau, some 18 miles from Vonzah, I found on the top of a hill a fine town, and large *plank* house, as yet unfinished. This was a great surprise to me. It was soon accounted for by the early appearance of the king, a tall, spare, fine-appearing man, who gave me a cordial reception. This man had lived in our settlements, and was once a servant of Governor Buchanan. On my inquiring concerning his house, he told me he wanted "to live like Americans."

The king here is one of the two chiefs who had sent for me to visit him. He offers to build a school house and a Mission house, and to give us *all the children* in his various towns, if we will take them, clothe, feed and instruct them. He will also give any amount of land for a farm for the boys to work. After I left the town, he assembled his headmen from the neighborhood, who readily acquiesced in his suggestion.

From Pau I pressed on three days through the wilderness; on the third day meeting but few towns. All through this region the elephant abounds. We saw their tracks on every side where they had passed through the night before. Evidences of the gross superstition of the people met us at every turn. I have never seen so many "Greegrees" before since I have been in Africa: in the towns, on the highway, in the valleys, on tops of hills remote from any town, in the rice and cassada fields, Greegrees, a tall gallows, with a huge rock slung to the cross-bar; or a stump covered by a cap made of bark; or a square reed box hung from a tree in the middle of the path.

On the fifth day of our journey we reached the Little Cape Mount

River, and taking a canoe, we went about eight miles up the river to King Bomba's town. This is the finest (not the largest) town I have seen in Liberia. It is doubly barricaded on four sides. On entering it I was struck at the completeness and finish of the huts; and in walking through the town I came across two couples, with their looms, weaving cloth. The sight was so singular and unique that I could not resist taking a sketch of the interesting sight.

The king was across the river at his country house, and a messenger went across and returned with an invitation to visit him. He received me in a most courteous and affable manner, and introduced me to his several wives, sons and headmen. Dinner coming on at this time, he very kindly offered me a large bowl of "rice and palaver sauce."

After dinner we at once had our "palaver;" first about the Gospel, next about schools.

Without entering into details, I will give the sum of the conversation in the *ipsissima verba* of the king: "Ah Mr. Crummell, I am too old for these things; but look at these children; take them all; put them in your schools, and train them as you please." I will build you a school, and a house for your Missionary, and give as much land as you please."

King Bomba is a little man, say 5 feet 5 inches in height, rather spare, with a large, round head, fine features, and keen, penetrating, restless eyes. He is very pleasing in his manners, and seems to live in great love and friendship with a large number of wives and a host of children. I spent two days with him, holding frequent converse with him and his sons and headmen. He is a man of much influence, and has a wide control through the country.

The Vey people are an industrious people, highly intelligent, polite and spirited. The women are beautiful, as well in face as in figure; and the king's wives treated me with great hospitality, providing me with everything pleasant and agreeable, preparing fire for me in my house, and a warm bath at night. As I sat in the town in the mornings, and saw these women—mere children—dressing themselves with their hand mirrors (*i.e.,* adorning their faces with clay paint), and heard their childish laughter and their glee, and observed their artless ways, I felt more keenly than ever before in my life the deep degradation of heathenism, and how that it is only by the evangelization of *women* we can ever break the chain of paganism in this land.

Almost everybody there spoke English, children as well as adults; some of the boys had learned to spell. My senior Warden spent the best part of a year here in '69, teaching; and he thus laid the foundation for future efforts should a Mission be established here. The youthful appetite of the children has been whetted; and there is a craving among them for letters and training. A Mission established at Bomba's Town would spread the influence of the truth in CHRIST among from 5,000 to 8,000 people in the immediate vicinity, and would thus eventually spread through the whole extent of the Vey tribe, up to the Gallinas.

One great advantage the Missionary would have at this point, and indeed through the entire Dey country which I have traversed: namely the absence of the Mohammedan influence. No Mandingo wars have raged through this region; the people have lived in their towns and villages in peace, comfort and industry, without the distractions and the bloodshed which the Moslems have carried through a wide region further north.

I found but *one* Mandingo man in all my route, at Bomba's Town—a keen, lively, talkative fellow, who was thought to be a spy, sent to find out the resources or the power of the country.

A week after my departure from home, I began my return. I spent Sunday at a new immigrant village near the Po river, where I found a small settlement, and a few disciples living on the beach. In the morning I held Service, and preached to this little company, every one of whom, save one, professed the name of the LORD. A long time had elapsed since a preacher had been among them; and their joy and gratitude was almost too much for me to bear. Poor, living in the humblest of cottages, yet they provided for me in the most hospitable manner. I shall not soon forget these people, and as soon as I can I shall visit them again. It is no common privilege to minister to GOD's saints cut off from the ministrations of the Gospel, and yet hungering and thirsting for the truth.

After a most tiresome walk of nigh thirty miles on the beach, I reached home on the eighth day from the time of my departure.

Allow me to mention two or three things which impressed me much in this tour:

1. First, in all my intercourse and conversation with the peoples I met, I saw very clear evidences of the presence and recognition of the main institutes of natural religion. The people are superstitious, especially the Dey people; not so much the Veys. But their superstition is but a thin incrustation; for immediately beneath a thin surface one finds the ideas of GOD, His providence, a sense of duty, consciousness of the sin of theft, and such like. And these do not have to be searched after. They come out easily, naturally in conversation.

2. But, in addition to this, I found a wide dissemination of the first truths of Revelation. Both the name and the mission of the LORD JESUS CHRIST are known by numbers of persons all through this country. Vast numbers of the heathen recognize with distinctness the difference between paganism and the Christian faith. This is to be accounted for by the apprenticeship of very many of the kings, head men and youth to the Liberians, who have lived in our families, and there got the germs of our holy religion.

3. I find that acquaintance, domestication, and trading have awakened a warm desire everywhere for schools. In almost every town the cry was for schools and teachers; and in two places, one of which I saw, houses are already prepared for the school and the teacher.

4. It is not right to leave the evangelization of this people to indirect influence. The Church of GOD should fulfil her mission by sending the Missionary to their towns, and villages and houses; but, from what I saw in my journey, I feel convinced that, in a wide region, Christianity is slowly, gradually undermining the paganism of the natives; and though the time would be long, yet eventually, by this indirect process, all the grosser forms, at least, must be broken down. Already our traders declare that, to find the more sanguinary forms of paganism, one has to go far in the interior; for the natives have become greatly modified in all their life and habits, by proximity to our towns and settlements.

5. One great lever is already in our power: *the sense of responsibility for their children.* I regard it no small, no trivial work that Liberia has effected among the heathen: that is, in creating a desire in the hearts of the parents for the improvement of their offspring. Nowadays, if one wants to hire native children, he has to go into the interior. It is almost impossible to get them from neighboring towns. But the parents cry out for schools and teachers; and when we establish schools among the heathen, we have no "code" to interfere, and lay down a course of secular instruction; we can make the Bible our grand text-book, and teach these children, if we place nothing else but "JESUS CHRIST and Him crucified."

Letter on Ethnology

You may judge of my interest in your letter from the fact that I myself have been endeavoring to secure interest in the same subject your letter suggests, in my circle in this city. I wished last year to enlist two or three friends of mine in the attempt to organize an "African Society" for the preservation of traditions, folk-lore, ancestral remembrances, etc., which may have come down from ancestral sources. But nothing came of it. The truth is that the dinning of the "colonization" cause into the ears of the colored people—the iteration of the idle dogma that Africa is THE home of the black race in this land; has served to prejudice the race against the very name of Africa. And this is a double folly: —the folly of the colonizationists, and the folly of the black man; i.e. to forget family ties and his duty to his kin over the water.

I, for my part, give my full adhesion to your plans. But I can do but little. The shades of evening are upon me. Age is fast relaxing my powers; —I am constantly up as it were to my eyelids in work and duty; but what assistance I can give I shall gladly render.

You are right in your reference to the ancestry of my dear friend Garnett and I have myself, distinct remembrances of the African (tribal) home of my own father, of which he often told me.

I have the impression that wide and telling information will fall into the hands of persons interested in the project that you wish to undertake; and I shall look for your circular at an early day.

You give an admirable and orderly list of topics in your letter and my impression is that among the class you rely upon—students and graduates, full up to this day, of the remembrances of southern homes and parents, you will find a larger number of inquiring minds than among a more ambitious and pretentious class of our people.

I wish you great success; and I shall be glad to hear from you again.

From *The Southern Workman*, January 1894.

Statement to the Congregation of St. Luke's Church

*This statement was made after the sermon and benediction, the
congregation remaining behind to hear it.*

Although I have been your rector now over twenty years, you will all bear
me witness that never, during this whole period, have I, under any
circumstances, brought any matters of a personal nature into this church
or pulpit. We have had trying times here, now and then; but I have always
refrained from putting any of my trials or troubles before you.

But an event occurred yesterday which I think ought not to be passed
over, without calling the attention of the good people of this church to it.

As I sat in my study yesterday morning, I saw a buggy drive up to the
door, and a person alight from it. The bell rang, and soon I was sum-
moned to the room below.

On entering the room I was met by a person who said he came to see me
on important business. On being seated he* began in this manner, and
with these words: "Dr. Crummell, I have come here to inform you that
there are *one hundred* of us who have concluded that we will no longer
worship in St. Mary's chapel, nor in St. Luke's church. We intend to
commence a new work somewhere on Fifteenth Street, between M Street
and the Boundary, and not far from St. Luke's church. I have just come
from the richest man in Washington and two of the leading clergymen of
this city. I have come to inform you about it, so that you cannot say we
have done this without your knowledge."

From pamphlet, Alex. Crummell, *Statement to the Congregation of St. Luke's Church,
Washington, D.C., Sunday Morning, 17th Sept. 1893* (Washington, D.C.: St. Luke's Church,
1893), 4 pp.
*I could not soil my lips, in making this statement, with the name of the vulgar creature,
who entered my house to insult and threaten me, and I will not stain this sheet with it.—A.C.

I immediately replied: "Well, this is certainly astonishing: what have I to do with your coming out of St. Mary's chapel, or the migration, of which you now inform me, from my church. I have nothing to do with St. Mary's chapel, nor with your purpose to start a new church."

His immediate reply was as follows: "Oh, yes, you have a great deal to do with it. Dr. Crummell, the whole thing is in your hands. You have been here many years, and you know you are a failure. Now, if you will resign from this church, all this movement will come to an end. You can settle the whole difficulty. I think you must know that the Bishop of the Diocese will look after you. I have no doubt whatever that Bishop Paret will provide some other work for you to do, and you will be taken care of. But if you don't we shall take this step."

Here I again interrupted him and said: "Well, this is indeed a wonderful thing! You are neither the Archbishop of America, nor the Bishop of this Diocese, nor the most eminent layman in this neighborhood; and yet you have come here to my house to give me 'notice to quit;' and you warn me that if I don't you will start a new church near St. Luke's."

Here he interposed with the words: "Oh, I don't mean to offend you by what I have said." And then, with what provoked a smile from me, he began again, with the most ludicrous gesticulations and gyrations of his body, both hands flying above my head, his alcoholic breath in my face: "Oh, I want you to understand that I have the greatest respect for your gray hairs, for your talents, and your character. I only came to let you know what we intend to do, if you won't take the step I have mentioned. It is all in your own hands. You can easily settle this whole matter. If you will only resign you may be sure it will be the very best thing."

"Look here, sir," was my answer. "Now I have heard enough from you. This conversation must stop right here." And I arose at once to my feet and showed him to the door. On leaving the room he turned and said to me: "Well, Dr. Crummell, you can't say that we haven't told you fully what we intend to do."

Who do you think was the Thing who dared thus to come into my house, and insult and threaten me in this manner? Why, a creature notorious for his licentiousness from his boyhood. A Leper, who got in peril once for the ruin of one woman, and shortly afterwards was publicly beaten for the ruin of another. A fellow, once snatched from a house of infamy, and with his victim brought before a city magistrate. Noted at all times for his drunken bouts; famous for his filthy amours and his gross blasphemies in the streets of Washington.

And this demoralized and broken down thing flaunts the atrocious falsehood in my face that *you,* the quiet, loyal people of my church are going to follow *him* into a new church organization, if I do not quit my post. A man who decent people in this city won't associate with. He, the depraved Moses to lead the saints of God in this city, into the worship of God, and into the ways of holiness.

Why, my friends, we who call ourselves disciples of Christ, never think of rushing into saloons and gambling halls, and houses of infamy to become the chiefs therein. But how do you account for the fact, that demoralized and licentious men are so anxious to become headmen in our churches, the first officers in the house of God.

Here is a wretched and disorganized creature, full of zeal to get hold of St. Luke's church, and to be a "big man" in it. And he thursts himself into my house, gives me "notice to quit," and warns me of the consequences if I don't obey him. And all because he wants this church for himself and his boon companions. Well, we will wait and see who "the rich man" is who is going to bolster up this precious character, and who the *"two leading clergymen"* who are his allies.*

*There is a handwritten note at the bottom of this printed flyer, which may have been added before the document was donated to the New York Public Library. I cannot vouch for its accuracy, but it seems to read: "J. W. Cole Clerk in Pension Office. Escapade with a female named Lena [Armee] was cowhided and both parties arrested."—Editor

Letters on T. Thomas Fortune, Booker T. Washington, and Others

1522 "O" Street Washington, D.C.
26th November '95

Dear Mr. Bruce:

I am up to my eyelids in work and at the same time, am feeble from a late attack of illness.

I must however snatch a few moments to acknowledge your favor of 7th.

I must, first of all, congratulate you on your marriage. May God bless you and your wife in all ways. I am sure you will be a true lover to her, *after* marriage: and so she will certainly court and charm you ever, and make you a happy home, and a more efficient public man. I am only sorry that I can't run over to Albany and tender you my felicitations in person. I wanted very much to visit New York during my summer tour, and stop at Albany, downward to New York City. I wanted much to see two or three old friends who, like myself, are not far from the times of eternity. One of these is Dr. Elkins. Do you know him? Matthews and Johnson the Democrats par excellence, etc, etc.

I am exceedingly anxious to *see* your castigation of Henderson. For sheer, outrageous and brazen impudence I think this fellow exceeds everything I ever heard of. Here is a man preaching to black people, living off of them; and yet writing and publishing the most outrageous and degrading descriptions of them; and withal utterly false! These sneaks, kicked, cuffed, scouted by the whites, are crazy to get into the society and associations of the very people who repel them. They know there is

---

Transcribed from manuscript, Schomburg Collection, New York Public Library, and printed with permission.

nothing legitimate in associating with the whites; they know it can only be by the humiliation of the black woman, and the bastardizing of her offspring; and yet this seems the very height of their spurious and impure ambition. And these men affect to be *leaders!* Henderson's article in the "Age," and Fortune's endorsement seem to me thoroughly demoralizing; and some way or another, such men should be called to account, and made to halt in their career.

I am watching the current of the debate anent Brown and the Reformers, on the one hand and the "Planet" on the other: —but I take no part in it. I shall be glad when it comes to its end. I can't desert Brown; for he is a grand genius. He has done nothing wrong; he has only made a mistake, and so given his enemies a chance to pinch and worry him. His resources, however, are great; and I think, if he would only act as a great mastiff does with little dogs—pass on without any notice of them, he would husband his resources, and soon secure quiet all along the lines of his activity.

You call upon me to bring myself more in evidence before the people. I am afraid I am too old for lecturing; for, albeit my voice is well preserved, my eyesight is much impaired.

Moreover I can't afford to travel and lecture for nothing. I must be paid; and where do our poor people pay for anything save for entertainments and pic-nicks?

I am writing a deal; but writing does not pay, i.e. in our colored papers. Just now I am preparing two papers for a missionary congress at Atlanta, whither I expect to go next month.

Dr. Blyden was here for a fortnight; and has gone back to England to take, I think, a government appointment under England, in the West Coast of Africa. I am very glad of his thrust into the ribs of that truculent screeching and screaming creature—Bishop Turner. Did you see Turner's contemptible sneer at what he calls—"*the good for nothing Negroes?*"

Do you remember a young man by the name of "Stephens"—from France? Can you tell me anything about him? His conduct, in certain matters, was exceedingly shabby; and now he has passed into oblivion.

But I must close. Thanks for the papers you send me. If you get hold of a copy of The "New York Evening *Post,*"—I shall be glad to see it.

With best regards to Mrs. Bruce, in which my wife joins me, most truly yours

Alex Crummell.

1522 "O" Street Washington, D.C.
7th April 96

Dear Mr. Bruce.

I have only time to thank you for your fine photo, and to acknowledge your welcome and cheery letter, "The times are out of joint;" and there seems just now a crisis in our condition. American (white) prejudice is relaxing. Divers indications evidence this fact: but lo and behold; just at this juncture, up rises a fanatical and conceited junto, more malignant than white men, pushing themselves forward as leaders and autocrats, of the Race; and at the same time, repudiating the race! And what is the basis of their superiority? Bastardy! A friend told me yesterday that "Charles Morris" told her to her face—"You blacks are a dead weight on us. It is you who keep us out of the Hotels and the saloons etc."—US! And who are us?

This ephemeral caste is sure to persist, as well as the other; only we must be true men.

Faithfully
Alex Crummell.

England
August 97

Dear Mr. Bruce.*

I have been struggling for the opportunity to thank you for your kind favor of 30th July, so full of meaty matter, but traveling and sight seeing are so engrossing and so tiresome that I have been sadly hindered.

I put off, today, an engagement to say a few words to you. When I read your letters it seems at times as though you were carrying the whole burden of the race in America. For indeed I know no two other persons— the *one* who feels so deeply upon race questions and the other yourself who does the work of vindication and knightly valour for the race. God bless you! You will [two lines are illegible] but you will be the great champion of your Race in your day; you will secure the honour of all genuine and philanthropic white men; and when the great [illegible] and our rights secured; then the race will applaud your name and memory as one of its chief benefactors.

*This letter provides singular insight into the personality and values of its author, although the original manuscript is fragmentary and largely illegible, and some portions have deteriorated beyond repair.—Editor

I have read Fortune's diatribe against the Negro and am not surprised at it. It is but one part of a wide movement which I have seen tendencies [illegible] for a long period [illegible] to tell you all my apprehensions concerning it. But this malignant Negro annihilator has his co-adjutors and followers; all endeavoring to segregate our people into antagonistic classes, and to promote the amalgamation of our men with white women. Our Negro women can go to the dogs or to the devil. As long ago as 1882 I saw the need of upholding the race against this satanic tendency and [illegible] "The Black Woman of the South," which I intended as a warning as well as a vindication. The audacity of this creature Fortune is astounding. Here in England a man or woman with the bar sinister uses every possible [illegible] to keep it unknown. It excludes all men and women from poli [illegible] alliances. A man or woman however culti-vated and refined, tho laden with enormous wealth could not [illegible] Socie [illegible] 5th ave, N.Y. Phil. Beacon St. Boston. It would be a misfortune for which he would not be held responsible; but—aha that but! No man of position wants his daughter to marry a bastard!—his son to marry a bastard! But here in [illegible] rises up a Coterie of men with [illegible] at their head [illegible] that boldly and [illegible] strive to [illegible] the bastardy of [illegible] into an aristocracy.

Fortune has talent, but he is one of the strongest evidences of Dr. [illegible] dictum that with the talents of an angel a man may be a fool.

The man Durham is another of the same ilk. He is the man who two or three years ago asked a friend of mine "After all [illegible] is there any-thing [illegible] the Negro!"

[illegible] The happier for the race than dep[illegible] of such fellows. They are [illegible] front for office [illegible] They mount backs of blind and willing Negroes, to get position and pelf; *and* so soon as they think themselves thoroughly [illegible] they at once repudiate the Negro.

Well, we are slowly getting sense. It takes time to open the darkness, [illegible] but soon we shall [illegible] see these fellows clearly and dis-tinctly.

If I mistake not some of our white friends begin to see that these fellows are only "opportunists" utterly ruthless in [illegible] principles; ready on the instant to use the Negro and the Republican Party for self and pelf. Is not this the significance of the McKinley policy to [illegible] Post Office seekers? And as the eyes of the administration are opened so is disappointment of these "Leaders" If men will only wait, they will see how Providence always

"Justifies the ways of God to man."

I have read with the greatest of [illegible] your articles in *Washington Post;* but yesterday, I received your [illegible] letter to the New York [illegible] concerning "Lynching and Rape" Capital! If we only could tend to whole [illegible] concerning the "Mrs. P[illegible]lers" of the South [illegible] What [illegible] they would yet cry of "Rape"!

Since my return to London I have been visiting the galleries, the great churches, the Law courts. The other day I fell upon an English friend, a Barrister at Law, who took me to "Lincoln's Inn," and gave me a sight of the Hall [illegible] the ancient legal Foundations. As we were passing through the Library, we saw two black gentlemen reading at the table. On our introduction to them we found that they were native Africans, [illegible] from the Gold Coast. We had a most interesting conversation. A few days later they called for us at our boarding house, and renewed the interesting conversation of the previous interview. How delighted I am to meet these fine fellows, full of strength and manliness; full of high hopes and lofty expectations for the race. A few days afterwards we had a [illegible] West India gentleman. [illegible] How hopeful are the incidents of travel! I send you by mail a few [illegible]. You will find them "heavier" than our American papers and far less newsy and sparkling [illegible] make my humblest apologies to Mrs. Bruce; but you must tell her that we [illegible] when we get deeply interested "topics" are wont ofttimes to forget persons; not through indifference, but owing to absorption. We are drawing our visit to a close, expecting to leave England on October [illegible] Meanwhile let us have a line [or two] Mrs. Crummell joins me in sincere regards to yourself and wife. [illegible] to hear acclamations on reading your articles and perusing your letters. I am an old man standing nigh to portals of eternity; dying daily. Should we never see each other again;—be good, true, faithful, heroic

Very truly

Alex Crummell.—

P.S. What a fine fellow is the Editor of the "Standard" [illegible] Is his name "Johnson?" If so what is the nature of the book—he announced for publication, some [illegible] who addresses our people [illegible] their condition

16 Percy St. Liverpool, England.
5th Oct 97.

Dear Mr Cromwell.

I am unavoidably a tardy correspondent. I have been wishing for many days the opportunity to keep up with my correspondence, and especially, to write to you; but what with constant charge, hospitality, continual daily, sometimes hourly, engagements; talking, speaking, and sight-seeing, I have fallen greatly in the rear!

Here I am, at the last, in Liverpool, and for a few days I have a little rest; but I have been journeying from the East, in Lincolnshire to the West, in Somersetshire; going to and from London, on divers engagements and visits to friends; until I have become exhausted. One of the hardest things in life is sight-seeing, entertainment and visiting; for, not seldom, the exhaustion begins to overbalance the delight; which certainly, in our case, English hospitality has constantly given us, during our four months sojourn in this land.

The tardiness of incoming Fees is what I anticipated; and, for some time, this will be a difficulty and a hindrance to our work. We have as yet no wide, stable basis of race-feeling to work upon; it has got to be created. Take the average black man in America, and you will find that he thinks that the creation of races was a superfluous act on the part of the Almighty; and that that superfluity is to be corrected in America.

I am very glad to get Mr. Kelly Miller's very able article; and with my two copies I am trying to draw attention to it in England. This morning I sent it for perusal to Sir Edward Russell, Editor of "Post;" formerly a member of Parliament: a man deeply interested in the dark races of the earth. He sent a Reporter to me this morning; and I am to see him on the morrow for a talk on the "Academy" and the "Negro Cause" in general. Some Negro gentlemen from Africa, are doing good work for the race in England. Two or three articles I have seen, are excellent.

The difference between the African and the West Indian black man, versus the American black, seems to be *this*—the *former*, works and writes for his RACE,—the *latter* for politics and an office.

I find very much interest in our cause in clerical and other circles in England, in the general, and in Liverpool, in particular. An English friend, resident in Paris, sends me an earnest request for full and frequent information concerning "*lynching*," after my arrival home. Yesterday I was talking with a noted and somewhat famous English clergyman. He told me he had visited the States several times; —had, indeed just returned home in July; and that he was deeply interested in our race. Speaking of lynching, he said "he could not see the end; for it appeared to him as tho the evil and savagery of it was increasing, and widening in its scope and extent." I remarked that few English people knew the true [illegible]ardness of the charge of rape. Much to my surprise he said— "O I found that out while in the States, in private conversations." Much to my surprise again, I found that he knew of the solicitation of white women!—and then the bitter vengeance of white men!

A still stranger utterance followed this. He remarked, "You have a tremendous fight before you, but one great difficulty in your way is the "white man's nigger." Some of your own men will betray and sell you. There is that Booker Washington, who constantly betrays your cause to please the South!!"

You ask me to give you a few topics for our annual meeting. I have been so overbusy that I have not had time to frame a theme, but I send you the following:

1. The intellectual loss of the Negro, and the mode of recuperation
2. The deficiencies of our race scholarship; and the remedy for the same.
3. The present value of Negro scholarship.
4. Have we any tokens, or the promise of literary eminence.
5. The duty of a ready and hearty recognition of genius in the race.
6. The need of a scholarly journal

We expect to sail hence on 13th and please God we shall likely reach Philadelphia on 23, 24, or 25th. The sea, thus far in October, has been quiet, and the arrivals of Steamers have been swift and early, on both of the ocean.

I shall be glad to reach home again, and once more to enter upon work. It is [illegible] little that I can do; but my appetite for labour and duty is as strong to day, as it was twenty years ago. It may be that I may still be permitted to tender a small contribution to the grand cause of freedom, righteousness, and the race, which Almighty God has put so distinctly before our contingent of the American people. With best regards to Mrs Cromwell, —in which my wife joins me, and with remembrance to Friends, I am truly and cordially yours.

Alex Crummell

1215–17th St Washington D.C.
9th Dec. 97.

Dear Mr Bruce.

I am dissatisfied with myself that I am *obliged* to be a tardy correspondent. The dissatisfaction is a selfish feeling, as I am forced to confess; for the tardiness serves to rob me of the letters I should otherwise be receiving from Albany and other places. But it can't be helped, i.e. so far as *I* am concerned. Bad eyes, over-occupation, age and constant weariness rob a man of his old-time nimbleness and elasticity.

Many thanks for "Star of Zion," and many more for pitching in to Fortune and Bishop Turner. These fellows are simply opportunists, and can't see a web before them. The white man has, in the past given us a brood of the "mixed multitude" and for a century past, but chiefly in the last generation since Emancipation, given them letters and culture; while the Negro, man woman has been a mere [blank space]

But a whole host of cultivated Negroes are soon coming on the stage of action; and *in your day* you will hear from them in no uncertain tones, vindicating the race. The indications abroad as well as here, in America, are encouraging. All we need is opportunity.

Are you coming to the annual meeting of the Academy? Why don't you come? It will be Holiday time; and surely you can spend two or three days away from Albany. Come! Bring with you a strong paper as a contribution. The Academy has done noble work in its one year of existence, albeit it has been limited to its *two* publications—Du Bois' and Miller's. But they have been sterling and telling ones, and have been noticed and recognized in Europe, Africa, West Indies, as well as in scholarly circles in America.

We need a few more thinking, race-devoted members. Can't you come prepared to nominate one or two; but they must be genuine fellows, Simon-pures.

I am working hard on two articles: one, a tract, which I will send you in a few days. Don't let anything from your pen escape my eyes. God bless you and your spouse. Mrs. C's regards.

Very truly Alex Crummell.

1215—17th St. Washington D.C.
15th December 97

Dear Mr Bruce.

I haven't the time to say all I desire anent your most valuable letter of 13th. When the "convenient season" arrives I will say what I have to say.

My special object in writing is to request that you will send a copy of "The Star of Zion" (which contained your article), to the following named person:—

Miss Impey.—
Street.
Somerset.
England.

Mark your article. When I see you I will tell you something more about it.

It is well you are not deceived by the Editor of the "Age." This is no new movement on his part. He has been at it the last four years. Last summer he thought he would shew his hand in that contemptible, jesuitical, and lying article in the "Sun," in which, without any justification, he drags in, the private and domestic affairs of individuals, into a public newspaper. Just think of the gross mendacity of the creature in calling my wife a mulatto. What if she were? Do I lose my race devotedness if I marry a mulatto, any more than the Prince of Wales loses his robust British feeling—his strong Anglicanism by marrying a Danish woman? But my wife is *not* a mulatto; and the fellow knows she is not. He thought he could make a point by his lie, in revenge for a telling thrust I gave him for his propagation of his absurd theory of "assimilation."

I hope to see you in August or February. With best regards to Mrs Bruce, and Mrs Crummell's kindest remembrances. Very truly yours

Alex Crummell.—

Sermons Revealing the Theological Basis of Crummell's Social Theories

"Keep Your Hand on the Plough"

Luke 9:62

The plough, in eastern countries, such as India and Persia and Egypt, is a very light and trifling thing. So small an instrument is it that a little boy can easily carry it. When used in ploughing it only scratches the surface of the earth. You can judge of its littleness by the command of God—"beat your ploughshares into swords." It was so small a thing that it could easily be turned into an instrument of warfare. In using such an instrument it was necessary, as is evident, to use care and caution: for it could easily be broken to pieces. A stone, the tangled root of a tree, a jagged old stump, if brought into contact with it, could easily destroy it. Hence the plough-boy or the farmer was unfitted for his calling, if he failed to attend to the business before him.

The Saviour seizes upon this illustration, easily understood by his surrounding hearers, to enjoin upon His followers, carefulness and assiduousness in their calling as Christians. "Devotedness and oneness of purpose," He seems to say, "are indispensable, in guiding a plough; so likewise, you, who are my disciples—if you would steadily pursue the high and holy calling of men of God: you must draw off your attention from vain and trifling things; and address yourselves, most scrupulously, to the great duties of the Christian life."

The primary reference of this passage was to ministers, but it may, without doubt, be regarded as addressed to disciples of every grade and calling. The declaration of the Saviour may be taken as impressing the following general doctrine: —"The man who professed the news of Jesus Christ, and yet yearns after the world and its objects, shows that he is unfit for heaven and its blessings." This statement it is my purpose this morning to illustrate and apply.

Transcribed from MS.C. 26. Untitled. The Schomburg Collection, New York Public Library, and printed with permission.

1. His unfitness may be seen in that his work is not well done; and this is discovered in *two* particulars, by observing the respective fields of a Christian's duty. For first he has his own soul to save and by this I mean that, with the gift of divine aid, God has also thrown personal responsibility upon every man to achieve his own salvation. "Work out your own salvation, etc." We are not saved passively, in a state of effortless inertia. We, ourselves, have got to ward our own spirits from the power of Satan to shield them from the poison of sin. And this is an arduous work: *not* the light easy effort which many suppose it to be.

And yet there are many who think it the easiest simplest of all things to save their souls. The earnest constant labour which is demanded, they can't understand. The ceaseless watchfulness which is required, they esteem fanatical. The announcement that the way is straight and the road narrow, they disbelieve as though it were a fiction. With false views of the character of God, with profound ignorance of their own nature and their depravity; they deem themselves capable of meeting all the moral responsibilities of life; of answering all the demands of the divine law; by the force of their intrinsic merit of securing the blessedness of the righteous.

But all this is a great error. There are tares to be rooted up from the human heart. Can this be done without labour? The soil of unbelief is to be broken up. Is this a playful pastime? There are passions to be repressed and uprooted, worldliness to be consumed, lust to be annihilated, gross desires to be quenched. Is all this an easy achievement? Can all this giant effort be performed without sweatful toil, without anxious watchfulness? Can a man—a disciple of Jesus, engage himself in all manner of temporal, carnal, godless concern, and be, at the same time wresting an immortal soul from the grasp of Satan, confident of presenting it, at the last, cleansed and sanctified, at the judgement?

Look at the man who, with his hand upon the plough, suffers himself to be constantly led off from his work. How irregular are his furrows! How devious his paths! Every stone throws him out of his course. The smallest tangled root or an old knotted stump could turn it over and thus, looking back, his hand still upon the plough; —everything goes wrong! His work is imperfectly accomplished; tares still remain in the ground; stones are scattered in every direction; and the field of effort which should have given evidence of his skill and faithfulness, indicates, in all directions, carelessness, sloth, inexcusable neglect!

So much then in regard of the individual himself. The man who has his hand upon the plough; but is always looking back, does the work of his own soul's salvation illy; and shows unfitness for the kingdom of heaven.

(2) How will this man do in the world; in the circles of family and society? For we do not live for ourselves only. To live for others is another part of a Christian vocation. He has, indeed, to save his own soul, but he was placed in the world, to subserve the interests and to secure the salvation of other souls.

How will such a man, his hand upon the plough, but his back upon his work, his eyes wandering anywhere and everywhere save upon the work which demands his sight and thoughtfulness; how, I ask, will he succeed, in the field of Christian labour? Will his furrows be straight? Will he make a good visible impression? Will the tracks he makes be such that all, in his own times, and the many who may follow him; shall be able to see and to know that a *man* has been there; that those are *his* footprints and that *that* is the line, clear, straight, well defined, which resulted from *his* constancy, his faithfulness, and his effort?

Such a supposition is an absurdity! Can a man be engaged in the follies and the [blank space] of society; engrossed with the cares and anxieties of the world; lost in the vortex of earthly pleasure; swallowed up in the perplexities which attend the selfish pursuit of fame or honour; crazy after popularity or mad in the race for wealth; and at the same time, be eaten up with a zeal for God's glory and the salvation of men? Why you might as well look "for thorns of grapes or figs from thistles."

That Christian man's work then is illy done alike with regard to his own soul, and the souls of his fellowmen, who while he has his hand upon the plough; has still cares and anxieties after the beggarly elements of the world; and is ever looking away from the work which his master has laid out before him.

And yet without doubt, precisely this *is* one of the hallucinations which has taken possession of numbers who call themselves disciples of Christ Jesus. You have but to observe the friendship, the alliance, the habits of multitudes; and you can see at a glance that while they have a name to live, they are dead. In one direction, a school of professors, gay and trifling as the vainest, amid scenes of frivolity in which the world delights: in another a whole class of disciples, the faithful and scrupulous devotees of fashion, and absorbed therein with passionate zeal and devotion. Here is a set who can't consort with the pious and sober: They make their closest friendships with the godless and the Christless; and there is a group calling themselves Christian, who can't abide the prayer room, or the visitation of the sick; they think they can serve God best at the ball-room or amid the exhilaration of the wine party! And these are the people upon whom the conversion of the world depends! These the people who are to

train little children for the glory of Christ Jesus! These the disciples who
are to illustrate the true genius of our holy religion and the spirit of Christ
Jesus! The trendy, the trifling, the fashionable! They, with their puny
hands and nerveless limbs to glorify God and to establish His Church!
Why a whole generation would sink down to ruin if their salvation
depended upon such fickle and characterless ciphers, in the work of God!

2 But, in the second place, notice another characteristic of this man, viz
that he has never made thorough consecration of himself to his work. For
what business has he to be looking back when his work is before him,
demanding all of his attention? A man's thought and interest are demanded *there* where his work lies; and nowhere else. It is the duty of every
man to find his proper sphere. His only appropriate position therein; and
there to keep himself; *there* to make his activities; *there* to put forth his
energies. It is this finding ones place and keeping it which *is* integrity,
character, honesty, and humility. No man can make a claim to either of
these qualities unless he is thus distinguished. A farmer, for instance, has
no business amid the gaiety of the city, when broad productive fields at
home call for active cultivation. A lawyer has no business amid proper
legitimate festivities; when his clients are at the bar; in the court room,
awaiting his defence and his pleadings. A clergyman has no business in a
wine party when the sick need the consolations of religion; and inquirers
are seeking the way of salvation.

It is every man's duty to attend to the duties and responsibilities which
are imposed upon him in the relations which he sustains. The duty of a
Christian man to subserve the spiritual interests of man; to advance the
glory of God; to live and to bear himself as a soldier of the Cross: —with a
mind raised above the world, looking into Jesus; pressing forward to the
mark. "His conversation is in heaven." Why then is he looking back? The
end which he is seeking is the crown of salvation. Why then does he busy
himself with a worthless muck-rake? He is reaching forth; he [illegible] to
the inexhaustible riches of Christ Jesus. How then can he be so greedy
after gain? He claims to be a soldier of the Cross. Why then is he battling
in the dark leagued bands of Satan? —Now take another view of the
situation. What is he looking back for? What interest has *he* in mere
worldliness? Of what importance are the schemes, and triflings of the
world to *him* if he is truly seeking the inheritance of the saints, the city, not
made with hands, in the upper heavens?

(a) Does he look back to see how the world is moving, or how it is
delighting itself? Is he so concerned in its doings that he must rest from

his duties, in order to acquaint himself with its follies and its ways? Then, in his case it is clear that he has a greater interest in the world, its purposes, and its plans, than a Christian has a right to have. (b) Or does he look back to see that his temporal concerns are not injured by his confession of the name of Christ Jesus. Or is he anxious to learn whether society will yet give him a place, since he has become a disciple of Jesus? Then he plainly shews that he has not fully obeyed the command to keep *first* the kingdom of God, believing that all other things will be added to him.

(c) Or suppose he looks back to see how far he may indulge in the fashions of the world, its foolish pastimes, and its trifling ways. Then he shows that he has not truly devoted himself to the cause of Christ Jesus; that he carries a traitorous heart, amid the hosts of glory and of grace.

A man in whom religion has made a fixed and abiding lodgement; who has turned with all his heart from sin, with all his heart has fastened himself, by faith, to the Cross of his Saviour, strives to rise above the world; and aims to live, by spiritual communion, with his God. Such a man will not allow himself to become entangled with the snares of the world; will not be hindered in his heaven-reaching course, by the weight of fleshly regards or sensual desires; but fastens himself upon God, upon the right, the true, the beautiful, the eternal and there stands invincible and uncorrupt. But in doing this does not every disciple set himself against everything opposed to his preference and his love?

To choose the greater is most certainly to reject the less. To reach forth for the solid and substantial realities of heaven implies, of necessity, the renunciation of the fleeting fading objects of earth. The election, as our portion, of the Lord our righteousness most surely signifies the rejection of the worthless.

Inconsistencies, opposites, contrarieties are irreconcilable. Light and darkness, are everlastingly distant. Truth and error, are made, by the fixed economy of God's moral government. Separate and adverse. You take up the whole category of moral distinctions: —right and wrong; vice and virtue; holiness and sin; purity and pollution; God and Mammon; and I declare to you on the highest authority in the universe that as they have ever in the eternal past been mutually alienate and repugnant, so *now*, so ever shall they be in the divine mind, and in God's moral government— perpetually, everlastingly distinct and antagonistic. For it is, in the very nature of things impossible to make evil good and good evil; to put darkness for light and vice versa, to make the bitter sweet and vice versa.—

Just the same distinctions should be lodged deeply in *your* moral consciousness, Christian friends, if you would obtain the abiding favour of God, and secure the inheritance of the just. Entire self-consecration is God's requirement. God will not tolerate a half surrender of your heart to him. He bears indeed with our weaknesses and infirmities; but He must have a whole heart. He will not accept a half devotion to him. And if He discovers the lingering of the desires after the world and its beggarly elements, the tardy reluctant flow of the affections; He will reject that man. When a man puts his hand to the plough, but, notwithstanding, is intent upon looking backward, anxious and solicitous concerning the pomps and vanities of a sinful world; all his profession of the faith of Christ Jesus is mere emptiness. He gives the clearest demonstration of utter unfitness for the kingdom of heaven.

Now my friends and brethren this reluctation of disciples, this spiritual dilly-dallying is most pernicious and destructive. It is one of the chief reasons why the ungodly turn with aversion from the Church and the Cross, and lose all faith in true religion. They see professed disciples with their hands upon the plough, but they themselves are constantly looking backward: —and the world is confused and bewildered; it stands in doubt whether truth is fiction, or fiction truth; it hesitates whether or not to believe whether the tremendous acts of the Christian *have* any reality in the conviction of Christians themselves.

For this is the mode of learning adopted by the world. It says, "If religion is as important as you allege it is, why do you not yourselves treat it as such? But, on the contrary you are just as much carried away by the objects which delight our souls, as we ourselves are." And they demand, "Is this consistent?" And the world reasons rightly. If it has no piety, it has common sense! There *is* a distinction between earthly, carnal desires, and affections, on the one hand; and spiritual and godly sentiments on the other. And, if the worldling, and the godless can see it; surely the children of the light should have sufficient discernment to discover this most manifest incongruity. If it lacks godliness, it knows a clear logic!

Let me be understood. I do not mean that Christianity divorces any of us disciples from our earthly relations and duties. I have no faith in that sort of piety which is so divine and unearthly, that it can't attend to the concerns and responsibilities of life. Christianity makes no such requirement on us. But this is what I say—if you are a Christian man, —if religion is the most important concern that can come home to the business and bosoms of men, —if it is the grandest object of thought that can be entertained by the human mind; treat it as such. Make it, in all things the highest. Be sincere. Do not belie your profession. Prove your manhood. Quit you like men. Vindicate the holy name by which you are called. Main[tain] your integrity, through Christianity, against all odds. Let God be the *first* in the whole category of thought.

3. But I proceed in the third place to say that this irresolution is likely to result in decided open apostasy. The statement of the text is a representation of an undecided man—a man going one way, and looking another; doubtful where he ought to go, no heart decided for either. The likelihood is he will go the wrong way. The irresolute man, i.e. in the things of God, perils his soul by putting his hand to the plough, his mind still wandering through all the mazes of earthly care. The ripest Christian is liable to fall.

> The Gray haired saint may fail at last
> The surest guide a wanderer prove
> Death only binds us fast
> To the bright throne of love

There is no absolute certainty this side of heaven. We shall be safe and assured only then, when we plant our feet upon the battlements of heaven; when we put on the celestial armour for the fields of glory above. But here on earth we are in a state of probation, and in such a state every man meets a point which is a crisis; we all come to a juncture which is decisive. The irresolution referred to in the text hastens such a contingency.

When the habit is formed of looking back upon the world, and of becoming absorbed in its cares and interests, the man may be looked upon as lost! This disposition is an unfailing sign of a falling, failing Christian.

Observe now the stream of tendency. Some men at the first in the work of Christianity work well. They are then in first flush of religious excitement. They are enjoying the exuberance of a new-born profession. But the sun waxes hot; the burden becomes heavy, and they begin to fail; they stagger in their course; they look behind, instead of before, and then at the last they leave the plough-share in the sod and rush headlong into vices and follies of the world. And the man who relapses falls, almost invariably into worse errors and grosser habits. He returns back to the world with urgency, the haste of a starveling. His temporary absence whets his appetite for iniquity. The last state of the man is worse, etc. He rushes into the vortex of sin, with an ardour of fire and soon becomes steeped in profligacy and corruption! The grossest scoffers, the most abandoned rakes, the vilest infidels, are your men who have fallen from grace—who have made shipwreck of the faith of Christ Jesus.

The condemnation of the recreant will be worse. He has upon him the guilt of broken vows. He has become faithless to the most awful trusts. He has shown himself a traitor, in the most solemn relations; a traitor to God and to man; a traitor, where to be a traitor, is to trample like an infidel upon the Cross, to do despite to the spirit of grace; to make shipwreck of the eternal interests of his fellow creatures.

His influence will be more pernicious and pestilential than [illegible]. Hundreds stand ready to seize upon *his* professed experience as a Christian, to confuse their own minds, to deride the truth of God and, to bring down wrath upon their souls. And they do use and exaggerate his experience to their own [illegible]. Youth who can hardly do a simple problem in Arithmetic [illegible] their thought from him and talk flippantly of themes which their fathers approach with fear and reverence! Gay young men speak slightingly of religion and the Bible, and will none of its ways! Men of years and maturity quote him as authority, in proof that there is no reality in religion; that the idea of God is a fiction! That the saints are a fable! that hell is a figment of the brain! that heaven is a creation of the imagination! And so they all, old men and boys, maidens and godless women, —all through his recreancy, rush into sin and haste on the road to ruin and to wrath. This is the influence of a slippery, vacillating professor, when he comes out a full-blown Apostate!

This subject we have been condemning suggests two or three considerations which deserve your notice and attention:—

First of all we are taught by the text the importance and the necessity of character in our Christian calling. And by character I mean something which inheres and is abiding. I mean a quality which, while it implies regulation, is, nevertheless deeper and more personal. For, desirable and commendable as it is, it does not follow that because a man is virtuous or a maiden chaste, that therefore they have character. What I mean by character is, the knowledge in their depth and fulness, of the Christian principles which you profess; with the will, both punctual and earnest, to act from those principles; to be rooted and grounded in the truth; and to live in the truth and for it, deriving all your vital power from its undying substance. To know where you are, and what you are, amid all the wonders and mysteries of this grand spiritual life of ours, under God's moral rule; not to be like the plain surface of a sheet of paper, meaningless and inexpressive; not like the vane upon the steeple top, shifting and unstable; but to be possessed of abiding principles and eternal truth: —to know God, and therein to know yourselves; know what you are, and for what you are living, and what you intend to do, in this world, for God and man: —men of truth, men of principle; upright, downright, with regard to every question of morals and every requirement of Godliness:—

—Men through grace "able to comprehend with all saints, what is the breadth, strength, and depth and height; and to know the love of Christ Jesus which passeth knowledge, that ye might be filled with all the fullness of God! This is what I mean by character.

And therefore, in the name of God, I beseech you take your stand firmly for your maker. Convince yourselves fully of the principles you have professed. Reject and drive out all the rootlets of vacillation from your moral constitution. Aim after a deep and vital consciousness of the noble truths of our blessed religion, which are spirit and which are life:

> Be strong;—be worthy of the grace
> Of God, and fill your destined place
> Above by force of [purpose] high
> Uplifted to the purest sky
> Of undisturbed humanity

2nd. To the demand for character I join the exhortation to *faithfulness in your Christian profession.* You have begun the career of holiness; do not tire. Your hand is upon the plough; don't look back! Difficulties and trials you will most surely meet; but not nigh so many, not nigh so disastrous as sin is ever breeding, in time and through eternity! Remember your obligation to your Lord and Saviour; and stand bravely by them. Forget not the urgency of His most magnificent cause. Forget not the sensualist, the blasphemer, the inebriate, the infidel, ever subverting the foundations of truth and virtue, and dishonoring the Lord who died for them! Amid the thickness of God's great battle, beware of turning your back or throwing down your arms. Stand up for Jesus! "resisting unto blood, striving against sin!"

3rd. Finally, remember the reward of Christ Jesus's faithful soldiers and servants, which lies beyond, and which is now awaiting you. Even now, if you have reached the delectable hills, if you have tasted "how sweet it is to love the Lord"—Even now you may catch glimpses of the promised land. O let the sweetness of its oftimes coming airs, and the sunshine of its gleaming skies subdue you to patience, to endurance, to perseverance.

The time is but short. Press on Christian pilgrims. Angels attend you in your labours. Jesus smiles upon you. The Holy Spirit stands ever ready to strengthen and refresh you. And God the Father awaits to receive and welcome you. Prove faithful; and at the end thou shalt receive a crown of life.

"The Day of Doom"

Matthew 24:30

This verse and chapter is one of those strong trumpet calls of our Saviour; which He at times delivered, which roused men from the death-like slumber of carelessness, and filled them with astonishment and awe. Doubtless you remember some two or three of the Saviour's discoveries in which His burning wrath, and deep dislike of sin show themselves; and wherein we may also see that if He *was* the "Lamb of God," that He was also the "Lion of the Tribe of Judah." His general wont was mildness, gentleness, love; but at times we see that most awful thing—"the wrath of the Lamb." When He drove the money-changers from the Temple; when He turned upon a crowd of Jews, and frowned upon them; when He looked the Pharisees and Saduccees seeking a sign, in the face, and called them hypocrites, and an adulterous generation, and refused them any sign, save the sign of Jonah the prophet; when He pronounced those awful woes upon the Scribes and Pharisees and Lawyers; and denounced [chorazin] down to hell; and when in this and the following chapter He describes the awful scenes of the judgement; —in all these cases He gives us clear and significant evidence that the eternal throne of the Messiah, has Justice and Retribution, as its pillars, as well as Love and Mercy!

The meaning and purpose of our Saviour's discourse in this twenty-fourth chapter cannot be mistaken; it points to the Judgement. I know it has a double meaning and that it refers also to the destruction of Jerusalem. But its *chief,* its main, its most prominent pointing is to the coming of the Son of Man, in awful pomp and power, to the judgement of men. And though this is a painful theme for all men, for we all are sinners, yet we ought, at times, to enter fully into it and *think!* We all have to die. We all

---

Transcribed from MS.C. 234. Untitled Sermon. Schomburg Collection, New York Public Library, and printed with permission.

have to go to judgement; we all have to be tried at God's awful bar. Why hide our eyes from awful things which we must face? Why not be wise and look them fully in the face; and ponder them?

There are three suggestions clearly presented in this text which you will notice. (1) The *fact* that He shall come again (2) That the *manner* in which He will come will be with power and glory; and (3) That the *end* for which He will come will be to judge the quick and the dead; the *fact,* the *manner,* the *end* of Christ Jesus's second coming. In the consideration of so solemn and so personal a theme as this, let us pray God to make us thoughtful for our soul's salvation; and to give us grace to be prepared for the awful day of the Son of Man's second coming.

First of all, let us consider the *fact* that Christ Jesus will come again. This you know is an assertion frequently made in Scripture, a declaration that may be read on almost every page of revelation. Not only is it spoken of and affirmed by our Saviour and His Apostles; but it is one of those facts connected with the life of Jesus, which stand out with peculiar prominence even among the prophecies. And without doubt the *fact* that Christ Jesus's coming to earth for judgement is prophesied; —that it was frequently spoken of and declared by our Saviour, Himself; —that it is repeated frequently by His Apostles; is *sufficient* for all persons here. Believing in the word of God, bowing with reverence to the utterances of heaven, we have no perplexities nor doubts; and we feel satisfied of the fact that there is yet to burst on this world a fact of stupendous power, a panorama of wondrous might and glory; in which shall be involved the decision and the issue of all human hopes and destinies! We believe in this fact of Scripture that the Lord Jesus Christ "shall come again in the clouds of Heaven with power and great glory."

But a fact always becomes more distinctly a fact to the human mind, when the reasons which give it verity and reality are set distinctly before us. Now some of the facts of Scripture are declarations, without any reasons given us whatever; yet they are to be believed. But it has pleased God to give us the *reasons* for certain other of the great truths of Scripture; and, herein, we are privileged to have a deeper assurance here of what God certifies to us, *before* the greater evidences which shall be revealed in the Kingdom of grace and glory above. The Doctrine of Christ Jesus's second coming is one of those.

There is a passage in I Corinthians which bears upon this point.

> I Cor. iv.5. Therefore judge nothing before the time, until the Lord come, who both will bring to light the hidden things of darkness, and will make manifest the counsels of the heart; and then shall every man have praise of God

Now this passage is evidently based upon a fact which is apparent to all, that is that the world is in a distracted state; that wrong and error prevail; that sin maintains an ascendancy; and that justice and right are loose and relaxed in their hold upon the consciences of men. For we have but to open our eyes and we cannot but see that "the dark places of the earth are filled with the habitations of cruelty." Take even civilized society; take the communities that are called Christian; and even amid such scenes and associations we see, most clearly, the confused, misshapen, and painful elements which compose human society. There is the orphan robbed of his rights; the widow despoiled of her inheritance and driven out to the cold charities of a heartless world; the ingenuous youth deceived and ruined at the very period of highest hopes and his most reliable expectations; the honest and successful citizen, just on the eve of retiring with wealth and affluence, suddenly defrauded by villainy, and sent down to his grave in want and poverty; the tender maiden seduced and beguiled by treachery, and made the mark of shame and the object of infamy; and honest men and innocent women persecuted, belied and traduced by foul slander, until at last, all reputation gone, they seek the shades of death, and the covering of the grave, as the protection of a dear mother to her weary-worn and heartbroken children!

Now these are some, a few, of the numerous cases of "wrong and outrage with which earth is filled," and which are never settled in *this* world. I have not spoken of the countless masses cruelly wronged and murdered by slavery, —mothers robbed of their children; children sold from their parents; of all the devastations of war; of the many thousand tender, youthful hearts bruised and broken by seduction. I have spoken of what we see so common in civil society; and of the fact that they live, they suffer, and they die without redress!

And now the question arises—"Does not human nature require *satisfaction,* mind I do not say *revenge:—satisfaction,* for all this wrong?" Are you contented that all this misery should be inflicted upon wretched humanity, and that there should be no retribution? Can you quietly sit or read and see the wrongs and evils of the world and not require redress?[1] Does not your soul rise up with mine, aye and with every man who has a soul; and does not the fervent utterance go up to Heaven "How long, O Lord, how long!" *Shall* crime and cruelty always have sway? Shall the groans of nature forever go unheard, of Thee? Wilt Thou not come with

---

[1]Here, for instance we have, just now the case of Juda [illegible] before us, with the murder, the treachery, and lust of incarnate fiends!

power? Wilt Thou not stretch forth Thy right arm? Wilt Thou not come forth, Thou that sittest between the cherubim, and shew Thyself?

Surely these are natural desires. Surely these are but native aspirations, and holy expectations. There *is* a requirement in our nature—the nature given us by God—that the evils of the world should yet be settled by Divine justice! But the evils of the world *are not* settled in the world, and yet still our moral nature makes the requirement for justice; and the pale and troubled shades of the mighty millions who have gone down to the grave, unredressed; aye the whole creation; and the angels on high; and the cross of Christ Jesus; and the broken moral Law; and the very attributes of God Himself, cry out, to the Eternal Throne—Justice! Justice! O God. And God meets and satisfies that demand and requirement of the universe, which His own moral economy has created; and "He has appointed a day in which He will judge the world in righteousness by that man whom He hath ordained." By *that man* [is meant] the Lord Jesus, who shall [words left out] and that day is the day when the foul slanderer, who has crushed the heart of the maiden shall be exposed, and she shall stand up pure before all men; when the villainy which ruined and destroyed the orphan and the widow, shall be avenged; and the rich bad man shall have his true portion meted out to him in shades and darkness; when the cruel bondage which tore husband from wife, and broke the hearts of tender children, shall be condemned and the heartless slavetrader shall have as *his* portion the grinding chains and the bitter slavery of eternal wrath; aye that is the day when all the wrong, and darkness, and injustice of man shall be exposed; and the innocent shall be cleared; and quietly brought out to the open gaze of the universe; and that which is hidden shall be made light; and the darkness and doubt and confusion which sin has bred so many thousand years; shall be stripped of their chaotic mysteriousness, in the perfect light of *Him* who "shall come in the clouds of heaven with power and great glory."

Second: We have shewn the *fact* of Christ Jesus second coming, and given the reasons which seem to demand His august appearance, once more among men, here on earth; and now we are to consider the simple but grand description which is with us in God's word, of the *manner* of His coming. "They shall see the Son of Man coming in the clouds with power and great glory."

This is the mode in which the Son of Man shall manifest Himself to the sight of man at His second coming: and when we think of the awful majesty of the Lord Jesus, or look up to the fleecy clouds, which daily float ✓ over our heads, in such gorgeous masses; we cannot do otherwise than wonder at the manner of this His second appearing. But brethren we may verily believe in the awful prediction, singular as it may seem to us; for it is a literal description of the grand coming of the Lord. For here, you should remember, is no fanciful description, no imaginative conceit; it is the revelation of a wondrous fact. We are to have no semblance of the Lord, but the Lord Himself. The glorious body of the Lord, visible to human eyes; the corporeal presence of the Redeemer, in our human form, *that* is the sight which is to meet our gaze, of a sudden, "in the twinkling of an eye," on the "glorious appearance of the Lord Jesus" to Judgement. Yes that same Jesus who was taken up into heaven, shall soon come in like manner, as He was seen to go up into heaven. It is not the power only, or only the brightness, or the glory, or the magnificence of the Redeemer that we shall see, but it is Himself! That very same mild, marred visage, radiant with divinity, which the Jews looked upon in the streets of Jerusalem, but could not recognize as their Messiah, through spiritual blindness; that same visage, that same form, that same body will come again, in glory. "Behold He cometh in clouds, and every eye shall see Him and they also which pierced Him."

Not less veritable and worthy to be believed is the fact that He shall come in the clouds. Not in some triumphal car; not in some stately chariot; but He shall come in the clouds of heaven. Those beautiful fleecy masses, which look like angel wings at times; which now are white and etherial in appearance, which in the morn often glide through the majestic heavens, so clear, pellucid and transparent; and at clear noon shine with such bright and burning lustre; and again at sunset change in all their colors, green, blue, scarlet, golden—these form the splendid and gorgeous vehicle on which the Son of Man chooses to shew Himself to the eyes of men, on the day of doom. And fit and meet is the form of manifestation; the clouds of heaven, the creation of Him who "made all things, and without whom was not anything that was made;" far more become His glorious coming than any device of art, or any skill of genius. Says the Psalmist of Jehovah Jesus "Thou comest thyself with light as with a garment; who maketh the clouds His chariot who walketh upon the wings of the wind." St John in his wondrous vision in Patmos saw the Lord of glory, and he says He was clothed with a cloud, and both he and the Psalmist describe His throne in the same manner: "He bound the heavens and came down . . . He made darkness His secret place. His pavillion round about Him were dark waters and thick clouds of the skies." He went up into heaven in a cloud; while the men of Israel stood looking up at the bright and wondrous vision, with ardent gaze and astonished minds; in like manner shall He come again in the clouds of heaven to judge the quick and the dead.

Ah but how different will be the signs of His coming, *then,* compared with His former advent to Earth. He came helpless; an infant, humble in condition; without signs of power or authority. Then He will come with every insignia of Divine Royalty and kingly might. The mighty hosts of heaven shall attend Him in state. The elements of heaven shall be stirred with unusual power; and the winds and the waves of Earth shall send for the loud report of His coming. "There shall be signs in the sun and in the moon and in the stars: —the sea and the waves roaring: —the powers of heaven shall be shaken." Aye the Lord Himself shall descend with a shout; and at the utterance of that Almighty voice the sounding of the trumpet of God, the Earth and the sea shall give up their dead; and all the masses of the living will come to Judgement!

Thirdly THIS is the *end* and the object of our Saviour's second coming: He comes to judgement; He comes to call men to account for the deeds done in the flesh; He comes to render to every man according to what he has done during the period of his earthly test and trial. He comes in the clouds of Heaven, with power and great glory to summon men to judgement!

Now I have already shewn, in the commencement of this discourse that there is a requirement in our moral constitution, for such an event as the judgement; and hence, I have no need to enlarge upon this point; but rather have to fasten our minds upon the *Judgement* its *nature, character* and *peculiarities.* The judgement is an event unlike anything that has ever occurred in all the past eternities of our God; which never has the world witnessed in all her histories; which never after this event shall occur again through all eternity. The Judgement is the assemblage of the quick and the dead, on the day of the Son of Man's appearing; the gathering together of all the sons of man that ever lived, at the judgement bar of God. "I saw the dead" says St John, in prophetic vision, "I saw the dead great and small, stand before God; and the books were opened . . . and the sea gave up the dead which were in it; and death and hell delivered up the dead which were in them; and they were judged every man according to their works."

The judgement is that appointed assemblage of men, at which, in the presence of the universe every man will have to render an account of the thoughts, deeds, and words of his mortal life. There is to be an unfolding there of all the secrets of the heart, all the hidden purposes of the soul, all the concealed designs of the mind, of which the world was not aware; and also of all those outward deeds and those shameful passionate words, which have done harm to man and dishonored God. There is to be a revelation there of the *entire* of the inner life of every mortal man that ever breathed. Memory then will be called upon to do a work which it never did before; for in a *moment* it must perforce reveal, in every individual, the guilty details of thought and word and deed of a whole life time. Ah there can be no holdings back; no concealments; no suppressions of the truth on that day, and in that presence, for beside the quick action of conscience, forcing the sinner to his dread confessions, there is the dread and awful book of God, open before the dense masses of the Judgement, in which the recording Angel has inscribed all the sad details of a sinful life.

The judgement is that awful event at which God intends to mete out to every man the full rewards for all his deeds and life, in just and exact measure, according as they were good or evil, and as they are clothed and covered by the broad mantle of the Lord Jesus, or stand up naked and exposed, in their sin, to the keen awful eyes of the Judge. Aye brethren, the hour is coming, and now is when the dead shall hear the voice of the Son of Man:— "The hour is coming in which all that are in their graves shall hear His voice, and shall come forth; they that have done good unto the resurrection of life, and they that have done evil unto the resurrection of damnation."

And when that awful day arrives then shall be witnessed the fear and the terror and the weakness of those [illegible] men who now neither care for man nor yet fear God. But they shall fear *Him,* and while little children and tender youth and weak and fragile women, trusting in Christ Jesus, shall stand unmoved amid the crashing of worlds; *their* lips shall be blanched and their knees smite together in fear and quakings; and there shall take place that scene of mortal terror and anguish which St John saw by prophetic vision (See Rev. vi:12–17) But brethren, no mountains, no rocks, no scheming, no art, no devices, shall be able, on that day, to hide us from that eye, which at one glance, sweeps the universe; or to aid us in an escape from the judgement. We shall all have to be there! and what an assemblage will it not be of countless numbers, and of varied nations. They shall come from every quarter of the globe; and shall be gathered in from all periods of time. Patriarchs and Priests and Prophets shall be there; Kings and Caliphs and Emperors and Czars and Sultans and mighty Dukes; and all powerful and destructive Conquerors shall come up on that awful summons. Men of all characters shall be there. There shall stand the proud man, who never in all his life could learn that pride was folly as well [as] sin, ungodliness, and ruin. The dead Tyrants of the world shall be there, stript of all their power; weak and helpless; fearfully awaiting their doom. The impure and corrupt shall be there; covered with all their filth and vileness. Thieves and Murderers and Adulterors and Fornicators, shall be assembled at that awful gathering. The deceitful, the lying, the slanderous men and women, whose trade was mischief on this earth, and who dealt in the soul-murder of their neighbors; they too shall stand up there before the open eye of the universe and see the awful presence of God. Unfaithful and wicked ministers shall be there; hypocritical professors, self-seeking and mischievous Demagogues, unjust shameless and corrupt judges too; men who loved interest more than right, and favor more than justice, shall stand, face to face, before that stern and inflexible Judge who then shall take justice into His own hand, and decide the fate of the universe!

Yes all men and all women, all kinds of characters, all sorts of moral agents shall be there, to judgement. Aye, and YOU shall be there my Hearers; ye who are living without God, and without hope in the world—you shall be there to give [illegible] your account; and if you will persist in sin, and will not trust in your Saviour; you shall be there for woe and wrath and eternal judgement. For that will be the great day of decision and there will be none, never more afterward. And every bad man and every wicked woman that ever lived, and who then is unwashed by the blood of Jesus shall hear the certain doom—"Depart from me ye accursed into everlasting fire, prepared for the Devil and his angels," and those other terrible words "He that is [illegible] let him be [illegible] filthy hell." "The whole world then," says one of the Fathers, "shall groan when the judge gives his sentence; tribe and tribe shall knock their sides together; and through the naked breasts of the most mighty Kings, you shall see their hearts beat with fearful tremblings."

And what will you do fellow sinner—brother man! for whom Christ Jesus died—what will you do on that dread awful *dies,* if you have no Saviour, and stand up at the judgement trusting in yourself. The Lord Jesus will then be no longer Mediator, but *Judge,* wedded to the Law; no longer the Lord of Mercy, but the Dispensor of Justice; Your Redeemer *now,* he will *then* be your accuser, and that mildness, tenderness, supplication to sinners, which he uttered on earth, and His tears will all be turned to rigidity and inflexibility. O sinful man. O guilty woman. O wayward godless youth; what will you do before *such* a Judge, at such an awful time!

> That day of wrath that dreadful day
> When heaven and earth shall pass away!
> What power shall be the sinner's stay?
> How shall he meet that dreadful day?
>
> When shrivelling like a parched scroll
> The flaming heavens together roll;
> When louder yet, and yet more dread
> Swells the high trump that wakes the dead
>
> O on that day, that wrathful day,
> When man to judgement wakes from clay,
> Be *thou* the trembling sinner's stay
> Though heaven and earth shall pass away

But besides the wicked and ungodly, in their various groups, there will be also the glorious groups, glittering ranks of the saints, washed by the blood of Jesus, and sanctified by the power of the Holy Ghost, —waiting, with unfailing confidence, and lively Hope, the joyous utterance of their Judge, which shall consummate their everlasting bliss. In that blessed company of the Faithful, shall be all the righteous of the past: righteous Abel shall be there; Father Abraham, and all the holy Patriarchs; zealous prophets like Elijah and Ezekial. The glorious company of the Apostles; the goodly fellowship of the Prophets; the noble army of Martyrs shall all be there. There too shall be the noble presence of godly Reformers, the adventurous missionaries of modern times; and all the pious and godly, who in more humble spheres have blessed mankind, and honored the name of the Lord Jesus. They shall all be there. And you too, beloved friends, who are in Jesus, you shall be there; and it will be your unspeakable delight to hear from the lips of your glorified Redeemer the welcome words—"Come ye blessed of my Father, inherit the Kingdom prepared for you from the foundation of the World!"

"The Episcopal Church in Liberia: On Laying the Corner Stone at St. Andrew's"

FRIENDS and Fellow Christians.

The act in which we have just engaged, shows most significantly that the conviction is held here, that there is both need of, and room for, the Episcopal Church in Bassa County.

I congratulate my brethren, both clerical and lay, that they have seized upon such a sound conviction; and that, amid many difficulties, they have clung to it for several years.

And now, without any further remarks, I proceed, at once, to vindicate the position assumed by my brethren of St. Andrew's Church, in this town. I shall not, however, limit my remarks to this particular locality. What is desirable for the people of Grand Bassa, is equally desirable for any other section of Liberia. We are one people in every quarter of this country: one in training; alike in habits and acquirements; equal in necessities, yearnings, and aspirations. If then, the Episcopal Church is a needed thing here; if she does indeed supply a vacant place, and meet a spiritual want, in this section of the country; then I infer that this Church is a good for the whole land.

My theme then is this, viz: THAT THERE IS A PLACE FOR THE EPISCO-PAL CHURCH, IN LIBERIA. I shall attempt to show that the Doctrine, Discipline, and Polity of the Episcopal Church, are special needs of the people of Liberia; that there is a peculiar work for souls, in this country, for which the Episcopal Ritual and Regimen, are specially fitted.

From Alex. Crummell, *Place for the Episcopal Church in Liberia: An Address Delivered at the Laying of the Corner Stone, of St. Andrew's Church, Buchanan, Bassa County, Liberia, West Africa, on the 24th February, 1870 by the Rev. Alex. Crummell, B. A., Rector of St. Peter's Church, Caldwell, Missionary of the Prot. Epis. Ch. U.S.A.* (Preston: H. Oakey, Caxton House, Fishergate, 1870).

1st. With reference to DOCTRINE. I fall back upon Scripture in the assertion that the presentation and enforcement of Doctrinal Truth, is a matter of the greatest moment, in the cure of souls. Dogma, heaven-descended, life-giving, soul-mastering, dogma, is the pith and marrow of the Gospel. This is most manifest in the preaching of our Lord. Almost every statement He made, well-nigh every utterance, is the embodying and setting forth of a great, cardinal truth. The Apostles followed implicitly in the clear track set before them by their Master. In their sermons and epistles, they dwelt, almost exclusively, upon a few distinct and prominent truths of the Gospel. In the Acts of the Apostles, we see how they went from place to place, holding up, repeating, and continually enforcing, some of these prime and fundamental principles of the Holy Faith. Hence St. Paul's emphatic charge—"Take heed unto the Doctrine." 1 Tim. iv.16.

Now what I claim for the Episcopal Church is, that she obeys this Apostolic injunction. The whole arterial system of the Gospel is made a matter of constant sight and observation in this Church. Such is its rule and practice, that no man can attend one single service of this Church, without having brought under his notice, the entire group of fundamental Scriptural Truth. Just run along the line of living, saving Gospel Doctrine, and mark these primal ideas of the faith: The Incarnation of our Lord; the Atonement; Justification by Faith; the Doctrine of the Holy Spirit; Sanctification; the Intercession of the Redeemer; the Resurrection of the Body; Everlasting Life. Each of these grand truths is dearer to the heart of a believer, than the life blood which fills his veins. And yet how seldom, in many systems, is the distinct presentation of them to the people! How infrequent the compliance with the Apostle's command!

Just the reverse in the Episcopal Church. Here we cannot escape this duty. I give you an illustration: —We have just had the Christmas season; and of necessity, the attention of our people was directed to the Incarnation of our blessed Lord. Ere long we shall fall upon the Lent Season, and Good Friday; and then all the great truths which pertain to the vicarious suffering of our Lord, and the great Atonement of the Cross, are brought in the most solemn and striking manner, to the sight and hearts of our people. Then Easter-tide with its light, its lustre, and its glories comes upon us; and the great doctrine of the Resurrection is preached, in divers ways, to our congregations, from desk, and pulpit, and the Holy Table. A few weeks afterwards, we come to Pentecost; and we are then reminded of the abiding presence of the Holy Spirit, in the Church of God, and crave his gracious presence, and seek his seven-fold gifts upon us. And then, the several fasts and feasts of a half year's cycle culminate in the presentation of the Doctrine of the Holy Trinity!

Thus, and in this manner, Holy Doctrine is the very warp and woof of our system. Truth, divine, soul-saving TRUTH is its most pervasive element. Whether it be that we humble ourselves in lowly confessions, or repeat the ancient creeds, or unite in the utterance of pathetic litanies, or pour out before the throne the prayers of ages, or lift up our voices in sacred anthems, or send up to heaven the praise of accordant glorias, or join in, on earth, with the hallelujahs of angels; TRUTH, not mere sentiments, however holy, not mere feeling, however deep and sacred, —but the Truth of GOD, is the animating, the vitalizing element of all our sacred services.

2nd. Another special work to which the Episcopal Church, in this country, seems called, is to MAGNIFY GOD'S WORD. And this, without doubt, is a most important duty, and a most solemn trust. The Church is the conservator of the Word. To her is committed the Oracles. She is to preserve and guard them; to honour and to magnify them, in doing this, she favours God. And them that honour Him, He will honour; and they that despise Him, shall be lightly esteemed, 1 Sam. 2, 30.

But brethren, and friends, the Word of God is, I fear, not unfrequently dishonoured, and neglected, even by some who venture to proclaim it.

When men will get up before congregations, to preach God's Word, who do not know it; when they boast, as though it were a thing of pride, that they cannot read it; when they give out, as texts of Scripture, words which are *not* Scripture; when they set in opposition, the Spirit, which they claim to have, as making unnecessary, the Holy Word, which that same Spirit has given, as His guide to the Church; what is this, I ask, but to dishonour God's Word? And it is thus dishonoured in the land, especially with the rising generation. I know many a case, where the well-educated and lettered youth of the land, are turning away with dislike from pulpits, where ignorance and stupidity, and blundering Scripture readings, are thus enshrined, and thus exalted.

But further, another evil result of this state of things is, that the Scriptures are but little read in our Churches. Men will not do willingly and with alacrity, that which is a difficulty, and a burden. When to read a chapter becomes as great a trial as to tread a thornbush, or to wear a blister, what wonder if men at length, choose to give up the reading of it altogether? Contemplate the continuance of this evil, and in what can it result, save in the ultimate banishment of the Holy Scriptures from the

Churches; and the setting up of the empty conceits, or the fantastic imaginations of passionate minds, as the rule of life, or as the Word of God; and the fanatical claim of direct, divine, personal inspiration, in the place of the sacred oracles?

Now just here is place for the Episcopal Church in this land. Here is room for a special work of this Church, among the religious bodies of the country.

The Bible is at the foundation of our whole system. The Prayer Book is not only the reproduction of Scripture, on its every page, nay, almost in every sentence, but it is saturated, if I may so express myself, with the very spirit of the Bible, and expresses the mind of the Spirit.

And it is the *whole* Bible, and not a portion of it, which receives the reverent regards of this Church, and is read constantly at her altars.

And herein we differ from some Christian societies. They declare, at times, in words, and if not in action, that the *New* Testament is the religion of Christians. The dictum of *this* Church is, that "the Bible is the religion of Christians." We believe that "*all* Scripture is given by inspiration of God," 2 Tim. 3, 16; and we cannot chose a portion of it only "for instruction in righteousness," and reject the rest.

It is the cleaving to the *whole* Bible, as the revelation of the mind of God, which accounts for very many peculiarities of our rites, worship, and services. The objection, that many of these things are not found in the New Testament, is no objection to us. We believe that *some* things, under the Old Covenant, were *not* transitory; and that *such* things were settled, once and for all time, —that they reach over to this, the New Covenant; that they need no repetition from the lips of the Saviour, nor from the pens of the Apostles. They were once settled and established, as the mind and will of God, and hence they are ours, as well as the Jews', and we feel safe and satisfied under their guidance and direction; for, as I have said, they express God's will, His purpose, and His holy choice. We *keep the Christian Sabbath*. We seek no specific command in the New Testament for this observance. We know that it was God's will of old, that one day out of seven, should be kept holy, as a day of rest. It matters not to us, where we find the expression of that will. Having received it, we honour it, and strive to obey it. We honour it as one of the sacred "proprieties" of Scripture, which have an abiding fitness and authority. We *maintain a Liturgical form of worship*. We seek no specific command in the New Testament, for this practice. We find that it was, without doubt, God's will of old, that His chosen people should worship him by the means of a responsive, precomposed service. This we take to be one of the things settled under the Old Covenant, as the divine choice. And we honour God's will in this matter, and adjust our system in accordance with it. Who can go wrong in abiding by a preference of the Almighty? Here, moreover, is another of the divine "proprieties," which we cannot but respect and perpetuate. Indeed, it is one of the *everlasting* "proprieties." Liturgical, that is, responsive worship, is to be the worship of eternity! Why should we concern ourselves about the jests which are aimed at a "form of worship"; or the sneers, which we often hear, against our "reading prayers out of a book?" We walk herein in the steps of our fathers; and our lot, in this matter is the same with "Cherubim and Seraphim, and all the glorious company of heaven," chanting for ever, the same eternal anthems, and endless hallelujahs, around the throne of the Lamb!

Another of these things which we take to be settled, by the Old Testament, for all times, *is the fact of a difference and disparity of offices, and prerogatives in the Ministry.* And therefore, without looking for any specific command, as the olden Church had its three orders, High Priest, Priest, and Levite; so we in the Church of Christ, have Bishops, Priests, and Deacons, as the several orders of our Ministry. This we maintain is in thorough accordance with scriptural analogy, and agreeable to the mind of God.

And still another of these things once settled by the will of God, is *the privilege of children to receive the seal of the covenant, to be incorporated as members of the Church of God.* And hence it is a matter of indifference to us that we find no specific command for the baptism of children. The great organic *principle* in this matter, was indicated centuries ago by the Almighty, in former covenants; and this is, without doubt, of far more importance, than specific rules. We have, besides, both the terms and the acts of the Abrahamic Covenant, and we have also the singular repetition of it, in the gracious words of St. Peter, —"The promise is to you and your children." Acts 2, 39.

In some other systems these divine "proprieties," with the great truths they clothe and symbolize, have been broken down, as though they did not show forth the mind of God; as though they were only fantastic conceits of Moses's brain, or, the fanciful notions of Aaron, and his successors.

People who read only a *third* of their Bibles; people who hold the Old Testament, as merely an old and useless legend, thus treat the divine mind as though it were an ephemeral mind. What wonder that they always live in a state of moral confusion, that they can grasp but petty rules, but cannot comprehend large and lasting principles, that their constant cry should be—"Where, in the New Testament, do you meet with this thing, or find the other?"

The truth expressed in the following paragraph, cannot be too often pondered:—"That the Bible is one whole, steadily progressing and growing from the beginning to the end—the New Testament resting upon and being the perfection of the Old, the Old pointing forward to and finding its prophecies fulfilled in the New—is one of the great foundation truths for which the Church must contend. It is also one of those truths which must be fully appreciated before we can enter into any proper understanding of God's plan, or any right and reasonable study of his word."—*The New Englander*. Most pregnant too, are the words of Dean Goulbourn, when he insists "on the necessity of believing the Old as well as New Testament, our Lord constantly quoting "the former with the words—'it is written,' as positively conclusive."

Now we hold the *whole* Bible as the fundamental law of our religion, as the revelation of the mind of God. We regard the things we have referred to, as divine arrangements, based upon divine ideas; not unworthy of the august mind of Deity, and fully deserving the unchanged reverence of all ages. Some of them, as you may see, show God's idea of the fitness of things. Some of them are "everlasting proprieties," dropped from heaven, for a time, under the Old Covenant, for the uses and training of men, but everlastingly maintained by holy angels—"amid the sanctities of heaven."

Now, if these principles are correct, then the Episcopal Church has a specific and a mighty work to do in this country, in maintaining the honour and authority of God's Holy Word full and entire.

This, moreover, is in every way, a matter of the deepest importance. There is every probability that, as Christianity pushes its conquests among the heathen, we shall have re-produced here, that, which, if I mistake not in my historical reading, was the characteristic of the early African Church: namely, warm, emotional, and impulsive energy, which was at once, both its failing, and its virtue. Every indication of religious sentiment in our race, the world over, shows this. No one can fail to see it here in Liberia. Such a race-peculiarity, needs a strong corrective, or, otherwise, the flame of religious life, however intense for a time, will blaze with unhealthy violence, or else "soon burn itself out," and then the ultimate result must surely be, heretical decline again, or a new outburst of revived heathenism.

The antidote to such a danger is a divine one. The corrective to such a tendency is the Bible; and it is inwrought, as an integral and vital element, in all our church life. In the polity of this Church we commence one system, in Africa, as we purpose, by law and custom, to have it continued for aye. As "Moses of old time, had, in every city, them that preach him, being read in the Synagogues every Sabbath day" Acts 15, 21; so the Holy Scriptures, in larger portions than among any other Christians, are required to be read to our congregations. At every service, you are sure to hear, in equal portions, God's Word read, as well from the Old, as the New Testament. We bow down at the utterances of the Holy Spirit, with equal reverence, whether from the pen of Moses and the Prophets, or from the lips of Apostles and Evangelists.

3rd. Another use of the Episcopal Church in this country, is the call for, and the MAINTENANCE OF THEOLOGICAL KNOWLEDGE, AS A REQUIRE-MENT FOR THE MINISTRY.

She treads, in this respect, in the footsteps of the fathers. She follows the leadings of the Apostles and Prophets. Under the olden Covenant, so deep was the conviction that "the Priest's lips should keep knowledge," Mal. 2, 7, that they had their schools of the Prophets, and their seminaries of the Rabbis, to train men for the service of God, in the Priesthood, and the Prophetical office. And we know that, immediately after the days of the Apostles, there arose, in primitive times, the great schools of Theological learning, which were established at Ephesus, Smyrna, Alexandria, and Edessa. The nearness of their establishment to the time of the Apostles, gives probability to the suggestion, that they were founded at the order and direction of the Apostles themselves.

Thus, holy learning has ever been a prized and cherished thing in all the ages of God's Church, both before and since the coming of our Lord Christ. It is so now in all the lands of Christendom, and the greatest Preachers of God's word; the most successful Evangelists from the days of St. Paul; the noblest Missionaries, have always been men from the ranks of the learned.

This, too, characterizes the mission efforts of Christians, of all names. Wherever, in heathen lands, they set up the standard of the Cross, and strive to save souls from heathenism; one of their earliest aims is to set up seminaries, for the preparation of men, by holy learning, to propagate the faith of Christ. The Christian Colleges which they have established in India, in China, in the Sandwich Islands, in New Zealand, in South

Africa, at Malta, at Mt. Lebanon in Canada, among the Indians of Red River, indeed everywhere, where Missions are set up, and the heathen are to be reclaimed; all shew the fixed conclusion of universal Christendom, of the need of early, careful preparation, in sacred Literature, for the future conquests of heathen lands, for Christ.

Unfortunately for our country, we have as yet no such order of men, as we have referred to in the Ministry. Our theological attainments, our acquirements of learning, are but small. And perchance it may be best, that for the time, we have no learned ministerial order; for possibly they would be ill prepared to face the opprobium, which learning—learning in the pulpit, has to bear. For indeed, it is a most trying thing to hear, aye, even from the pulpit at times, sneers at "learned men, who have to go to college, to learn to preach"; or the rude utterance—"We don't need any *learning* to preach the Gospel; we have got the Holy Ghost"; or to listen to the travesties, of Scripture, which are not Scripture at all, made the mock of rude and witty boys, unable to repress the ludicrous, even in things sacred.

One thing however is most certain, that this state of things is, and is acknowledged to be, injurious to the people of the country; and I am glad to find, excites apprehension concerning the future of the children, and the youth of the land.

But even here, in Africa, we feel that we must be true to these customs and holy instincts of our Church. It is our purpose, God helping us, that our Ministry, in the future, shall be a well-trained and scholarly order. The home-authorities of this Church, are using earnest efforts to train superior men, for Holy Orders. Thoroughly agreeing with this purpose, we her ministers, and missionaries, earnestly desire that all candidates for Orders, should know more, in the future, than they have in the past. Our endeavour is to prepare men, well read in theology, and who know the *Word* in the original. Ashamed as we are of our own acquirements, we shall try to advance men, who are our superiors in holy learning, for the edification of the saints, and the glory of Christ, by the preached Word. It would be a dastardly shame, a disgrace, unpardonable and without atonement, if, when our Lawyers are taking in law journals, from foreign lands; and Doctors are sending for the newest works on medical science; and Statesmen are reading profoundest works on political economy; and thinking men are subscribing for the great quarterlies; that the Church of God in this land, should become the abode of ignorance; the pulpit, the refuge of broken English, and of vulgar and inaccurate remark! This cannot be in Liberia. We have the most cheering assurances, in each of the bodies of Christians, among us, that the future will be brighter than the present.

4th. Again, I remark, that the Episcopal Church has a place in Liberia, as THE CONSERVATOR *OF* A HIGH STANDARD OF MORALS.

I beg to repeat here, that the Bible, the whole Bible, is the religion of this Church. We cannot afford to give up the Old Testament. It is the revelation of the Law, and this wicked world still needs to hear the reverberations that rolled once so awfully, from the top of Sinai. We bless God indeed, that "grace and truth came by Jesus Christ"; but we feel that men still need to know, that the "law was given by Moses."

And it is just here, upon this rock, that so many religionists split. Rejecting the Old Testament, and confining themselves exclusively to the New, they pass over those preceptive laws, set at naught those regulating principles therein laid down, and renounce that special religious providence and its suggestions, which it was the design of the Old Covenant to set forth, once and forever, with emphatic significance and authority.

And what are the results of such neglect? What, but that dark congeries of moral evils, crudities, and heresies, which indeed assume the name of Christian, but which subvert the faith, deny a visible church and ministry, and undermine morals:—Half truths, wrenched from their proper relations, and perverted into moral monstrosities; great fundamental principles set aside, because not specifically enjoined in the New Testament; MYSTERY, a sacred dispensation of the Holy Spirit, made light of, and superseded by a hard, icy, unenlightened, and lawless reason; indifference to, nay a questioning of the WORD, allied to a blind reliance upon feelings, emotions, and personal convictions; a pseudo spiritualism, at times, set up, affecting such heavenly minded rays, that it cannot attend to earthly relations, and ordinary duty; the rejection of moral precepts, because of the claim of spiritual freedom; antinomianism; and, in the end, moral corruption and ungodliness.

Such are some of the deadly fruits of this untheologic system, so much in vogue in our days, which with affected holiness, casts aside the Old Testament, makes the Law, in its every aspect, a nugatory thing, and claims to itself, superior spiritual freedom.

"License they mean, when they cry liberty."

But this Church declares that the "law is holy, and the commandment holy, and just, and good," Rom. 7, 12; that the law has still its uses in the evangelical system; that "the law is good, if a man uses it lawfully," 1 Tim.

1, 8; that any system which passes over the law, and rejects it, is a system of confusion, contains in itself the seeds of rottenness, and must soon end in spiritual license, and moral grossness.

As a preventive of such evils, also to regulate the lives of Christians, and to maintain the law of purity, as well for individual personal rectitude, and the spiritual health of the whole household of faith; this church maintains the discipline of the law amongst her members. At the very same altar, where, by appropriate symbols, she reminds us of Calvary, she carries us back to the stern remembrances of Sinai. Every Sunday, when we assemble for holy worship, she pours into our ears the Ten Commandments of the Law.

And I bless God for this moral yoke, this spiritual discipline, which, in her master's name, the Church lays upon the necks of her children. I thank God for a Church, which, while constantly proclaiming a gift of life, through the blood of the Cross; thus constantly reminds her members of the validity of the law, as a rule of life. I bless God for the fact, that though indeed "free grace" is the breathing of every rite, every service, each sacrament, and every office of this Church, she holds up, with prominence, a most effectual barrier against antinomianism, and carnal license.

I am thankful for the authority this Church thus gives her ministers, to wage a ceaseless warfare against all lewdness, grossness, irreverence, Sabbath desecration, and dishonesty. In communities like ours, where the strongest influence is heathen, how great the temptation to forget everything high-principled, holy, and reverent! How widely forgotten indeed, are many of these principles in our country. See the gross disregard, at times, of the divine law of marriage; of marital rights; of the laws of purity; of the rights of property! How could we otherwise, a mere handful of Christian people as we are, surrounded by dense masses of heathen? Now, what, under such circumstances, can be a greater temptation to feeble men, albeit they be ministers, than to pass by these evils; and from fear of man, or a dread of losing popularity, or, on the plea that their duty is to preach the gospel; pass over the damning improprieties of the times?

The Episcopal Church lays her interdict upon all such subterfuges, and all such moral cowardice. She herself, in her corporate authority, utters her voice, Sunday by Sunday, in the ears of sinners, and in the name, and by the authority of God, declares—"Thou shall not make to thyself any graven image"—"Remember that thou keep holy the Sabbath day"—"Thou shalt not kill"—"Thou shalt not commit adultery"—"Thou shalt not steal"—"Thou shalt not bear false witness."

You are thus assured that, if, in any other communions, men forget the law, they cannot in this. No Episcopal clergyman could hold his place among us, whose squeamishness or personal immorality, might keep him from reading the Ten Commandments to his people.

And this gives this Church a vast advantage in the work of God, if she be but true to her mission. For see how Churches are becoming demoralized in our land, upon this very point,—the fear of discipline. Indeed it is not too much to say that *the* great cause of the occasional failure of missions, on this coast, and the moral fall of ministers, has been owing to the timid dealing with sin, and, at times, the actual parleying with iniquity!

Now my brethren, contest with sin, is a great mission of God's Church. If she fears this strife, or avoids, or repudiates it, both judgment and ruin is her portion. In this matter there is no election, no alternative. The love of peace, the desire for "godly quietness," can furnish no excuse. There is but one course before the Church of God, that is, rigid duty and cheerful acquiescence. "Now is the judgment of this world: now shall the prince of this world be cast out.'" John 12, 31.

Duty in this matter, brings with it blessing and success. Grapple in with sin, as an offensive thing, in the love of God and holiness, and victory perches upon your banners. Go back in the history of God's Church; read the great contests of the Church with evil, and see how glory descends from the clouds, upon the faithful witnesses for God's truth; and angels cluster, with approving delight, around faithful confessors; and God makes bare his arm, in defence of his Church; and sinners are converted, and press in crowds, through her porches, and surround her altars.

Read the narrative which tells how gloriously God's infant Church of old came out of Egypt, and when pursued, left the hosts of her infidel enemies, overwhelmed in the midst of the Red Sea: See how God protected His Church, and destroyed her enemies in the days of Joshua, and Gedeon, and Barak, and the Judges: Go back to the wondrous achievements of Elijah, and see how God and his holy angels, came to the succour of holy Prophets: Turn to the New Testament, and mark the wondrous deliverances of holy Apostles, in dangerous straits, and the uprising of God's Holy Church, like a thing of life, from the deadliest persecutions, from baptisms of blood, and the cruel slaughter of the sword: and then run down the track of history, and see this Church of God, to all outward seeming, feeble as an infant, yet triumphing in God's might, over kings, and emperors, and the grandest empires; and by the power of the cross, drawing them away by tens of thousands, and bringing them into allegiance to the King of Kings, into subjection to the "Lamb of God, who taketh away the sins of the world!"

And now, just here, I pause. I might indeed go on, and muse and meditate, and call upon you to meditate and muse still further, upon the fair proportions, and the fine features of this stately structure, of which, many of us here, are ministers, and members, —the Church of God. But what I have already said, will serve to show fitness and adaptation, of this branch of God's Church, for the work of grace, here in heathen Africa.

I have pointed out, in a four-fold manner, the peculiar appositeness of our system, for instruction in saving truth,—the setting forth of Doctrine; for the honouring of God's holy word; for the maintenance and perpetuity of holy learning, in the ministry, and in the Church; for the correction and chastisement of rebellious sin. These four items, include, if I mistake not, every thing that is requisite for a Church, under the guidance of the Holy Ghost, to fulfil its mission, in a heathen land, to the glory of Christ, the salvation of sinners, and the edification of saints.

To the carrying out these grand and august purposes, the Episcopal Church in the United States, commenced many years ago, a Mission on this coast. The building of a new Church here, is, as it were, but the contribution of another polished stone, to that grander spiritual edifice, which the Holy Ghost purposes to erect on this Continent, to the discomfiture of Satan, and for the ingathering of multitudes of precious souls, now naked in body and soul, brutalized and denuded, by the great enemy of souls. But you know brethren, how our blessed Lord, when one, naked, frenzied, demented, well symbolizing, in many respects, this wretched, blinded, heathen Africa, was brought to Him, how He said—"This kind goeth not out, but by prayer and fasting," Matt. 17, 21—so brethren and friends, be well assured that the heathenism of this land can never be subdued; the devil will never be driven to release his grasp upon this Continent, until the Church of God maintains a most holy persistance in righteousness, and rises to the highest sanctity.

And this, my brethren, makes manifest our foremost and master duty. This act to-day, symbolizes this duty. It is the offering up to God, these earthly creatures of brick and stone, of gold and silver, which you merchants of Bassa, have so nobly, so generously given, for the glory of Christ.

But this brethren, is but a partial performance of spiritual duty. We must indeed give of our possessions for God's glory; but the real gift, which is most pleasing to God, is ourselves. Let us here this day dedicate ourselves, all that we are, and all that we have, to Christ our Saviour. Let it be a sacrifice so complete, so entire, that it shall pervade every shade of our thought, every atom of our blood, every breathing of our lungs, every word of our tongue, all our thought, word, and action; until holiness to the Lord, shall be the vital element of our being. *Then* shall we be able to rise up, and advance forward; our banners flying; the Cross of Christ glistening in the sunlight; to take possession of the heathen; to bring them into the obedience of the faith, under the yoke of Christ! To Whom, with the Father, and the Holy Spirit, be all honour and glory, might, majesty, and dominion, henceforth, and for ever! Amen.

"The Greatness of Christ"

Christmas

And when they were come into the house, they saw the
young child with Mary, his mother, and fell down, and
worshipped him; and when they had opened their
treasures, they presented unto him gifts; gold, and
frankincense, and myrrh.—Matthew 2:11

It was a little child, nay, a feeble, helpless infant, to Whom all this
reverence and devotion were given. And it is, by imagination, the same
little babe that all Christendom to-day turns back to and approaches with
joy, and salutations, and profoundest worship. The point of interest in
this little child is not simply that its body was small and weak, but that His
person, diminutive as it was, was the germ of wondrous power, was the
fountain-head of a world-wide ocean, was the root of prodigious reality
which reaches from time over into deepest eternity.

It is one of the wide, general facts of nature, that the things of magnitude throughout the universe spring from small and minute causes. It is so
with plants, and trees, and forests: tiny seeds are the parents of vast and
formidable wildernesses; so with beasts, and birds, and fishes; so with the
stars of heaven, whose brilliant bodies derive from the impalpable nebulae
of the spheres; so with the nations of the earth, with families and individuals. All the great things, all the great men we see, hear, or read of, passed
from littleness up to magnitude and importance. It is, then, strictly in
accordance with the analogy of all the things of God, that He, whose
Advent we celebrate to-day, began His wondrous life in the feebleness of
infancy. But our joy springs from the miracle of His life, which was divine,

From Alexander Crummell, *The Greatness of Christ and Other Sermons* (New York:
Thomas Whittaker, 1882), Sermon 1, pp. 1–19.

✓ and the majesty of His mission, which was princely, beneficent, and godlike in all the minutiae of His work.

Nothing but this greatness of Christ could cause, from year to year, from century to century, this world-wide anniversary. Nothing but majesty, most august and profound, repressing the pride of reason and its sceptic doubts, could thus kindle the imaginations of men, start their united affections, and, on one day in the year, sinking their separate nationalities into oblivion, join their common sentiment into united adoration before the manger of Bethlehem!

I wish to speak to-day of the greatness of Christ. It is a greatness which has constantly manifested itself through the ages by a gracious but irresistible revolution, which has never, at any time, known a moment of cessation. We talk of the influence of Christianity; and men ofttimes seem happy when they can thus drop or deny a personality and make a catchword of a system. But it is best, at all times, to speak the real facts of a case. No system, of itself, produces results. It is, in its results, the work of either devils, or of angels, or of men, or of God. There is a personality behind every organized institution, behind every bank, behind every insurance company, every mercantile house, every manufactory. So, too, of Christianity. It does not work itself. It is not the work of men and ministers. It is a result, in all nations, societies, families, and persons, —a result that is produced by Jesus Christ, present in this world by the power and energy of the Holy Ghost.

Let me point out a few things which the Lord Jesus has done, and which never would have been done if He had not come into this world, and which He alone, of all the intelligences, had the power to do.

First, see the great change our blessed Lord has made in the domain of thought. I refer to this special point at the first, not because I would exaggerate the intellect, as superior to the moral nature; for I do not. I speak first of our Lord's work in the realm of thought because the life of man and the life of society is determined chiefly by the convictions which are reached by the intellect. As a man "thinketh in his heart, so he is." According to the ruling ideas of an age or a nation, so is it.

Now the power of every being, in the sphere of mind, may be seen in three special respects, viz.: (1) In the ability to stimulate thought; (2) in the specific weight or quality of the thought expressed; (3) in the practical or active nature of the thought put into human souls. In these several respects, you can see how unique, and how exalted, has been the force of the Lord Jesus, in all human history.

You will remember that always and everywhere the mind of man has been active; for activity is a native quality of mind. It was active at the period of our Lord's Nativity; active in its show of greed; active in philosophy; active in war and conquest; active in the ambitions and dominancy of great men and great nations. It was an era of great luxury; it was an age of prying and abstruse philosophies; it was a period of subjugation of provinces and empires. The mind of men, at the time of the Saviour's birth, was seething, burning, with large and important problems and gigantic undertakings.

But previous to the time of Christ, notwithstanding all the activity of the human mind, there was a whole class of subjects, subjects of vast importance to the human soul, from which the mind of man was universally divorced. Religion was the possession and the practice of all peoples. But those noble features of religion which flow in lofty truths and sacred precepts from the lips of Jesus had never before circled the brains, nor agitated the hearts, nor stimulated the sensibilities. I read the histories of men, pick out the annals of the noblest Pagan nations, select the writings of the most elevated of their sages, but search in vain, in the most abstruse and most elaborate of their treatises, for the grand divine conceptions which Jesus of Nazareth has put into the minds of men and of nations, and which have awakened them to life and energy.

I turn to the Scriptures, and find there the grandest ideas and principles which ever entered the mind of man; which did not come from the human mind, and which could only be of divine origin. The grand thought of Christ may be analyzed and presented somewhat under these three aspects: (a) That of His sovereignty and rule. He tells us of a divine and eternal government set up in this world, founded upon righteousness, sustained by heavenly affections, generated in our sinful nature by divine influences. "I establish a kingdom," says our Lord; and the Church, "the Kingdom of Heaven" on earth, the "Body of Christ," springs into existence; higher in authority than all the kingdoms of this world, mastering governments and dominions; and never has it failed; "and the gates of hell shall not prevail against it." (b) Another phase of this truth of Christ is that of a reconstructed and spiritualized humanity, produced by the operations of the Holy Ghost in the kingdom of Christ. Our Lord promises a righteousness put into our being, of which man had never before conceived. He guarantees us the reality of a regenerated humanity. He shows us, in His own life and excellence, the possibility of disinterested virtue as the possession of exalted men here on earth. He encourages us with the idea of a benignity and brotherhood among men, which shall destroy everywhere the spirit of revenge, national enmity, and fiery war, and usher in the reign of universal peace. And (c) He crowns these teachings and instructions with a phase of His truth which is at once celestial and transporting. He holds up to view a future state, where the everlasting craving of the soul shall be for the treasures which are incorruptible, and the riches which are eternal. That state is a state of eternal well-being in another sphere, in which men shall company forever with angels and archangels, and eternally enjoy the presence and glory of God!

These are the grand thoughts, yet only partially presented, which Christ has put into the minds of men: earthly in one aspect, working out philanthropies and enterprise in human society; heavenly in another and higher view, because reaching onward to eternal issues. See the wonderful revolutions they have produced among men! See the grand impulses they have started in all the lines of human action! See the great mastery they have given to select peoples, whom they have elevated and invigorated! Note, above all, how, that, having once entered the soul of man, they have taken to themselves the law of heredity, and come down not only in the polity, in the governments, in the liberties, in the letters and literature, and in the laws, but actually in the blood of mighty nations, from age to age! Generations come and go, but these great thoughts of our Lord abide and reproduce themselves. Aye, and they are destined to stay here till the crack of doom! Persecutions like those of the Caesars could not destroy them! Revolutions like that of France in 1792 could not crush them out! These thoughts are thoroughly vitalized with the life of God Himself. They are the thoughts of eternity, and have become so incorporated with our humanity in its very best conditions that they will work, quicken, and animate the masses of men, until, by and by, they get the ascendency over all the thought, reasoning, and reflection of mankind.

Brethren, Jesus Christ is the most powerful thought, this day, in the intellect of man. The person, the claims, the idea of Jesus Christ, are producing more thinking, more philosophizing, as well in the infidel and pagan as in the Christian world, than all the science and politics of the nations. More thought, more speech, more works and treatises are inspired by the one single name of Christ, than by all the statesmen and kings of the entire world. One great personality has entered this earth and thoroughly mastered its intellect, and thrown utterly into the shade all its other thought, reasoning, and speculation, in all the ages.

Second, I turn to another evidence of the greatness of Christ. I refer to that broad transformation of man's civilization which He has wrought. We have only to go back into the past histories of nations, and we shall see the nature of this achievement.

We all know somewhat the cultivation of Egypt, Babylonia, Phoenicia, Greece, and Rome. We know how various were the forms of this cultivation in these several peoples; but we find one broad generalization that may be made of them all, that is, that they were saturated with the spirit of brutality, lust, and murder. When one goes into the museums of Paris or London, and looks at the monuments of ancient art, dug up after centuries of dark repose from the ruins and debris of Nineveh, or Cyprus, or Greece, or Rome, it is difficult to say which form of astonishment is the greater, the astonishment at the exquisite perfection of the art, or the astonishment at the moral debasement they discover. The same contrast and disparity constantly come to mind, in reading the poetry and the histories of pagan writers. The paintings and the sculpture are too often vile and infamous. The condition of woman among them was degrading. Their family-life was barbarous and not seldom shameless. Their social state presented the varied aspect of great luxury, dazzling splendor, allied to gross license and unrestrained indulgence.

While it is difficult to define with exactness the term Civilization, the several items thus referred to may be taken as representing its prominent elements; and it is evident that the civilization of man, at the time of Christ's Advent and previous thereto, was not a power for good and elevation in the world.

See now the great work which has been done by our Lord in changing the moral complexion of human civilization. This revolution began in the family. It destroyed, first of all, the pagan status of womanly life. The Gospel law was a proclamation of equality to woman. In the Church of God she found at once, and for the first time, her place as man's equal and his companion. The elevation of woman in the Church was, at the same time, the reconstruction of the family. The household, thus sanctified and elevated, was a "Church in the House"; and it became an organic unit for wider, nobler uses beyond itself. As Christian households increased, the whole structure of social and domestic life became changed and purified. The saints, in heathen communities, carried the divine principle into their traffic, business, trades, professions, civil relations, and service; and so, gradually, the old, impure, pagan elements of society were everywhere antagonized by the Cross, and beaten down from supremacy. The leaven of Christianity spread into every section of society; it seized upon every occupation; it entered every relation of life; it penetrated the army, the civil courts, the senate; and at last it reached the seat of Imperial Caesar. "We are a people of yesterday," says Tertullian in his Apology; "and yet we have filled every place belonging to you, —cities, islands, castles, towns, assemblies, your very camp, your tribes, companies, palace, senate, forum! We leave you your temples only. We can count your armies; our numbers in a single province will be greater." And about the middle of the second century, says Justin Martyr: "There is no people, Greek or barbarian, or of any other race, by whatsoever appellation or manners they may be distinguished, however ignorant of arts or agriculture, whether they dwell in tents or wander about in covered wagons, among whom prayers and thanksgivings are not offered in the name of the crucified Jesus to the Father and creator of all things."

When the Gospel had done its work in the Roman Empire, it stretched out for new conquests in the other states of Europe. Nay, the Roman Empire was God's instrument and agency for the spread of this newly-created Christian civilization. The empire conquered tribe after tribe, province after province, one barbarous nation after another; and subjected them to Roman law and authority. And then the Church seized, in Christ's Name, upon the Empire, and made it her agent, whereby a chastened Christian civilization was spread throughout Europe. And this day every one sees the grand outcome of the whole process. Christianity, at this moment, is the masterful power in every European state, and through their laws, colonies, and commerce, wields the sceptre of the globe.

Let us pause, just here, for a moment, and make a reckoning of our Master's great work this nineteen hundred years, in the renovation of the world's civilization. You will recall what I suggested as the elements of civilization—the family, the status of woman, dress, culture, manners, social life, art. Art, however, may be taken as the crowning point, the criterion of civilization. See, then, herein, the wonderful change Christ has made in this regard. I will speak of but two or three of the chief of the arts, —painting, sculpture, and music.

In 1851, in the first world's "Great Exhibition," I stood up in the Crystal Palace in London, amid groups of statuary. I walked through long avenues of painting gathered from all the great galleries of Europe; and there was not a picture, not a statue there, which the most innocent maiden might not look at, with as much peace and purity as she would at the midday skies. At the Advent of Christ, if such an exhibition had been held, almost everything would have been smirched! If you go this day to

Pompeii, and ask for the gallery which contains the pictures recovered from the lava of Vesuvius, no decent man, I am told, would dare to ask his wife or sister to gaze upon those pictures! To this may be added the other telling fact, namely, that no woman is permitted to see the art treasures of antiquity, in the Vatican, at Rome!

See now the change. The Lord Jesus Christ has been laying His Cross upon art, as well as upon law, the family, and social life; and wondrous transformations have taken place in all the elements of the world's civilization. Nothing has escaped the influence of our divine Lord, nothing evaded His miraculous touch. Invisible, indeed, to sight, He has been passing through the centuries amid the choicest, most delicate craft wrought out by human genius, and touched them, and by this touch driven out the vile possession of paganism, and put into them the life and beauty of heaven; and so all art has been more and more sanctified to most sacred purposes. The churches and cathedrals of the world, are grander in their structure and their style, than the palaces of kings and emperors; and they are erected for the glory of Christ. The very finest paintings in the royal galleries of kingdoms tell, in magnificent colorings, the story of Bethlehem; the temple scene among the Doctors; the agony in the Garden; Christ, as Da Vinci represents Him, at the Holy Table; the Cross of Calvary; and Christ amid the clouds of glory ascending into heaven. The pencil of the artist has no such touches, his brush no such hues as those lavished upon the Crucified! So, too, that other art, which through the ear stirs the soul with deepest sensibilities, —that, also, has been chastened and sanctified by the touch of the Cross! The highest, noblest, holiest raptures of the harp, the organ, and the human voice, have been evoked by the life, the sufferings, and the glories of Christ! All along this Christian era the saints of God have been pouring forth their praises in the loftiest strains, and the tenderest love to the Lamb, in "psalms and hymns and spiritual songs," "singing and making melody in their hearts," out-rivalling therein the grandest secularities of human song. Yes, music rolls forth its deepest tones, sends out its sweetest melodies in the grand Te Deum, the plaintive Miserere, and the majestic Magnificat. Everything beautiful in earth has been more beautified by the Cross. For, as Keble sings:

> The base earth, since Christ has died,
> Ennobled is and sanctified.

Third, your notice is called to one other striking evidence of the greatness of Christ, —the humanizing influence He has put into, and diffused throughout the world.

We mourn, day by day, at the brutal acts which are chronicled in our newspapers. We are horror-struck at the fearful murders which are constantly committed. Our souls sink when we read or think of the ravages and slaughter of the battlefield, which still disgrace this Christian era.

Bad as all this is, contrast it with the state of the world before and at the coming of Christ, when war was the trade of nations; when nothing but extermination was the end and issue of their fierce and interminable conflicts; when one nation would lift up with hoarse, univocal, brutal tones against another, "Carthago delenda est"; when such a thing as arbitration was never known nor even thought of by the noblest pagan thinkers; when the Temple of Mars at Rome was kept almost perpetually open; when "fire, famine, and the sword" devastated vast empires and swept colossal nationalities so completely out of existence, that even their foundations are now undiscoverable!

My contention, be it noticed, is not that Christianity has abolished war. Christianity, in its best results, is not an extemporaneous affair. God, in His providence, moves with majesty, and not in a flash. To use the words of Guizot, "He hurries not himself to display to-day the consequences of the principle that He yesterday laid down; He will draw it out in the lapse of ages, when the hour is come." Christianity has not yet entirely abolished war. But the greatness of Christ is seen in the fact that He *has been abolishing war* all the centuries through, by the humanization which He has introduced into the policy of nations. All along the Christian era His faith has been lessening the frequency of wars; diminishing the cruel, pagan slaughter of war; extinguishing the brutish, heathen love of war; and, above all, counteracting and extirpating the *idea* of war as a motive of national and personal action. So that now, in the nineteenth century, we have reached this state of the case, namely: that nations are hesitant about entering upon war; *when* war does take place, it is under the most urgent, absolute necessity; *while* it is carrying on, everything possible is done to alleviate its horrors; and especially that, when a Minister of State, in any land, proclaims in any way to the world that the trade of war is a prime policy of his country, the Christian world rises up in indignation, and by the voice of a Burke, or a Channing, or a Gladstone, blasts that statesman to utter ruin, and drives him to disgrace and confusion. Added to all this is the notable fact that, in our own day the principle of arbitration has become a part of international law, as a preventive of the slaughter of men, and for the promotion of national peace, equity, and justice!

See, too, the humanizing influence of Christianity in the suppression of the slave trade, in the destruction of piracy, in the abolition of slavery, in the reformation of prisons, in the progress of the temperance cause, in the improvement of tenement houses, in the increase of hospitals and infirmaries; in the care of the blind, the deaf, and the dumb; in the godly efforts to prevent the ravages of licentiousness; and in the merciful endeavours to save the victims of prostitution! In all these generous, gracious ventures which one sees throughout all Christendom, we recognize the working of that quality of mercy, the special attribute of Christ,

> It droppeth as the gentle rain from heaven
> Upon the place beneath:

This spirit has been working its way nigh two thousand years, against the deep depravity of mankind; but only in this age has it succeeded, to any large degree, in the exercise of its fullest power. We have now, at last, reached the age of missions and noblest charities. In these times we are permitted to see, not only in Christian lands, but in the pagan quarters of the globe, whither the Church of God is speeding, all the fair humanities, the large philanthropies, the saving appliances which are fitted to restore, uplift, and regenerate the most degraded of the human species. Never before in the history of man has the thoughtful mind been so alert and active as now, in ingenious effort for human good. The beneficence of man is instinct with curiosity. The spirit of benevolence, and even of evangelization, is no longer confined to the Church of God. It is the spirit of the age. Our Lord Christ has put this spirit into insurance companies, and mercantile ventures. It stimulates adventure. It prompts geographical research. It vitalizes science. It gives coloring and tone to literature. Just take this single, simple fact, and ponder on it. The poetry of the ancients has come down to our day with a finish and a glow, which holds for centuries, the admiration of the schools, and which has given them the title of "classic." And yet you may sweep the entire field of Grecian and Roman poetry in vain, to find a poem of such genial human sentiment, of such real hope and brotherly aspiration for man, as the simple song,

> There's a gude time coming,

or the fine stanzas of Burns which give us the noble refrain,—

> A man's a man for a' that.

I have thus given you a few tokens of the greatness of Christ, in words that may seem somewhat as though a man should take a single ray from the burning lustre of the midday sky, and hold it up as a specimen of

sunlight. The evidences of our Lord's greatness and majesty crowd the
eye, and overcome both mind and memory. It seems impossible but that
they should impress us all with the deepest sensibility and the greatest
reverence. Here is a Being who comes into the world in precisely the same
manner as every one of us has entered it. He was born of woman. His
infancy was helpless and feeble. But all His after-life was unique, separate
in its influence and power, from every other being that ever lived on earth.
He lived some thirty-three years, a life of blessedness, labor, suffering, and
insult, and at last died an ignominious death! And yet His divine face, the
odor of His sanctity, the glories of His nature, and the mystical power of
His resurrection come streaming down the centuries, neutralizing the
might, majesty, and splendor of kings, statesmen, and warriors, and,
casting them all in the shade, attracting to Himself the homage of the
centuries! Mine is not the task to-day to produce evidences of the truth of
Christianity. It is no purpose of mine to vindicate the Deity of my Master;
but I submit, that this singular fact in human history, the greatness of
Christ, is unaccountable, if it be not divine! There is no room in the mind
of any devout believer for misgivings. All will admit that the instinct
which looks to Christ as a Saviour, as the world's regenerator, must be an
universal one. We go to Bethlehem to-day; we approach Him with the
reverent homage of the Magi, as the fontal source of all this majestic
power of the Christian era, to see God manifest in the flesh, to see the first
manifestation of that interference which God graciously effected for our
rescue and deliverance. We have no gold, frankincense, and myrrh to offer
the infant Jesus; but we would fain present Him that which is far more
acceptable, the best devotions of the heart, the lavish outpouring of the
affections. We go to Bethlehem, and remembering all the wonderful
works of Jesus, by apostles and martyrs, by holy men and women, by
missionaries and evangelists, by philanthropists and churches, by gifts,
and charities, and offerings; we acknowledge Him as the originator of all
the blessedness of the Christian faith, and hail Him "Wonderful, Coun-
sellor, the mighty God, the everlasting Father, the Prince of Peace!"

"The Work of the Black Priest"

Psalms 51:5; Job 15:15; and Romans 7:24.

. . . In a most signal sense the work of the black priest in the church of God is a revolutionary one. For *first* of all we have to uproot very much the roots of religious extravagance, and to check the outburst of senseless enthusiasm, to lessen the growth, not seldom, of ignorance and error.

And, then, next (b) we have to begin upon a basis of deep conviction and stable reason to *build* up these precious souls, our own kith and kin, in the most holy faith of the Gospel. Set free from mere sensibility, it will be ours to lead them out beyond themselves: to fix them in faith and assurance, in Christ Jesus, the rock of ages, and so guide them to the imitation of Christ Jesus, in all the ways and habits of heavenly morality.

Join to this another important feature of spiritual reconstruction. The religious training of our race has been *one-sided* and *disproportionate*. It has fastened upon the race abnormal ideas of heaven; it has substituted rhapsody and hallucinations, for spiritual service and moral obligation.

The time, however, *has come* when they are to be taught that the Kingdom of heaven—to every righteous soul—is *now* at hand; —right here, touching us at every point; and *we* constantly in contact with it! —In the family; in the relations of husband and wife; in the rearing of children; in the duties of citizenship; in the circles of society! That no man need to die to realize heaven! That it is holy duty, the ardent, loving service of Christ Jesus amid human relations which is the beginning of this glorious kingdom; and hence that not a stunted lop-sided, but a full rounded manhood is to be the grand acquisition to be striven for in this work of [the] soul; the grand consummation of this ministry of Christ Jesus.

Transcribed and excerpted from MS.C. 340. Untitled. The Schomburg Collection, New York Public Library, and printed with permission.

"Piety, Moralism, and Enthusiasm"

Ephesians 4:20–21

You have all heard, I am sure, the expression from the lips of some overzealous Christians—"Now we don't want your morality. Give us the Gospel; what we are seeking is religion!" This is the language of enthusiasts; the saying of excitable and hysterical pietists, people who think that godliness consists in emotion, and manifests itself in feeling.

The unfortunate thing in all such language is that it is a repudiation of moral obligation, as a cardinal element in the religion of Jesus. This religion does not set aside the emotions and feelings. They are an important feature in the Christian system. But it should be noticed that they are only *secondary,* alike in place and requirement; while, on the other hand, the spiritual and moral qualities of our nature are the *primary* and foremost. It is *truth,* and not feeling which is sought by the Holy Spirit. It is *conviction,* not emotion; sacred *principle,* and not excitement; high morality, instead of glowing sentiment; solid character in the place of vivid sensation, which are the prime characteristics of our holy faith. And hence the demand for religion, to the exclusion of morality is all a delusion and a farce.

The text which I have announced as the theme of discourse, this morning, is pitched in another key. It is characterized very largely by the elements of moral character. After alluding to the conversion of the Ephesian Christians, the Apostle goes with pointed directness to the end and object of that conversion. "But ye have not so learned Christ Jesus; if so be that ye have heard Him, and have been taught [by him] the truth as

Transcribed and excerpted from MS.C. III. Untitled; dated "12th Oct. 90." The Schomburg Collection, New York Public Library, and printed with permission.

it [is] in Jesus." *What* is the special truth here referred to? Plainly simply, *this:*—"That ye put off the old man, and that ye put on the new man, which after God, is created in righteousness and true holiness," and then immediately he enjoins the four precepts of the text.

1st putting away lying;
2nd intolerance of malicious anger;
3rd abhorence of theft;
4th repudiation of filthy speech.

Here then are four practical things in the school of morals, which are held up as the fruit of spiritual conversion. There is not a single allusion to a man's frames or feelings. There is not even an incidental reference to the emotional sentiments. "If you are in very deed a disciple of Christ Jesus," says the Apostle, "shew it by righteous living; manifest it by holiness of character." Saintship is characterized by truthfulness; by charity; by honesty; by purity. There are two or three principles which spring from this subject to which I shall briefly call your attention:—

1st I remark that godliness does not consist in mere sentiment or feeling. How could it consist in these emotions? For what is true religion? It is the bending back the errant mind of man to the majestic mind of God—who is a spirit. And when we speak of the mind of God we refer to that fountain of truth from which all things real proceed; to that everlasting Reality, which excludes all that is fitful and changeful to that eternal Reason, which is the spring of every grand idea and every lasting principle, to that celestial beauty which is the source of all light and excellence in the universe.

Some way or other, godliness must have some measure of these qualities of the divine Being; and on the other hand these qualities, again, can only touch and tinge elements in *our* nature which are of an abiding nature. But sentiment, feeling, emotion don't spring from the depths of our nature. They are not the offspring of the most solid basis of our nature. Moreover, useful as they are, they are not abiding features of our constitution. They come from an *inferior* side of our nature. They are more allied to the physical than they are to the rational or spiritual of our being. And then notice, they are fitful and transient qualities. Easily excited, they as easily depart. And, at the best the feelings come and go, ofttimes independent of the will; dependent, not seldom upon health, or some peculiar physical condition; and hence evidently they are not the soil in which the Holy Spirit plants the seed of Gods wonderful grace.

Now religion, or godliness is the grandest, most elevating, and the most awful state of our existence, and exercise of our faculties; and it thus becomes evident that it cannot consist in sentiment or feeling.

2nd. The question arises here—what *is* true godliness? My answer is that it is the reconstruction of our humanity. This reconstruction is the deepest of all our necessities. When dread calamity comes, by any disaster, by storms or hurricanes or cyclones, to any of the great structures, any of the grand edifices built by man; the only way to save them is by building them up again. Two or three months ago the "City of Paris," the swiftest of all the ocean steamers, met with a perilous accident in her machinery, jeopardizing the lives of all her passengers. The company owning her could not think of such a thing as giving her up to ruin. She was the finest of steamships, and she had cost well nigh one half million of dollars. What were they to do? Why, reconstruction was the only resort; and so she has been in the docks of Liverpool ever since, under extensive and expensive repair.

So too our humanity has suffered a tremendous fall, unhinging every joint in our moral constitution; and everywhere one goes, one sees in young and old, in man and woman and child, the dread and awful results of man's spiritual ruin. You go into a community of human beings in any quarter of the globe, in civilized or barbarous countries; and on every side you see the awful criminality of human beings, in lust and theft and falsehood and murder. The inky tide of depravity, like a gigantic river, outrivalling, in its volume, the Niger or the Oregon [?], bursting through all barriers and sweeping along in destructive force, is constantly carrying on millions of willing victims, into the wide ocean of endless ruin. You go into numerous families and you have there, on a smaller scale, a revelation of the same deadly forces, which one sees in the wide world of human wretchedness. There are households innumerable, where strife and malice, and cruelty and impurity are the staple of the lives of fathers and mothers and children, and brothers and sisters. "The whole creation groaneth and travaileth in pain together until now" "They know not neither will they understand. They walk on in darkness. All the foundations of the earth are out of course." Indeed we stand up amid the columnar ruins of a fallen world! Moral desolation abounds on every side! Strong pillars of truth and righteousness lie prostrate before us, in every quarter!

Now, as I have just said, the Apostle points out (4) four cardinal principles of man's depravity. Everywhere, on earth we see lying in the dust, truth and peace and honesty and purity; and men unblushingly lifting up, in their stead, Falsehood, Malice, Knavery and License. These are the main pillars of the guilt and sinfulness of man. These are the master works of the flesh. They may not inaptly be called the quadrilateral of human depravity. Nothing could have been more apt and telling as a revelation of the nature and effect of sin than the warnings of the text. It is as though the apostle had said—"Do you want to know what *godlessness* is?— Look around you and see the lying, the malice, the theft, and the impurity, of the wicked city of Ephesus; and see what we mean by sin! On the other hand, do you want to know what we mean by repentance and faith? Do you wish to learn what we call conversion? Put away lying! Give up malicious wrath! Steal no more! but live by honest labour. Let no corrupt communication fall from your lips!"

Here you see the basis of the new life, set forth by the Apostle. Not a single reference to sentiment or feeling is discernable! No appeal is made to the emotional side of our nature. When St. Paul preached at Ephesus he preached repentance from sin, and faith in our Lord Christ Jesus. When men repented and believed, he separated them at once from their pagan associations, and asked the immediate fruits of their conversion. This was a revolution in character. It was a change in *living; not* simply in feeling; but a change in *living,* to the glory of God. He took these miserable, demoralized Greeks and Jews, and first of all demanded, in God's name, renunciation of the gross evils of Ephesian society. There was to be an immediate and a thorough departure from those evils; and then the Apostle would fain begin the uprearing of another and a higher life and character. On the basis of the new faith he attempts the reconstruction of the whole fabric of their spiritual being. You will notice the process of this reconstruction. The wording of it is unique, pointed, most positive. It is the sloughing off of an old sore; the excision of a poisonous ulcer! — "That ye put off the old man who is corrupt according to the deceitful lusts." Here we see that unrobing ourselves from the filthy garments of sin, which is the demand of righteousness and there in opposition, comes the injunction— "that ye put on the new man, which after God is created in righteousness." Then come the special injunctions of the text—putting away lying; speak every man truth with his neighbor.

> Be ye angry, and sin not: let not the sun go down upon your wrath:
> Neither give place to the devil.
> Let him that stole steal no more: but rather let him labor, working with his
> hands the thing which is good, that he may have to give to him that needeth.

Let no corrupt communication proceed out of your mouth, but that which is good to the use of edifying, that it may minister grace unto the hearers.

And grieve not the holy Spirit of God, whereby ye are sealed unto the day of redemption.

Let all bitterness and wrath and anger, and clamour, and evil-speaking, be put away from you, with all malice:

And be ye kind one to another, tenderhearted, forgiving one another, even as God for Christ's sake hath forgiven you.

Eph. 4:26–32

3rd. You see from this, my brethren, that a high morality is the direct and immediate fruit of evangelical faith. This is the third point and the last, to which I desire to call your attention, the plea of hysterical enthusiasts— "We don't want your morality we want religion," is alike delusion and unscriptural. The demand of the Scriptures, everywhere, is "cease to do evil, learn to do well." In other words, *conduct* is the evidence of grace. The yoke of Jesus binds disciples, binds them to the strictest obedience and to the highest excellence of life. And for the attainment of this excellence, we have every possible inducement, and every conceivable aid. In the advent of our Lord; in the gift of His life blood for our salvation; in the succor and assistances of His Spirit for the strengthening of our souls; in the example of His holy life as the pattern of our own saintly living; in the spotless purity of His stainless character, we can see, at a glance, the sacred obligation for us to depart from all iniquity.

He came into the world to save men from sin. It is an effectual salvation, or else it is nothing! It *is* effectual! Men *can* be good and holy!—for Jesus was good and holy. Does any man plead that Jesus was so separate from sinners, that His life cannot be a standard for *us?* I present the fact, first of all, that Jesus took upon Himself *our* humanity, and was as truly a man as you or I; sin only excepted. And then, next, that the spirit of Jesus, all through the ages, has been given to multitudes of converted men, who have lived the life of Jesus. The saints are countless in number who have been chaste and pure, and honest and truthful, and full of love, and uncorrupt in life; walking the pathways of existence free from carnality, scattering blessings and charity around them, to the glory of Christ Jesus their Redeemer; for it is all His work. The virtue and excellence of the saints is no mere human product. It's spring is not the heart of man. It flows over from the open wounds of Jesus, into their souls; cleansing them from sin, and purifying them to moral excellence and heavenly
[blank space]

If the gift of grace to our souls does not lift us to severe and lofty morality, then it is clear we have never received that grace. "We are yet in our sins and our faith is dead."

Conclusion:

What then is the conclusion of the whole matter?

1st First of all, we see how thoroughly Practical is the religion of Christ Jesus. It is a religion, which, rising above mere theory, subordinating sentiment, setting aside passion; seizes upon the most real and abiding features of our moral being, and marshalls them into service, for the purposes of holiness. The great aim and end of the Christian system is the production of holy character, for the destruction of the world's evil and for the honour of our God. Its strongest *human* forces, in this endeavor, is the priority and excellence of true and faithful men and women. The Holy Spirit of God spends his wondrous power in human society, in raising up a generation of sincere, honest, truthful, God-fearing people; shining as lights in the sinful world. Mere profession is chaff. All the sighs and tears and dreams of excited people are vanity, if they are deceitful, truthless, impure. Men may boast never so much of their inward joys and heavenly hopes, but if they are not pure, honest, chaste, and upright, they are *not* children of God! No man can serve God, and at the same time, serve the world, the flesh, and the devil; and hence

2nd We see the demand, on disciples, of rigid rectitude of life and character. "Let your loins be girded about and your lights shining," is the command of the Lord Jesus. Eschew all looseness of speech and action. Be upright and do right in all your conduct. Make no compromises, with the lewd and lying. Hang out your banner on the outer-wall, for truth and righteousness. For *this,* grace, the everlasting fountain of Christ Jesus's righteousness is poured into your souls. You have no lack of ability. All things are [illegible] All the things of Jesus, and the Holy Ghost! For the grace of God, which bringeth salvation hath appeared unto all men, teaching us that denying ungodliness and worldly lust, we should live soberly, righteously and godly in this present world:—

> Looking for that blessed hope and the glorious appearing of the great God and our Saviour Jesus Christ;
> Who gave himself for us, that he might redeem us from all iniquity, and purify unto himself a peculiar people, zealous of good works.
>
> Titus 2:13–14

Statements of Social and Political Ideology

"No Man Cared for My Soul"

Psalms 142:4

"No man cared for my soul." This is the language of extreme desolateness, the utterance of absolute and utter wretchedness. No terms could be coined, and no expression used, more indicative of misery and forlornness. There might be large mental attainment and abundant intellectual resources. There might be a fullness of physical vigor, of temporal comfort, and earthly prosperity and satisfaction. But if with these there should be the absence of spiritual enlightenment, and the lack of divine grace—if the soul should be conscious of its poverty and should know its need; and there should be no quarter to which it could turn, no resource which it could make, for its needed good and blessedness, but must still go on in ignorance and benightedness, in guilt and unholiness; then there would be a sense of poverty, a conviction of wretchedness, a consciousness of misery and desolation, the most tormenting and agonizing, and in lieu of which, all the stores of wisdom, and all the comforts of earth would be as vanity. For amid all the plaintive utterances and all the pathetic appeals which express physical want and anguish; if we know there is no *spiritual* want, no lack of sacred influence and comfort, then, both in the mind of the sufferer and the observer, there is a neutralizing of the suffering and an assuagement of the grief. Or when we hear of the intellectual destitution of large masses of our fellow men, or even of the awful severities of slavery, if we have likewise the assurance that they have the Gospel, that amid all their needs and miseries they are taught of the precious Saviour, then lament as we may, as we *must*, over their destitution and their sufferings, still we have gratefully mingled with our sorrow the feelings of thanks and joy to God, for His unspeakable gift! We care not, on the one hand, what

Transcribed from MS.C. 310. "No Man Cared for My Soul." The Schomburg Collection, New York Public Library, and printed with permission.

may be the refinement, the affluence, the erudition, if added there to these should be spiritual benightedness and moral darkness. —The soul without God and without hope in the world—lost in the gloom of sin, and pressing on in the way to ruin: —For we know that with all his other advantages, the human being without God in Christ Jesus is wretched and miserable and poor and blind and naked. And so, on the other hand the grace of God, through Jesus, Christ Jesus, our Lord, we can become comparatively indifferent to human deprivation and human want and suffering; nay we can glory in tribulation if we can only see the triumphs of redeeming grace, and the abundant manifestations of the honour of the Spirit. For the soul is above everything in man; and there is nothing human—nothing created that can be placed beside it. The body shall decay in the cold mould of the grave yard, and return to its original elements, earth to earth, ashes to ashes, dust to dust. And the hoarded wealth of the intellect, the splendid monuments of genius shall grow dim and fade; for the Apostle declares that prophecies shall fail, that tongues shall cease, that knowledge itself shall vanish away. But the soul is immortal; and lives on forever after, all temporal decline and all human decay. And the soul has wants, which are unbounded, and they must be met. The soul has thirstings quenchless, and they must be satisfied. The soul has longings and aspirations, that are infinite; and they must be satisfied. The soul has graspings and yearnings, and upward-reachings, that are eternal, and must be answered.

And this we learn from the superiority of the soul, that physical want and misery can be endured; and intellectual narrowness be tolerated; — But oh if the *soul* be impoverished and unfed, —if its needed food is lacking, and the refreshing waters for which it sighs and thirsts, are withheld; then we have expressed the most intense human suffering, and the greatest human woe.

So that it comes to this that of all kinds of want and misery—of all kinds of need and wretchedness—the want of the soul, the barrenness of the heart—*spiritual* need and destitution, is the most absolute; and that no expression of wrong or outrage or neglect is so urgent and so sorrowful, as the cry of poor, lowly, depressed human nature—no man careth for my Soul.

My friends and fellow Christians, the object which I purpose presenting to your notice this evening is one which has connected with it all the wretchedness and the woe, which are breathed forth in the words of the text. I stand before you, a representative in my own person, of the most forlorn and degraded race of human beings on the face of the globe. The history of my race, especially during the last three centuries, you are all well-acquainted with. The agitation for the Abolition of the Slave Trade, which shook this country to its centre, and demonstrated the tremendous moral might of England, with the recent Abolition of Slavery in your colonies, the grandest moral event, and the most magnificent spectacle of love in the history of the world, saving only *that* other X; —both left a track of light behind them, which opened to the eyes of Englishmen and of Europe, the almost inconceivable suffering and anguish which had been visited upon Africa. The revelations thus made you are all aware of, and by them you have clearly seen that this is a people robbed and peeled! Perhaps it is not too much to say that no nation no class no race of men have ever been called to such outrages and afflictions as my race. None have ever had to pass through such a fiery trial. None ever been subjected to such murderous, such ingenious cruelties. Earth has had its beauty marred by the bloody track of the cruel men who have robbed my fatherland of its children, firing villages, burning hamlets, and putting the resistful to the sword. And the choral voice of ocean, which should be an everlasting jubilant in the ears of angels and of God has been made harsh and dissonant, by the shrieks and moans and the agonizing cries of the poor victims, who have either chosen a watery grave in the preference to slavery in a foreign land, or else have been ruthlessly cast into its depths, the sick and the emaciated, by the heartless slavers. And then, when landed on the distant strand, the home of slavery and the seat of oppression—then has commenced a system of overwork and physical endurance, incessant and unrequited, a series of painful tasks, of forced labor, of nakedness, and thirst and hunger, of whippings and lashings and scourgings and of premature deaths—continued from generation to generation, transmitted, as the only inheritance of poor hapless humanity to children's children. In your own American colonies, this wretched system, to the glory of God, and to the immortal renown of England has been brought to an end. France and Sweden have followed in the glorious track you have marked out for the nations. Denmark has given the irreversible declaration that she will soon follow in the same bright and honorable career. But far across the Atlantic main, there is a nation, young and vigorous, fresh born among the nations, which commits herself with the whole fervor and energy of her being to the maintenance of this institution, and to the most pertinacious persecution of the poor and abject Negro race.

I have come from the United States of America to ask the aid of English churchmen, in behalf of a congregation of poor black people to whom I minister in New York, who are anxious to raise, found, and build themselves a church. Some may think it strange that one should come so far across the ocean, from a rich protestant country like the U.S., in order to obtain the means for church building. It *is* strange. Tis marvelous. And part of my duty this evening is to set this matter before you in a clear and distinct manner. In the United States of America there are 3,400,000 persons of the Negro race; and truly and indeed may it be said of them in the mass—no man careth for their souls. Everything that ingenuity and legal device, and custom could project to keep my people from the fountains of knowledge, and the streams of life and salvation *has been* done.

First of all, three millions of my brethren are slaves. Three millions of men, women and children—a population larger than London, held as chattel, and treated as brutes. And oh the miseries and the cruelties of the system! They are bought and sold like cattle, at Smithfield. Every year upwards of 60 thousands by the sea board, by the rivers, and through the upland roads, men, women, and children, chained together are carried off into the cotton, rice, sugar, and tobacco growing states, to supply the plantations, where the waste of human life is so great, that they have to be supplied every six or seven years.

These wretched beings are whipt and scourged. Families are separated, and the dearest, tenderest ties cruelly snapt asunder. But all this is as nothing, cruel as it is, when we turn to the fact that these fellow creatures, are kept in the most absolute ignorance, and educated in the most thorough vice and bestiality. The instruction of the blacks is forbidden by laws of the most strongest character. In most of these states the man who should teach a black person would be liable to a severe fine, to imprisonment, and in two states to death. Their spiritual condition is of the most wretched character. Hundreds of thousands are literally heathens. According to the representations of ministers who live in the midst of this system, there are hundreds of thousands, who have never heard of the plan of salvation through a Redeemer.

In the part of the American Union where I live there is no slavery; and one would suppose that a free black man, in America would have the same privileges as any other man. Sorry am I to say that it is not so. There are 400,000 free blacks in the American states; and nearly every one of us could take up the sorrowful exclamation of the Psalmist—"No man careth for my soul." Very few persons in this country have an idea of the manner in which black men are treated in the U.S. In that country there is a wide gulf between the black and the white race, which is seldom crossed by either. The white race, Christian, and worldlings, entertain and cherish a strong dislike to men of my color, and carry out a system of exclusion of the most perfect character. The Brahmin is not further separated from the Soodra, than is the white race from the black in the American states. Caste of the most fearful nature. Caste, as strong as any that ever existed in India meets the black man, everywhere, in every relation of life. It is a system of perfect exclusion. It prevents our children from getting trades, for no mechanic will have a black boy in his workshop. On board of steam-boats, traveling night and day, we are forced to remain on the deck, because white travelers would not tolerate blacks in cabins.

We have no social intercourse. As a clergyman, I have never associated with persons of a different hue from my own until I came to this country. Our children are excluded from the schools, where white children are taught, and no entrance is allowed us to the academies and colleges and seminaries of the land. But oh the worst of it is seen in religious matters, and in ecclesiastical relations, for Brethren, I am sorry to say this spirit of Caste has its stronghold among the Christians of America. The blacks are excluded from the churches of the whites; and must worship apart by themselves. If they do enter the churches of their white brethren, they must sit apart in an obscure corner in the Negro Pew. But where the Holy Communion is administered the blacks are obliged to wait until their white fellow-sinners have communicated; then they may advance forward to the Table. Even death does not terminate this unholy prejudice. From most of the cemeteries, the cold bodies of deceased blacks are excluded. We cannot bury our dead, where the corpses of whites are laid.

I have not time to detail further the nature and the workings of this universal spirit of caste, and from what I have said you can hardly form an idea of it. It is universal and overwhelming, preventing the elevation of the Negro race, keeping them in ignorance and sin and darkness. Under it human beings, emerge from infancy into youth and from youth into manhood and womanhood; with no culture, no instruction—children, all their days, to bent and grey haired and decaying old age. They grow up in ignorance and vice and bestiality; and the way of life they know not; and the common salvation through Jesus Christ your Lord, they are not allowed to participate in. It sorrows the early tender life of little black children. —It makes fiery and bitter colored youth and young men. It turns many into malignant infidels. It takes away hope from the Negro matron. It brings on premature age, and drags my people down to early graves, in despair and wretchedness! Truly my people are a people robbed and spoiled. They are, all of them, snared in holes; they are hid in prison houses; they are for a prey, and none delivereth; for a spoil and none sayeth restore. And the sad utterance of the Psalmist is the mournful cry which we have to lift up in the valley of our humiliation: —Have mercy upon us, O Lord, have mercy upon us; for we are utterly despised. Our soul is filled with the scornful reproof of the wealthy, and with the despitefulness of the proud!

/ But my object is not only to state the condition of my people, but to ask your Christian charity in their behalf. And this gives me an opportunity of stating more particularly their spiritual condition and their spiritual needs. As a consequence on the state of things which I have thus related, education and religion are in a very low state among the Negro race in the United States. I have already told you that there were 3,400,000 of my people in that country. Well of these not 100,000 are receiving any sort of instruction either mental or spiritual. In the slave states, it is against the Law to teach my people, and consequently the few black ministers they have can neither read nor write. In the Northern states, being shut out of all the schools, our ministers are men of little, and very generally no education. The same spirit which shuts us out of white churches and white schools; makes Americans indifferent to our spiritual conditions; and as a consequence we have very few churches. In the city where I minister there are between twenty and thirty thousand of my race. There, as everywhere else in the United States, we have to worship by ourselves; and the places of worship for my people are so very few, [they] will not supply more than one sixth of the population.

To help meet the wants of this most needy people we form congregations in our houses, and in public rooms. My church is a congregation formed in this manner. It has been in existence ten years, and has always had to worship in hired rooms. To a poor people, mostly servants, the burden has been heavy. More than once have we been forced to suspend services on account of our poverty. The minister who preceded me, a coloured young man, on this account, the deadly force of this prejudice, left and went to the West Indies. In vain, have we appealed to our white Brethren. They will do nothing for us. They have no sympathy for us. They have no regard for our interests or our welfare. The existence of this all pervading prejudice of which I have spoken, fully accounts for their neglect and their coldness. —In these circumstances, and under the burden of these necessities, I was forced to leave my people and my family, and come to England to beseech English Christians, to aid us in this behalf. Christian brethren, we need the Gospel. I need not stand here, and demonstrate the intimate connection of sacred edifices, and our holy religion—the coincidence of Churches and the Gospel. The spires of your unnumbered temples, on the hilltop and in the grove; in your tree-shaded villages, and amid the close crowded mansions of your vast cities are sufficient to attest to this relation. We need the Gospel of salvation; as we need, all the means and appliances connected therewith. Education, we need and educational advantages; but one most absolute need is the Gospels. Amid all the sufferings and deprivations of the poor black race, in America, what gifts, what resources, what offerings, would be satisfactory, what would suffice for solid enjoyment, and abiding blessings, besides the Gospel?

The wretched black Father, the child of despair and nursing the dreadful appetite of death, —the Negro Matron, with Hope frozen in her breath, —the youth and maidens and little children, with young desire and aspiration *repressed,* even in their buds and blossomings; —what would mere intellectual wealth be to them or worldly affluence, while living under this crushing, soul destroying system of Caste? What, but to aggravate their distressses, and augment their griefs! So that even as policy and kindness, the gift of the Gospel would be the most acceptable and the most philanthropic; because the Gospel serves to produce contentment, and give comfort, and diffuse a celestial peace, even amid the most distressful allotments; the Gospel gives hope which oversteps the grave. The Gospel assures us of the better land where the wicked cease from troubling and the weary are at rest. But when we come to the consideration that man is immortal creature, —that these masses of our poor brethren are sinners before God—that the blood of Jesus was shed for them, that He has claims upon them—that these poor creatures are in danger of everlasting wrath; —then the purposes of policy yield and fade before the absolute necessity that these precious souls should be rescued, and be saved—that the Gospel should be preached to them, and its saving power be applied to their hearts.

To aid in this desirable work, I entreat your charities this evening. I ask them for the black and the white man alike in America; because in giving the means to establish religious institutions for the Negro in America, you will be blessing both the oppressor as well as the oppressed. You hush the cry of the African—that no man careth for my soul; because you help furnish him with the means for spiritual instruction and divine worship. But in doing this, English Christians, will do a good Christian work for white men in America. You enter your protest in this manner, against the rank offensiveness of Caste, against our Holy Religion. You demonstrate, that the unholy prejudice of color is not indigenous to the soil of the Anglo Saxon race. You give American Christians evidence, that the sorrowful crying of the poor black people of America is heard on *Earth* as well as in heaven. You shew that there *are* Christian people in the world, who care for the soul of the debased African race in America—that true Christian sympathy takes in the world in its regards—that its genuine manifestation is not restrained by the fact of race or lineage or color—that the bond of Christian love transcends all Earthly distinctions; and is based upon the great principle of the Apostle, that in the Christian Faith to use the words of St Paul so kindly read in my behalf this evening by your Pastor "there is neither Greek nor Jew, circumcision nor uncircumcision, Barbarian, Scythian, bond nor free, but Christ is all and in all."

Amid the almost boundless charity of this country which astonishes the world, I beg to put in a plea this night for my benighted race in America; in behalf of the cause of Christ and for his poor and lowly ones. The Almighty has given the people of this land the means by which, with His blessing, the mighty fabrics of error and oppression throughout the globe may be made to reel and totter to ruin; and to erect thereon the glorious institutions of Religion and of freedom. A blessing is on your land by the dispensation of which to the nations the souls of men may be saved and the cause of Christ advanced and honored. In the Divine Providence, this Kingdom [illegible] has been raised up to be forever for a people and for a name, and for a praise and for a glory in the whole world. And in fulfilling the divine providence in this respect you have secured your own peace prosperity and happiness, while the nations have been convulsed and waning and sinking to decay. In caring for the heathen, the oppressed the needy in foreign lands, then, you are caring for yourselves, and promoting the cause of Christ Jesus. It is a law of God's economy that we receive as we give. I believe in your own day and generation you will hear of the blessing you may confer upon my people in America, by benefactions bestowed upon them. I hope and trust that God will dispose the benevolent sympathizing Christian minded people of this country to listen to the appeal of my congregation, and enable them to erect a temple in which to worship Almighty God—to reclaim the hosts sinful people around us whose souls are uncared for, and to the rising generation in the ways of truth and holiness.

So will you be hastening the day of the world's spiritual renovation; and securing to yourselves and country that favor which God always bestows upon those who seek the welfare of Zion, and live for the Divine glory God shall keep you and all the ends of the world shall fear Him.

"Address to the British and Foreign Anti-Slavery Society"

Rev. ALEXANDER CRUMMELL, coloured episcopal clergyman of New York, on rising, said, I am thankful for the existence of the British and Foreign Anti-slavery Society. I am thankful for its existence, because this society is opposed to slavery, and is pledged to continuous and unremitting efforts for its final extinction in every quarter of the globe. I am especially thankful for its existence at this particular period; for never were its exertions and its influences more needed than at the present time. There appears just now a general rising of the surges of slavery and oppression throughout the world, presaging wrath and destruction to the cherished liberties of mankind. Any one who has followed the movements of the crowned heads of Europe, during the last two or three years, cannot but have observed the "royal conspiracy" to narrow the limits of liberty, confine the boundaries of freedom, and to deprive their subjects, as far and as much as possible of their rights. If you look across the Atlantic to another continent, you will see a striking manifestation of the same spirit of tyranny in the recent passing of the Fugitive Slave Law by the United States of America. Thus you will see that some of the great powers of the world seem disposed, at one and the same time, to hinder the progress of man, and to retard the advancement of the cause of freedom. Of these powers two stand out before the world with distinguished prominence— Russia and the United States; and, Sir, I verily believe, the liberties of mankind have as much, if not more, to fear from the democracy of the United States, than from the autocracy of Russia. The acts of the former of these powers are brought before us this evening, and to them I shall call your attention for a few moments; and, as Mr. Sturge has raised the question— "What can be done best to promote the emancipation of the

From *The Anti-Slavery Reporter,* 2 June 1851, pp. 87–89.

slaves in the United States of America," —I will confine my remarks more particularly to that point. I shall not refer to some of the measures which have already been proposed. I wish rather to call attention to one other means, which has not been considered as much as I think is desirable. Sir, it seems to me that the friends of the negroes in the United States, during the last fifteen or twenty years, have partially forgotten one great fact, namely, that the origin of slavery is not, perhaps, to be found so much in any particular laws, as in the weakness, the benightedness, and the degradation of that particular class brought into slavery. It is the disposition, on the part of the strong and selfish, to use and employ the weak and miserable part of creation as their own instruments. How is this to be remedied? I cannot ignore the other plans which have been proposed and enforced here this evening; for I regard each of them as good and feasible. Yet I think there is one other plan which should not be neglected. I repeat—for myself, I do regard the employment of English influence, the free-labour movement, and the other measures presented, as excellent and desirable means for the promotion of the cause of abolition. But, in addition to these means, I do think, that if you wish to free a people from the effects of slavery, you must improve and elevate their character. And the negro needs this improvement. I do not pretend to deny that the people to whom I belong in the United States are, as a whole, weak and degraded. How could it be otherwise? For upward of two centuries they have, for the most part, been deprived of all religious instruction; debarred from all the means and appliances of education; cut off from all participation in civil and political prerogatives; shut out beyond the pale of humanity! And what could be the result of such a regimen as this, but degradation and benightedness? Sir, it is one of the marvels of the world that they did preserve so many of the high instincts of humanity as they do—that they have not become, long ere this, thoroughly brutalised and demented! But, Sir, it is full time now to begin to instruct this people, to cultivate their minds, and to instil into them good moral and religious principles. Extend to them the means of improvement, and allow them full opportunity for the development of their capacities, and oppression could not withstand the influence and the power thereof. The relation between the *free* coloured population of the United States and their brethren in bonds is close and intimate. The interests of the one tell strongly upon the other. The cultivation and the elevation of the one have a most decided bearing upon the other. As the *free* coloured population go up in the scale of intelligence, increase in mental capacity, and demonstrate their intellectual power, the whole fabric of slavery proportionably crumbles and totters. But, Sir, there are great difficulties in the way of the cultivation even of the *free* coloured race in America. In the Southern States it is forbidden by cruel and oppressive laws. In the Northern States the prejudice of the whites prevents a full participation in the advantages of schools and colleges; while, on the other hand, the poverty of the coloured people makes them unable to secure to themselves these advantages to a desirable extent. From these circumstances arises the necessity that the friends of the African in America should interest themselves in the educational interests of the coloured race in America. I do hope the friends of freedom in England may give their attention to this part of the subject. It is a matter of the last importance to the African in future times. Among the many means and agencies employed for the elevation of the negro, his culture and enlightenment should be a prime one, and it should be commenced at once; for it is a work of time. It was so in England, among the Anglo-Saxons. The fine monuments, the splendid and magnificent manifestations of material and mental advancement which surround one, on every side, in this great country—which excite the admiration of the whole world—which have placed England in the front rank among the nations of the earth, and which, in their choicest products, are now gathered together for comparison and competition with the choicest products of all other nations; these did not take any sudden and mysterious rise. These did not spring up in the brief period of a year or a century. No! they are the result of the long, the steadily-pursued, the unwearied and plodding industry and application of the Anglo-Saxon mind for long centuries, carried on amid many difficulties, at first faintly budding forth, then slowly progressing, at times disastrously retarded; but, amid all reverses and hindrances, carried on, gradually, but surely, until they have at length reached their present glorious manifestation. The same process must be developed and carried out in the negro race, and so they too would rise gradually into a state of higher and nobler civilisation and improvement, to the gratification of the friends of man, and to the glory of God. Mr. Sturge has desired some reference to the American colonisation scheme, from those of us who are from the United States. Before I conclude, I will make some few remarks in relation to this subject. Now, Sir, let me remark, in the first place, that I do not wish to say aught to the harm or hurt of my brethren who have been exiled from America to the colony of Liberia. I feel the utmost sympathy with them; for I, too, live under the influence of the same cruel prejudice, which almost broke their hearts, and drove them from their native land to the pestilential shores of Africa. Nor, Sir, would I have you suppose that I am indifferent to the evangelisation and civilising of Africa. Far from it, Sir; there is no spot, of all this wide world, to which my heart travels with more ardent affection than Africa. It is the land of my fathers. I feel the deepest interest in whatever may tend to the elevation of the mighty masses of that continent; and, Sir, although born in the United States, connected as pastor with a congregation of my own people in that country I should think myself privileged if it had been the providence of God that I could have been a missionary to that continent and spent the small measure of ability the Almighty has given me, in efforts for the salvation of those to whom I am connected by descent in that benighted land. For in this, under God, lies the hope of Africa—Africa is to be evangelised only by preaching the Gospel. No mere trading-institutions, no colonies, and no colonisation schemes are able to redeem and elevate the vast population of that continent. Sir, the Lord Jesus Christ intends to redeem the nations, and to save the souls of the different peoples of this earth, by the influence of the Cross, and by the power of the Holy Ghost; and not by colonies, nor by colonising schemes. And, Sir, when the Lord has evidenced this in all the results of missionary enterprise, it is surprising that men of thought, intelligence, and wisdom, should allow themselves to be beguiled and deceived into the belief that the hope of Africa is in the colony of Liberia—that the whole difficulty is now solved, and that the redeeming agency of Africa had been discovered in this colony! The idea that a colony, made up, as its advocates frequently assert, of ignorant, degraded, benighted slaves fresh from the slave-shambles and cotton plantations of the Southern States of America when once carried across the ocean, should become the hope of Africa! Sir, the idea is preposterous, upon their own showing, in the last degree that men, who have been degraded for centuries—that a people who have been made base and miserable by a most galling oppression—who had been almost brutalized, and kept almost godless; that these should be the men to lay the foundations of great states on the coast of Africa, of dispelling the ignorance of the nations, and of propagating virtue. Where was there ever such a marvelous sight witnessed in all the history of the world? Take up the history of colonisation, both ancient and modern, and on which of its many pages do you discover such a result, or can you find such a precedent? For my own part, I am ignorant of the instance. What do we see in the colonies of England, where there has been no such plan and system, and where there has been the lack of intelligent oversight and guidance? Are they all such models of good and beneficent influence to the aboriginal population, as to recommend the experiment for the children of Africa, on African soil? Where, then, I ask, is the aboriginal population, in the places where Anglo-Saxons have colonised? and where are the signs of a blessed influence? Let the Indian of New England, the native of Van Dieman's Land answer. Or, if you seek an illustration in the present time, look at the Cape of Good Hope. But it is said that black men colonising Africa will have a fellow-feeling for black men. I deny it, Sir; there is no evidence that the human nature of black men is any different, in its main features, from that of other men. And, Sir, if you will inquire into the history of Liberia, you see this fact abundantly evidenced. Sir, I say again, the true way to save and elevate Africa is by the Gospel of our Lord Jesus Christ. And if people in this country desire the evangelisation of that continent, let them instruct and evangelise African youth in Africa, in America, and in the West Indies; and from these would spring up men, full of an ardent missionary spirit, who would go to Africa, attempt the evangelisation of the land of their fathers, and engraft Christianity upon its nations, kingdoms, and governments; and thus, eventually, great and mighty Christian nations would arise in the midst of the institutions of heathenism. And now, Sir, let me say that although there are some things, in relation to the cause, which are indeed disheartening, all are not so. For my own part, I have no fears for the future of the African people. God has most singularly and kindly cared for this race in times past, notwithstanding all their fiery trials. I have the most trustful confidence in Him, that He will continue his care and mercy. I stand up here to-night, saddened, indeed, when I think of the pro-slavery movements in America, and the Fugitive Slave Law recently passed; but I am not disheartened. There are some facts, connected with the history of the negro, suggestive of most hopeful consideration. Wherever European civilisation has been taken in any country, it is a noticeable fact, that the natives of that country have receded and vanished away, as the morning mist before the rising of the morning sun. The Indians of America are fast fading away. The natives of Van Dieman's Land are gone. The many millions that once peopled the clustering islands of the West Indian archipelago have vanished before the presence and the power of the white man, and shall never return again from the deep repose of the tomb, until they arise at the final day, for accusation as well as for judgment. The aborigines of the South-Sea Islands, of New Zealand, and Australia, are departing like the shadow before the rising sun of the Anglo-Saxon emigrant. It is said, that no statesmanship, no foresight, no Christian benevolence, can preserve the Sandwich islanders. There is something exceedingly sorrowful in this funereal procession of the weak portions of mankind, before the advancing progress of civilisation and enlightenment. Amid all these melancholy facts, there seems to be one exception. The negro is an exception to the general facts. I have been noticing, Sir, the mid-passage alone is enough to destroy any people. It has not destroyed the vitality of the negro! They have increased in mental and moral importance, and have made themselves felt. Yes, Sir, they have made themselves so much felt, that they have made their cause and their interests matters of great importance to the nations enslaving them. In many cases they have worked out their emancipation—for emancipation has not been merely a boon. It has been, also, an achievement on the part of the black man. These facts I take and mention as indications that Divine Providence designs this people to play an important part in the future history of the world. They appear to me tokens and evidences that this particular section of the human family is not doomed to destruction. Sir, the elevation and civilisation of the negro appear to me determined purposes of the Divine Mind for the future. It may be tardy in its arrival; but I believe it is sure and certain, and bids fair to be peculiarly bright and distinct in its features and characteristics from any form of civilisation the world now witnesses. Sir, I remember, and, perhaps, you may remember, the half-prophetic lines of a lofty and profound intellect of a former generation—Bishop Berkely:—

> "Westward the course of empire takes its way;
>   The first four acts already past;
> The fifth shall close the drama of the day;
>   Time's noblest offspring is the last."

I believe the expectation and prediction of the last line of this verse will be realised in the African people. When I notice the endurance of this race, their patience and hopefulness, their quiet perseverance and humility; — when I contemplate their remarkable vitality and strong tenacity of life; —when I see their gradual rise from degradation and enslavement, and their transition in many quarters from a state of chattelism to manhood and freedom; —when I behold the capable men of this people coming forward to vindicate and redeem their brethren in Africa and in other lands; —when I observe the increased interest of the Christian world and especially of Christian England in Africa and the simultaneous interest of

African chiefs and Africans in general, in the Gospel, and all the zealous efforts of the civilised world in behalf of this people—I cannot but think that all these are the concurrent providences of God for good; that they are all tending to some great fact—some glorious manifestation of African development in the future—a FACT so high and lofty in its moral significance that it may justify claim to be the realization of the poet's prediction—

"Time's noblest offspring is the last!"

"The Progress and Prospects of the Republic of Liberia"

Delivered at the Annual Meeting of the New York State Colonization Society, New York, May 9th, 1861. *

"The Americans are successfully planting free Negroes on the coast of Africa: a greater event, probably, in its consequences than any that has occurred since Columbus set sail for the New World."—*Westminster Review.*

I have been requested, sir, by your Secretary, Rev. Dr. Pinney, to offer this resolution, and to make a few remarks upon it: and I have felt it a duty to comply with his request, and to come here to tell how great a work this Society is doing on the west coast of Africa, that is, in the Republic of Liberia. I shall speak of what I have witnessed with my own eyes; I shall detail the facts which are matters of experience; and I shall mention some of the blessings and advantages of social and political society there, in which I have participated. For, sir, I have been a citizen of the Republic some eight years, and a residence in Africa such a period affords one sufficient experience to speak from. When I went to Liberia my views and purposes were almost entirely missionary in their character, and very much alien from any thing civil or national; but I had not been in the country three days when such was the manliness I saw exhibited, so great

---

From Alex. Crummell, *The Future of Africa: Being Addresses, Sermons, etc., etc., Delivered in the Republic of Liberia* (New York: Charles Scribner, 1862), pp. 131–48.

*The reader of this speech will find considerable variation, in some of its statements, from the original publication of it. The reason is briefly this, namely, that on the delivery of it, in the Author's great anxiety to avoid exaggeration, he *understated* various items herein mentioned. More careful inquiry and investigation enable him to give the statistics, now brought forward; which will be found to accord with official documents.

was the capacity I saw developed, and so many were the signs of thrift, energy, and national life which showed themselves, that all my governmental indifference at once vanished; aspirations after citizenship and nationality rose in my bosom, and I was impelled to go to a magistrate, take the oath of allegiance, and thus become a citizen of Liberia. And I then decided for myself and for my children, so far as a parent can determine the future of his line, that Liberia should be our country and our home forever. Nor have I repented this election. As denizens of *all* new countries, so we have been called to the trials and some of the sufferings of emigrants; and sickness in my family has caused us to seek restoration in the land of our birth; yet, if it pleases God to open to me my field of labor, I shall soon be wending my way back to my home again.

The resolution in my hand expresses gratification at the signs of industrial, moral, and intellectual progress in Liberia. And this, sir, is the assertion of fact. In every department of life and labor in Liberia there are unmistakable evidences of growth. I feel the assurance to affirm here that in every quarter the most casual observer can perceive strength, confidence, self-reliance, development, increase of wealth, manliness, and greater hardiment of character. A glance at any of the facts indicative of national growth serves to show this. *Take the item of Agriculture.* When I went to Liberia the farming and husbandry of the country pertained chiefly to the home supply. But the case is somewhat different now, and the change, considering the small civilized population, is indeed wonderful. The productive capacity of the republic warrants this assertion. Look at our coffee-fields. It is, indeed, not generally known, but, indeed, I make a *moderate* statement when I say, that our citizens have planted, and have now in full growth, not less than 1,000,000 coffee trees. It is true that we are not telling as much upon the market as we are able to in this particular. Various reasons can be given for this, some arising from the state of the country; some from the condition and character of the people; especially from the fact that the acquisitive principle is latent, reserved, and sluggish in many men in the land; but the main reason is, that we have lacked suitable machinery for cleaning our coffee.*

But there are signs that even now serve to show that we are yet to have a large participation in the coffee trade of the world, and this is seen,

---

*I am happy to say that this last difficulty will soon be overcome. Through the warm interest and enterprise of Edward S. Morris, Esq., of Philadelphia, Liberia is likely to be supplied, this year, with "COFFEE-CLEANING MACHINES," capable of hulling over 1000 lbs. of coffee a-day, with ordinary hand power.

especially in the interest exhibited in this trade by the citizens of Bassa, and in the important and increasing exports which are annually made from that county.

Look next at the facts relating to our production of sugar. When I landed on the shores of Liberia, eight years ago, not a pound of sugar was exported from the land; I doubt whether as much as a pound was then made for home consumption. But, sir, since those days life, and energy, and power have been thrown into this branch of industry. The forest has been levelled; broad fields have been cleared; and hundreds of acres of sugar-cane have been planted, cut down, manufactured into sugar, and replanted again, and again, and again. Taking the Republic in the aggregate, we have between five and six hundred acres of land appropriated to the growth of cane. Some of the farmers on the St. Paul's River have thirty acres under cultivation, some forty, some sixty. This year there is unusual activity among the planters. Sugar-making is no longer an experiment among them; they have put forth their effort and it has succeeded; the market has welcomed their contribution, and *they have made money. This* stimulant has incited them to nobler efforts, and I have no doubt that some half-dozen men on the St. Paul's will, this year, enlarge their respective farms to one hundred acres each. At the last grinding season, some of these men manufactured and shipped to foreign ports, some thirty thousand pounds, some forty thousand pounds, and in one instance fifty-five thousand pounds of sugar, with a proportional quantity of molasses and syrup. These facts, with the strong current of industrial interest now flowing in this particular channel, warrant the belief that Liberia bids fair to become one of the greatest sugar-producing countries in the world.

These two staples, that is, sugar and coffee, are the chief staples produced by us; and having referred to them, I need not detain you by any special reference to cocoa, cotton, and other articles which have not as yet entered largely into the calculations and efforts of our farmers as sources of gain.

Take the item of Trade. All along the coast and in the interior, from Sherbro River to Cape Lahou, our merchants have set up their trading factories among the natives. This trade is a trade in CAMWOOD, IVORY, GOLD, COUNTRY CLOTHS, and especially in PALM OIL. In order to carry on this trade our citizens need the service, *coastwise,* of sloops and schooners, and those whose ambition has stretched beyond the home trade, have bought for themselves brigs and barks for foreign trade. And thus the merchants of Liberia are owners of quite a respectable commercial fleet. The number of vessels, small and large, owned by Liberia, and engaged in trade, is forty.

What the correct statement is of exports and imports, I can only say proximately. The imports at the single port of Monrovia, for the year 1860, amounted to near $150,000; but as there are *five* other ports in the Republic, and two of them of great importance, that is, with respect to native trade, I have no doubt that our imports exceeded $300,000. I am happy to say that our exports exceed our imports; we are factors and producers over and above our consumption of foreign products; and thus we are enabled to show signs of thrift and progress, and indicate increasing wealth. The report of exports from the port of Monrovia is about $192,000 in 1860, and I presume that the sum of $400,000 is no exaggeration of the amount for the whole republic.

Take next those items which pertain to the best and most abiding interests of man, those which pertain to civilization—I mean schools and religion. Through the provident care of the several denominations of Christians in the United States, all our settlements are provided with schools, and opportunity for securing a common education is afforded to a goodly portion of our population. The Methodist, Baptist, Presbyterian, and Episcopal missions have each their schools in all of our larger towns. In these schools are gathered together, under teachers of, in the main, respectable acquirements, our civilized children. But they are not exclusive. Numbers of native children, servants on the farms and in the families of our citizens, are also received in these schools. The Sunday-schools receive a much larger number of natives and Congoes for instruction, and the churches are ofttimes filled with them. I have seen, in some Sunday-schools, with our own children, thirty, forty, and fifty native children, under instruction in English and the Christian religion. Added to this, are the schools, exclusively for natives, under missionary direction, all which agencies are bringing forward a large class of natives of the soil, English-speaking in tongue, and civilized in habits and manners. Some of these already approach our own civilization. Many of them are respectable citizens in our towns and neighborhoods; men who not long since were heathen, but having been brought up in American families, are now civilized men. They live in our towns and villages; they go to our schools; they visit our families; they pay taxes; and they marry among our people. Some of them are teachers; a few have become ministers of the Gospel. One case of this civilized transformation is worthy of notice. It is the case of a native young man, who was brought up in a mission-school at Bassa;

subsequently he was brought to *this* city, and went to the second colored public school in this city, and afterwards returned to Africa. On a recent occasion, a vacancy having occurred in the representation to the Legislature in that county, this young man was pitched upon by the Bassa people as the proper person to be sent. I believe, however, that the purpose of his fellow-citizens was frustrated by some missionary arrangements; but from the way I have heard responsible citizens speak of him, I feel quite certain that the people of Bassa regard Mr. Pitman as one of their foremost men for character and ability.

I am endeavoring to show how in various ways Liberia gives evidences of moral, industrial, and intellectual progress, and I think the statements I have brought before you evince energy and progress among my fellow-citizens; but perhaps a more life-like representation of activity in Liberia may be gathered from a brief account of a recent journey along our coast. I left Cape Palmas, a few weeks ago, on my return to America, and on our journey we stopped at every settlement on the way to the capital. When we reached Sinou we found there the bark E. B. Roye, the property of a most enterprising fellow-citizen, Mr. E. J. Roye, merchant of Monrovia. In a day or two we reached the settlement at Bassa, and there we found a small craft trading, owned by another fellow-citizen. We went to Junk, and there we saw the fine steam saw-mill of Payne and Yates, their yard filled with plank, and a long distance along the banks multitudes of logs, which are furnished them by the enterprising natives there, for their mill. Off from the town we found there, lying in the harbor, two vessels, the property of Payne and Yates, Liberians, loading with lime and plank. We went on to Monrovia, and, as we turned the noble projection which makes Cape Montserrada, we found in the roads *six* vessels and the steamer Seth Grosvenor, all the property of our own citizens, and floating the Liberian flag. We went ashore and entered the streets of our capital; a city regularly planned and gradually filling up with brick and stone edifices. The next morning we were woke up with the early sound of martial music, and, hastening into the streets, saw a fine body of troops gathered from several settlements, and led by the Secretaries of State, and of the Treasury, on their march to the beach to embark for the southern section of the country, to put down a pestilent set of natives, who, for the last three years, have been giving us much trouble and defying our authority.

A few days afterward, I took a journey to the new interior settlement, Careysburg. I sailed up the St. Paul's and found everywhere the signs of progress. I had been nigh three years away from Montserrada County;

and great was my surprise to see large and extensive fields cleared, and planted with sugar-cane, which, when I went to Palmas, were a dense wilderness; new brick and frame-houses recently erected; brick-kilns at divers places, containing from fifty to one hundred and fifty thousand bricks. Great was my delight, as we sailed up the river, to behold wide-spread sugar-fields; the brick mansions of the farmers, ranged upon the banks of the river; and to see in the distance, the curling smoke ascending, and the floating steam from the sugar-mills, at several points, where the grinding of the cane had commenced, and sugar was in the process of making. Stopping a few hours at the farm of an old friend and schoolmate, who plies two noble packets on the St. Paul's; has a large sugar-cane farm; and at the same time is making, this year, one hundred thousand bricks, I mean Mr. Augustus Washington; I started thence, through the wilderness, for Careysburg. After a few hours' travel, we came first to a solitary log-house of a new settler; soon after we reached a group of good, substantial dwellings, forming a little village, surrounded by acres of recently cleared land. After a while we arrived at the neighborhood where large preparations are being made for the interior road. There I saw, at different places, the banks of some four different streams secured by neat, solid masonry of our own laborers, in preparation for the bridges, projected for the cart-road. In two places, fine bridges, symmetrical and substantial, had been thrown across these streams. At another spot I saw a company of twenty odd men, in busy activities, preparing a new bridge, and grading the road; and all this work was being done by workmen, emigrants from this country, citizens of Liberia and under the direction of Liberian officers and superintendents. Five hours brought me to Careysburg; and as I ascended the main street to a lofty elevation, I saw, on every side, the town laid out before me, with the precision of a multiplication-table. All around were visible more than a hundred mansions of the emigrants, surrounded by largely cleared patches of vegetables; their humble chapels in elevated positions; a large reserve in the heart of the settlement for a public park; not far in the distance were the larger farms of the settlers, while the air was filled with the cheerful sounds of labor, of conversation, of hilarity; and peace and happiness seemed to rest upon man and beast and nature!

I have presented these incidents to you, sir, as evidence of life and activity in Liberia. They show, I think, that men are alive in that country, and are moving the arms of industry. There are, you know, sir, incidental, but significant things, in all lands and among all men, which serve to show more clearly than more marked demonstrations, that society, in its different departments, is instinct with productive energy. So these facts which met me a few weeks ago, in Liberia, evince that an industrial impulse prompts the people of that country. They show, in fine, that the springs of action are at work in our communities, and give the promise of a not distant state of aggrandizement, of greater political importance, of commerce, and wealth and refinement.

I have been speaking thus far, sir, with reference to that part of the resolution which relates to the industrial, moral, and intellectual progress of Liberia. I wish now to show, in as brief a manner as possible, that as the Republic is growing in itself, so likewise it is telling upon the interests of the aboriginal population. I have already referred, incidentally, to this topic. I wish, however, to call attention more distinctly to one or two facts which will show more strikingly the work we are doing among our uncivilized kin in Africa. *Our diffusion of the English language illustrates this point.* A mighty number of native children have been brought up in our colonist families and in mission-schools. Many of these, it is true, on reaching their majority, return to country homes; but they carry with them good English utterance; in many cases capacity to read and write; in *all* cases many of the elements of civilization. I have had native boys working for me, who when they wished any article from their distant towns, would write an English note, in as good style as myself; and yet they dressed and were living in native style. Their habits, civilized necessities, and acquired wants assimilate to ours. Vessels sailing from American ports loaded with provisions, on reaching our coast, find a ready market in native towns, as well as among our civilized settlers. They buy meat, and fish, and sugar, and molasses, as well as cloth, tobacco, and beads. And thus, in these and various other ways, our different settlements are diffusing a civilizing influence among our native population, and gradually bringing them up to our standard of civility. There is also another large class of natives who live among us constantly: the youth who have been apprenticed to our families, have grown up in our midst, and who have been brought, more or less thoroughly, into civilized habits. These form an important and valuable accession to our population. You know, sir, that our population is often set down at 15,000 persons; but this by no means does us justice. *That* is very likely our *emigrant* population: but for every *American* citizen, you may safely put down another, either *native* or *Congo,* who has been trained in our families or schools, and who form, in the aggregate, an equal population to our own. They are indeed the *lower crust* of our civilized population; but we should have the full benefit of their enumeration, and we should be thus reckoned fully at 30,000 civilized people.

Let me now advert briefly to one more evidence of our influence among the natives, and the regenerating power of our people and polity: *I refer now to the civil and political influence of our government upon the natives around us, especially as it respects their rights, freedom, and civil elevation.*

You know, sir, that slavery is indigenous to the soil of Africa. Indeed, sir, it is indigenous to all soils on the globe, and is the cause of misery and distress wherever it exists. It is thus in Africa. But the hopes of freedom, the aspiration for liberty, work as strongly in the bosom of the native African as in any other man on the globe. The servile population of our surrounding tribes, even to the far interior, know where safety can be found from the oppressor. Hence, this class, when they find the yoke intolerable, seek the protection of our flag. Runaway boys and fugitive slaves come to us from the Bassas, the Queahs, the Veys, the Deys, and especially the Pessahs, who are the hereditary slaves of the interior. All along the banks of the St. Paul's, in the rear of our new settlements, are to be found a heterogeneous compound of people of all these tribes, living in small towns, enjoying the protection of our laws. I remember the case of two boys who escaped the slavery of their tribe, by coming to my own neighborhood; they were pursued by their native master. They were taken before a magistrate, who refused to return them to their master. The ground assumed was, that slavery was not recognized by our laws, and that fugitives from slavery could not be sent back to bondage. Thus, sir, our Republic is already a refuge of the oppressed. Thus, sir, are we demonstrating to the heathen tribes of Africa the highest laws of freedom, and the beneficent operation of Christian government. And thus likewise are we realizing on the soil of Africa, the words of one of your own poets:

> "No slave-hunt in our borders, no pirate on our strand,
> No fetters in Liberia, no slave upon our land!"

It is these realities, which I have witnessed, experienced, participated in, which have led me to commend the Republic of Liberia to those of my friends in this country, who, either from enterprise or the spirit of emigration, feel disposed to look to other lands. For a number of years past, a goodly number of American colored men have left this country, in order to better their fortunes. Some have gone to California, some to Australia; and, after accumulating wealth, returned again to their homes. A like feeling now influences many in these States, save that they are seeking *permanent* homes abroad. Some are going to Hayti; some have their attention turned to the West coast of Africa, especially to the Yoruba country, and the locality of Abbeokuta. And this latter class interest me a deal more, I confess, than those who are going to the West Indies. And this chiefly because the *need* of Africa—*her need of civilized emigrants*—is great, and because educated free colored men are *the* fit agents to effect the regeneration of Africa. We cannot, it is true, make great pretensions; our training and culture have been exceedingly imperfect. We have been deprived of many of our rights in this country. We have been debarred from many of those privileges and prerogatives which develop character into manhood, and mastery, and greatness. Still we have not been divorced from your civilization. We have not been cut off from the lofty ideas and the great principles which are the seeds of your growth and greatness, political, intellectual, and ecclesiastical.

On the contrary, we too have learned clearly and distinctly the theory of free speech and of constitutional government. We too have participated somewhat in all the vast wealth, both religious and civil, of your Anglo-Saxon literature. We too have learned the advantage, and have risen to the elevation of all those great legal charters which interest men in government, and which make government subserve the best interests and desires of its citizens. And these kindly though incidental providences have placed us in governmental capacity, and in fitness for the prerogatives of government, in advance of many peoples, who in other respects are above us. The freed black man of America is, I feel assured, a superior man, in the points I have mentioned, to the Russian, to the Polander, to the Hungarian, to the Italian. Notwithstanding our trials and burdens, we have been enabled to reach a clearer knowledge of free government than they, and to secure a nobler fitness for its requirements, duties, and guarantees. I speak from the facts which have fallen under my observation, among my brethren in Africa. And hence I feel desirous that those enterprising and Christian men here, who are looking abroad for new homes, and other fields of labor, should join us in Africa, for the regeneration of that continent. My own desire, moreover, is that instead of scattering ourselves thousands of miles apart along the coast, we should rather concentrate our parties and our powers. Of course, I cannot say a word in the abstract, against the mission which draws many men, and some of my own personal friends, to Abbeokuta. But I do regard it a mistake in policy. I have the impression that providence points out all that field to the freed and cultivated men who have been raised up and prepared by the English at Sierra Leone; and who, especially by blood and language, seem to me God's *chosen* messengers to the valley of the Niger and its far interior. And I have the conviction that we of the United States, with our peculiar training, and with our democratic tendencies, will find ourselves out of place, as well as in an uncongenial element, in the strong governments of interior Africa. And therefore I have thought that in every way, it would be far better for men leaving this country for Africa to join their fortunes with us in Liberia. Our training, habits, customs, education, and political experience, have made us—it is not, it is true, a dignified mode of expression, but I have used it in private, and may be pardoned its use here—they have made us "Black Yankees;" and I feel assured that in Liberia, we shall find a more congenial field, better appliances, a govern-ment more suitable to our antecedents, better fitted to a youthful nation and an aspiring emigrant population; to achieve *that* which seems to me the master aim of all our colonization to Africa, and the noblest duty of the Republic of Liberia—I mean the evangelization and enlightenment of heathen Africa! But, sir, I fear I tire you, and I close at once.

For three hundred years the European has been traversing the coast of Africa, engaged in trade and barter. But the history of his presence and his influence there, is a history of rapine and murder, and wide-spread devas-tation to the families and the homes of its rude and simple inhabitants. The whole coast, sir, has been ravaged wherever his footstep has fallen; and he has left little behind him but exaggerated barbarism, and a deeper depth of moral ruin.

Now, sir, we are there: we black men of America—we who have been trained in the severe school of trial and affliction—we who have been educated amid the free institutions of this country; and, sir, I pledge you in behalf of that able man, our national chieftain, and all the other leading men of Liberia, that we will endeavor to fulfil the duties which devolve upon men laying the first foundations of new empire; and to meet in a proper manner, the obligations which Divine Providence has brought upon us.

"Our National Mistakes and the Remedy for Them"

Delivered before the Common Council and the Citizens of Monrovia, Liberia, West Africa, July 26th, 1870, being the Day of National Independence.

FELLOW CITIZENS:—I have met somewhere with the remark that "man beats towards the truth." The meaning is that we do not reach truth directly, in a straight line; but that we arrive at it by treading the winding pathways of experience. The saying is a nautical one, easily understood by any one who has ever sailed upon the high seas.

The gallant ship that sets out upon a voyage rarely meets with those direct, propitious gales, which bear her along in a straight, undeviating line, to the wished-for haven. For, perchance, at the very outset, contrary winds retard her progress. Then the skill of her commander is put to the test. He does not reverse his course, and return again to the harbor from whence he sailed; but bravely meets the winds, adverse though they be. Now he turns his sail to the windward, and makes a tack; and now again he changes his canvass, and sails a point to the leeward: and so, by one tack and another, he bids defiance to opposing gales; *beats* towards the port desired; and sails triumphantly on his way.

So man beats towards the truth. We fall into an error, and then retrace our steps. In the very act of recovering ourselves we step, perchance, into a deeper maze. Once more we make the attempt to advance; and, possibly, at length, proceed aright.

The poet Young, doubtless had this fact in view, in penning the well-known lines:—

From Alex Crummell, *Africa and America: Addresses and Discourses* (Springfield, Mass.: Willey and Co., 1891), pp. 165–98.

"At thirty, man suspects himself a fool,
Knows it at forty, and reforms his plan."

Painful and embarrassing as is such experience, it is not entirely useless. We are learning somewhat the narrowness of the circle of our vision, the incompleteness of our faculties, the necessity of prudence, the worth of forecast and judgment. And thus it is, that, by one mishap and another; a tantalizing blunder, a blind miscalculation, a heedless misadventure: we learn the lessons of caution; we are sharpened up to sagacity; and gather to ourselves a harvest of wisdom.

It is such trials as these, for they *are* trials to temper, patience, and desire—that harden character; and, to quote the words of a master, "because they render being upon our guard, resolution, and the denial of our passions, necessary in order to that end."

The nation, as a man, beats about into one error and another; flounders now into this blunder, now in that; now halts or falls behind; rushes perchance, into a rash procedure and is made to smart most keenly for it; but by and by, after many bitter experiences, learns the truth; gathers, from divers mishaps, a masterful wisdom; falls gradually into a corrective prudence; and arrives, at length, at the policies which are wise, judicious, and restorative.

Such being the experience of both nations and men; you will not ask of me any excuse if I call your attention to day to "OUR NATIONAL MISTAKES; AND THE REMEDIES FOR THEM."

I take up this subject for the reason that, having done something, we thus show that we can do more. I am anxious that we should do more in the future; and hence I attempt to-day the discovery of some of the obstructions which have heretofore prevented a larger work. I am encouraged to this discussion by the universal desire in the land, for a broader, more statesmanlike policy, and the conviction everywhere freely expressed, that nothing but a complete, but healthful, revolution of plans and policies, can give this nation success and aggrandizement.

I am cheered to the duty before me by the fact, that the self-congratulation of former years, has passed away; and that the people of Liberia have become greatly sobered to duty. Thank God that the self-praise and the idle vanity of the past have vanished; the past and the present too, seem little, compared with the rising proportions and the bold magnitude of the future.

I. *One great mistake of the people of Liberia has been neglect of our native population*. I do not say that this has been universally the case; and I am glad to aver that it has been unaccompanied with a malignant will. The fault has been more relative than absolute. We have far fallen short of our duty, than is either justifiable or excusable. We have been guilty of a neglect, which has carried with it harm to the aborigines; and, at the same time, visited grievous wrong upon ourselves.

Our mistake in this matter has sprung, first of all from a too strong self-consciousness of civilized power. Nor is this to be wondered at. As a people we were "ferried over," in a month, or little more, from a state of degradation to a position of independence and superiority. In a little more than a monthly change of the moon, we were metamorphosed from the position of underlings to one of mastery; with a vast population of degraded subjects around us. We should have been angels instead of men, if the contrast, between ourselves and the heathen around us, had not made a most vivid impression upon our minds; had not somewhat in-flamed our imaginations. It has done both; it has led to an exaggeration of our own capacities. It has made us oblivious of our own humbling antecedents. It has blinded too many of us to the fact that we are but a few generations removed from the condition and the benightedness of the heathen around us. It has made us forgetful of the great duties we owe these people who serve us in our families and work on our farms. It has led too many to look down upon the native as an inferior, placed at such a distance from us, that concord and oneness seem almost impossibilities for aye!

Let us be just and candid with ourselves, and look this matter fairly in the face; for, if we cannot call ourselves rigidly to account for any of our policies, we cannot make any improvement, and must surely die. Look first at the *personal aspects* of the case, observe how few persons send their native boys to school; how seldom they are taught to read; how unusual it is to accustom them to proper habits of dress; how that it is only by dozens, instead of hundreds, they are so trained as to fall into our civilized habits; and that only individuals among them become ministers and teachers.

Next, view the matter in its *governmental* bearings. See how carelessly, thoughtlessly, we have ignored the *national* obligation to train, educate, civilize, and regulate the heathen tribes around us!

With a rigorous hand, caused, I know, by their own wilfulness or folly, we have made them feel, at times, our superiority and mastery. But what have we done—what, I mean, on a large and noble scale, to assure them of our sense of obligation to do them good; to impress upon their souls the awfulness of majestic law, as the regulating force of society; or to mold them, body, soul, and spirit, by the plastic and elevating influence of letters, civilization, and the Divine Word?

No native king has ever had sent to him, by the government, a teacher to educate his children and his people. No sons of princes have been brought from our native tribes to be educated by the government. No government farms have been established for the training of native men in the pursuits of agriculture. No native kings or head men have ever been invited to sit, as advisers or senators, in our Legislature, to represent their tribes, and to show them the advantages of civilized and responsible government. No commissioners have been sent from tribe to tribe, from king to king, to offer pecuniary inducements or government prizes, for the cultivation of coffee, cotton, pepper, or ginger. And, at the close of our several wars, no single effort has ever been made to bring tribes into closer neighbourhood to us, by the opening of roads as a condition of peace, and as a bond of friendship. Even native prisoners when discharged from custody, have gone forth from our control untrained in useful trades, and ignorant of profitable handicraft.

A SECOND *mistake in our policy has been our dependence upon, and our eager desire for, the foreign supply of our needs, to the culpable neglect of our native resources and of native skill.*

This point offers a wide field for discussion, and deserves to be noticed by itself as a single theme. I must not pass it by, however; but will compress it into as small a space as possible.

The mistake discovers itself in two particulars. (I.) Let me call your attention to the prodigality of nature in this tropical clime; in the air; in the teeming waters; in the marvelous productiveness of the soil; in the wild herds roaming the forests; in the priceless gums exuding from vines and trees; and in the rich woods, rotting down from century to century, worthless and waste!

Just go up to the St. Paul's river an hour or two's ride; and where, under the sun, can you find such myriads of fish as swarm its waters? Go across the level plains of Caldwell, and look at the wild prairie land, stretching out almost uninterruptedly scores of miles; with grass sufficient for multitudes of cattle. Go out an hour's walk, in the settlement of Virginia, and see, at night, the wild oxen, and the gallant deer, which come into the farmsteads, tearing up cassada roots, plucking potato vines, and stealing sugar canes.

Notice, too, the large quantities of corn, meal, and rice imported into the country; when we can easily produce two crops a year on our own lands, and largely export to foreign lands. Mackerel, codfish, and herring, in thousands of barrels, are brought to our ports; while the very same fish, sport in our own waters. And in less than ten years such will be here, as already in Sierra Leone, the valuable results of our own fishing operations, that our children will wonder at the careless neglect and lack of enterprise of the present day.

See, again, the large quantities of plank brought to Liberia; while we have, in our wilderness, the most precious of woods, cedar, saffron, mahogany, iron teak, and rose. And here too are the facilities of wind and water for mills; and yet there is not a single wind-mill in the country, and not half-a-dozen water-mills.

And yet, with all these vast opportunities for wealth, we lack a full supply of our needs, and send across the ocean for no small portion of the articles of family consumption, which are needed for our tables!

I said there were two aspects of the neglect of our native resources, and of native skill. I have referred to *one*. Now let me refer to the other.

(2.) That other is our slight grasp upon *the interior trade*. It is slight because we have less of it than any trading people on this Western Coast. Go to any of their settlements, and you will find their "factories" scores, sometimes hundreds, of miles in the interior.

The foreigner comes to the coast. For a few months he languishes under the influence of fever; but shortly he shakes it off; and now you hear of him far up on the banks of the Senegal, the Gambia, or the Niger, pushing his active trade.

How does not this contrast with our partial movements! *Our* operations but skirt the coast. We have not got a factory further inland than Vauzah! Every one here knows the grounds of this difference. The other governments send their protective and regulating power far into the interior. But while we can command as much personal bravery and endurance as any other people in Africa, our government influence is partial and limited.

Note another aspect of this case. Observe the small advantage we are taking of *native labour* in carrying on the work of improvement in the land. In this single county of Messurada we can count the names of no less than a dozen tribes. And yet notice (1) The limited contact of our communities with the aborigines; (2) The great lack of labourers amoung our planters; and (3) The comparatively small amount of trade we draw from the interior. Considering the period of our settlement here, we ought to be touching tens of thousands of these people on every side, and far in the interior, with a more plastic and regenerating power than we are now exerting. We ought, moreover, to be employing, by this time, many more thousands of natives on farms; availing ourselves of the vast riches of the interior; and training masses of them into civilized communities and enlightened citizens.

Look at the labour question. What is the most dazzling, anxious, problem to our large sugar planters? Labourers! Every farmer of any magnitude is constantly putting the query—How can we get a fuller supply of fixed, steady, trustworthy labourers, for the cultivation and the ingathering of our crops? And this question is put in a country where there are tens of thousands of unemployed, but vigorous men, unproductive; *but fitted, as well by the habit of labour as by physical power, to all the needs of our agricultural operations.*

For this, I maintain, *is* the nature of the case. The native man has not only physical capacity, but he has also the habit of labour. He is a WORKER; notwithstanding all that Mr. Carlyle and all his brother Anthropologists, may say to the contrary.* The criterion of industry is, if I mistake not, this, that is—*"Do a people work up to the level of their necessities and their cultivation?* If they do, then they are industrious, if not, not!

The native African *does* work, and that most gladly, up to the level of his cultivation and his needs; not indeed, I grant you, up to the civilized man's needs; for he is a barbarian. He does not work for a brick house, for carpets and chairs, for books and pictures. He has not reached that point of civilization, which requires such things. Neither did Mr. Carlyle's grandfathers when Caesar came to Britain. These things are not the native man's needs. His needs are rice, cassada, palm oil, and a hut; not awry, dirty, and ready to fall, like a thriftless Italian's or a rude Irishman's, but perfect and complete. And these needs are always supplied. Who ever heard of a famine in the country, caused by native laziness?

And, therefore, I say that our native population have the habit of labour, and are industrious. They are industrious according to their habits and training; we must teach them ours.

And yet, with all our needs, we have never taken the proper steps, either by a skilful increase of their wants, or by a generous mode of interesting them in the profits of labor, to avail themselves of their powers and fitness for wide and productive use! How great a blunder!

*See "Latter Day Tracts," by Thomas Carlyle.

Look again at our halting, national and individual prosperity. What is a common complaint throughout the length and breadth of the land! The slowness of our accumulation of wealth! Contrast this fact with the vast talent wealth of this part of the continent, or the revenues of the colonies and settlements which draw to themselves the riches of Lagos or Sierra-Leone.

Think of the forests of palm trees in the interior; their golden fruit falling wastefully on the sod, and then springing up again in crowded clusters, painfully pushing their feathery tops towards the skies! Think of the forests of camwood growing wild, hundreds of miles all through this country, and, in their maturity, going to decay and falling prostrate to manure the land for a ranker luxuriance! Think of the multitudinous vines, and shrubs, and trees, constantly wasting their exuding gums upon the ground—gums which, in foreign lands, would command millions of dollars! Think of the vast and valuable beds of precious minerals, rivalling, perhaps, the riches of California, now lurking, hidden from human sight, in bye and sequestered places through all the land! Think of the thousands of plants of matchless virtue, which science and pharmacy would gladly welcome to the laboratory, now growing up in the wilderness, but to wither, die,

"And waste their *richness* on the desert air!"

And yet, after all this, the liveliest imagination can hardly measure the wondrous riches which God has scattered at almost every footfall throughout this country to our very doors!

And yet the acquisition of these products, one of the prime conditions of our existence and success on this soil, has been only casually attended to, or, else, in too frequent cases, passed over with neglect or indifference!

II. I have thus stated some of the more prominent deficiencies of our national policy. And now I beg to remark that they are all, for the most part capable of remedy. It is in our power, I feel assured, to commence, at an early day, a new and effectual policy, and to enter thereby upon a career of growth, prosperity, and beneficence, parallel to the successful progress of many of the new-born states of modern times.

I know the smallness of our means. I feel too the need of aid in carrying on fully the processes of successful civilization, in such a wide territory as stretches out beyond us to the heart of this continent; for we must aim to touch graciously even that outer bound. And, as for myself as an individual, I do indeed covet that aid, let it come from any quarter. Not indeed for ourselves; but for the great work which we are to do, in civilizing and evangelizing the rude and benighted neighbours about us. I see, too, somewhat, I think, how great help could be secured for this mighty work.

For help we need. There is nothing humiliating in such an avowal. It is the common need of new nations. Wherever before did a handful of people, less in number than thousands of nameless American villages, set up the fabric, and assume the functions of national life? Even should Liberia fail, that is *in attempting such a vast undertaking,* there would be nothing inglorious in it; no evidence of race inferiority. It would be but one of the many instances of glorious *unsuccess.* It would only be the venture of a child to do the work of a giant, and he could not compass it. But we are, child though we be in form and power, we *are* compassing it; only our powers are overtasked; we miss provident opportunities; we ofttimes "beat the air;" we waste healthful energies.

We need help; and we must fain secure it, if aid and succour can possibly be secured. But not, I assure you, by a declaration that black men cannot carry on a nation; and then go begging some foreign people to take us as colonial vassals, or contemptuous appendages!

Now I do not wish Liberia to become a colony of any nation. I want her to maintain, forever, distinct nationality. After our experience of independence we could not endure colonial subjection. Well and truly says Lord Lytton, concerning liberty—"The first thing is to get it; the next thing is to keep it; the third thing is to increase it."* And so we, having got independence, must not give it up.

I hear, indeed, some talk of annexation to America. Why not to the planet Jupiter? Fellow Citizens—I am astonished at a proposition, at once so humiliating in its nature and so disastrous in its tendency; and I stand here to-day, and entreat you, with all my heart and voice—don't you have anything to do with such a wild and deadly scheme.

Fellow Citizens—the genius of free government, during the ages, visited in turn a few favoured spots of earth, for the gift of freedom and civil liberty. She visited, in ancient times, the states of Greece and Rome. She visited, in the middle ages, the Venetian territory and the Republic of Genoa. In our modern era, she long dwelt amid the mountain fastnesses of Switzerland; on the sea-girt isles of Britain; in the new-born, the virgin, territories of America. But never once did she visit this West coast of Africa; never take up her abode in any quarter of this vast and benighted continent.

---

*"Caxtoniana," by Lord Lytton.

Now, in these latter days of the world's history, filled with generous desires for Africa, she stooped from her lofty flight, and visited the lowly sons of Africa, painfully toiling on the farms of Maryland and Virginia, in the rice fields of Carolina, or amid the everglades of Florida; and whispered in their ears her good intents for this their fatherland. And when they, at her promptings, came o'er the seas, she accompanied them; and set up here, in this seat of ancient despotism and bloody superstitions, the first free, civilized, and Christian Negro government that Africa had ever known from the dawn of history!

And now, I ask, are you, because of some pain and toil, some trouble and poverty, going to unmake history? Because of some little suffering, will you put back ten degrees the dial of the world's progress? Well nigh every foot of land on this West Coast, which lies upon the sea-board, is in the possession of some European power? Will you give up every rod of this coast for foreign possession? Will you not retain a foot of land on this coast for Africa's self and her sons? Is there not to be *one* single free Negro government in the world. Circle the earth; and where can you find one single, responsible, representative, Negro government among the nations? And will you sweep this one lone, simple, star from the heavens?

The United States Government, however, can do great things, through us, for the regeneration of Africa. It would be immodest to assert that she owes *us* a debt; but the averment, is, without doubt, a proper one, that America is deeply indebted to Africa. And providence seems to have made us, who spring from her loins, the proper channels in Africa, of her prompt and generous Christian solicitudes, and, as I trust eventually, of her governmental succor and assistance. For it seems to me that now, as the United States has begun a colonial policy, it would not be unseemly in that great nation to extend to this nascent state the many advantages of a colony without its disadvantages, that is, by the offer and the guarantee of a PROTECTORATE to Liberia, for a lengthy period, for specific ends, pertaining to African regeneration; with those monetary helps and assistances, and that *naval* guardianship, which would enable us to commence a greater work of interior civilization, by the means of roads, model farms, and manual labor schools; with the definite condition that our internal economy, and our full national functions, should remain intact and undisturbed.*

Such a protectorate, or some such strengthening and assuring aid;

---

*Greece; the Ionian Isles; and the Sandwich Islands are examples of the compatability of national life with a foreign protectorate.

would supply that government patronage, of which Liberia alone, of all modern or ancient colonies that I know of, has never felt the fostering care and sustentation; and would soon enable us to enter vigorously upon that regenerating policy, in this part of Africa, which I will now endeavor to point out.

And *first*, I would suggest the duty of rising to a higher appreciation of the native man, his usefulness and his worth. I present this first, because all the great outer works of man come from an internal root; are the fruit of sentiment or principle.

I fear that we are lacking in that recognition of the native man, as a future element of society, which is desirable, as well for our needs, as for his good, and God's glory. And this assuredly should not be the case; for here is a MAN, who, however rude and uncultivated, is sure to stand. The hardihood of the race through long centuries, its quiet resistance to the most terrible assaults upon its vitality; its resurrection to life and active duties, after a ghastly burial of centuries in the caves of despair, in the graves of servitude and oblivious degradation, are all prophetic of a lasting future. Other races of men, in foreign lands, as in America and New Zealand, fall before an incoming emigrant population. But this is not our mission here; and, if it were, it is not in our power, that is, we have not the ability, to destroy the native. With all his simplicity he thoroughly feels this. You see that he does not lose his countenance in your presence; and he knows not fear. In his character you see nothing stolid, repulsive, indomitable. On the other hand he is curious, mobile, imitative. He sees your superiority, and acknowledges it by copying your habits. He is willing to serve you; and, after being in your service, he carries home with him the "spoils," which he has gathered in your family, by observation and experience; which makes him there a superior fellow to his neighbor. There too, in his own tribe, you see that he is sure to live, for he fully supplies his own needs; rears a goodly family; cultivates jollity; attains a good old age; and shows great vitality.

Now this being shows clearly that he has the needed qualities to make a proper man. Everywhere, where the trial has been made, he has passed out of his primitive rudeness, and made a step in advance of his former state.

Why then should we doubt the full and equal ability of the native man to become all that we are, and do all that we can do?—Indeed I can hardly maintain my gravity, while talking thus to *you*. For who indeed are *we*? Right glad am I that there are no Europeans here to-day; for surely they would see the almost ludicrousness of such an address from such an one as I am—and to *you!*

Have faith in the native. You *have* trusted him—trusted him to nurse your children—trusted him with your goods in trading—trusted your life in his hands, in fragile canoes—trusted yourself, unprotected, in his sequestered native villages. Go now to a farther length—trust him as a man, fitted to

—"Move and act
In all the correspondences of nature."

In the *second* place I would suggest the use of well-regulated and judicious measures, in order to secure the vast resources of the interior. What I desire to see undertaken is alliances with powerful tribes in the interior, to secure thereby permanently open roads, and the uninterrupted flow of trade; not indeed as an end, but for the ultimate purposes which lie beyond trade, but of which trade is everywhere a facile agent—I mean general civilization, and the entrance of the controlling influences of Christianity. Surely the command comes to us as a Christian nation— "Prepare ye the way of the Lord." And I have the deep conviction that this work is not a difficult one. What prevents our government organizing an armed police, and a line of forts to the interior, whose presence and power could be felt up to the border line of our territory? How soon then, especially in this country, would vanish those petty native fights, which annually obstruct trading operations six and eight months at a time, and which inflict the loss of thousands of dollars. What should prevent our government enjoining upon our subject natives the maintenance of peace, the constant opening of trade paths, and the bridging of rivers and streams?

Perhaps it may be said that we have no right to command, or press such regulations upon our native population. To this I reply that both our position and our circumstances make us the guardians, the protectors, and the teachers of our heathen tribes. And, hence, it follows that all the legitimate means which may tend to preserve them, which anticipate bloody antagonisms, and which tend to their mental, moral, and social advancement, determine themselves as just and proper.

All historic fact shows that force, that is authority, *must* be used in the exercise of guardianship over heathen tribes. Mere theories of democracy are trivial in this case, and can never nullify this necessity. You cannot apply them to a rude people, incapable of perceiving their own place in the moral scale, nor of understanding the social and political obligations which belong to responsible humanity. "Force and right," says a brilliant writer, "are the governors of this world; *force till right is ready.* * * * *

And till right is ready, force, the existing order of things, is justified, is the legitimate ruler." And he adds—"Right is something moral, and implies inward recognition, free assent of the will; we are not ready for right—*right,* so far as we are concerned, *is not ready,* until we have attained this sense of seeing it and willing it."* Out of this grows the necessary tutelage of children to the years of their majority. Hence also the stern necessity of assuming the nonage—the childhood of the natives; and, consequently, our responsibility of guardianship over them.†

Now, in our exercise of wardship, nothing can be more serious than that terminal exercise of force which lags at the heel of disaster, and is only supplemental to sanguinary calamities. You would despise a parent who postponed all the training of his children till moral ruin had seized them; and then only gave them vengeful retribution. So, likewise, is the nation despicable which claims the right of force over blinded heathens; but can only use that force as the instrument of retaliation for real or supposed injuries.

No, fellow citizens, force is, indeed, our prerogative and our duty with respect to the native; but I maintain that *it should be the force of restoration and progress*—the force which anticipates the insensate ferocity of the pagan, by demonstrating the blessedness of permanent habitation and lasting peace; which forestalls a degrading ignorance and superstition, by the enlightenment of schools and training; which neutralizes the bareness of a native rusticity by the creation of new wants and the stimulation of old ones; which nullifies and uproots a gross heathen domesticity by elevating woman and introducing the idea of family and home.

But you say that all this work, all the machinery for carrying on this work, will be expensive. Of course it will be. But then look at the other side of this matter. Is not *that* expensive too?

Look at our war expeditions and our tribal difficulties, and their great cost. The "interdicts" on trade, which the government has had to enforce, and the consequent loss of thousands of dollars; is not that a matter of consideration? Who can fully estimate that loss?

---

*"Essays in Criticisms," by Matthew Arnold.

†"To characterize any conduct whatever towards a barbarous people as a violation of the 'Law of Nations,' only shows that he who so speaks has never considered the subject. A violation of great principles of morality it may easily be; but barbarians have no rights as a *nation,* except a right to such treatment as may, at the earliest possible period, fit them for becoming one. The only moral laws for the relation between a civilized and a barbarous government are the universal rules of morality between man and man."—*Dissertations and Discussions, &c.,* by John Stuart Mill, vol. 3. *Art.: A Few Words on Non-Intervention.*

The Sinou war of '61 cost this nation 15,000 dollars. It occurred at the commencement of the planting season, and drew off hundreds men from their labour; which involved an additional loss of fully 15,000 dollars work.

In addition to all this, it included the loss of life of several sturdy, valiant, industrious men, whose places, as citizens, husbands, and fathers cannot be filled; and whose value cannot be estimated.

Look at our difficulties in '66 with King Boyer. Who of you here can tell me the full sum total of the loss the government "interdict" on trade, at Bassa, has caused this nation?

Now look at a different policy—suppose years ago, when we purchased that territory, we had sent a schoolmaster to teach King Boyer's children, and, at the same time, to act as a Liberian magistrate, to assist him in settling difficulties; —suppose Boyer, at every session of the Legislature, had been invited to sit with the Senate as an advisory chief, entertained, meanwhile, by the Executive and leading citizens; suppose that, at a proper time, we had followed up this policy by establishing a farm school, in King Boyer's neighborhood, for the growth of coffee and other products, and the training of boys in carpentering and other trades, and in the profits of which King Boyer himself should be a chief participant; —do you think that, with such a policy, we should ever have been troubled by that chief as we have been? Or, rather, do you not think that such a system would have increased Boyer's personal self-respect and conscious dignity; filled him with the moral burdens of responsibility; raised him, long since, almost to the point of civilization; put his people on the road to civilization; and spread the influence thereof to neighbouring tribes?

Put such a system into operation, and, in less than five years, you will see its magnitude and its magical operations all through our territory; in the alliance of strong chiefs and tribes; in the undisturbed opening of roads; in the constant flow of the treasures of the interior to the sea-board; and in the quest of powerful kings, and mighty men, even from the Kong range, for the education of their children, and the enlightenment which comes from the beaming rays of the Cross of Calvary!

You think still, perchance, of the expense of such a policy. But think also of the large export duty such a system would give you; —think of the capability it would give the people for meeting direct taxation; —think of the confidence and assurance with which it would inspire distant capitalists for adventure; —think of the gravitating influence of the trade and barter of great nations to Liberia!

Why the very report of such largeness, energy, and noble forecast, would bring the unsolicited capital of great nations to your doors, for your encouragement and support. Such a system would delight the heart of universal Christendom! It would attract the gaze of all the mission societies in the Protestant world! It would deepen the confident assurance of all the friends of the Negro, in every quarter of the globe! It would bring to your shores the congratulations and assistance of great nations and mighty kingdoms, intent upon the regeneration of Africa!

And, believe me, some such work of magnitude must be undertaken by us, or, otherwise, we shall lose all nobleness of feeling and endeavour; we shall become gross, sordid, and sensual; and so insignificant and trifling will be the life of this nation that, by and by, the declaration will become a common one everwhere—"That people are undeserving national recognition; they are only playing at government; they are not fit to live!"

To prevent such a degrading fling at us, we must give up the idle notion of dragging hither a nation from America, and go to work at once in the great endeavour to construct a vast national existence out of the native material about us.

And such a system you *can* commence. It has been done by other people with no larger resources than yours, and under circumstances not a whit more promising or advantageous. Some of you have heard of the early history of the Indian Empire of Great Britain, and of its marvelous after-growth from a seed of insignificance. Some of you are familiar with the trials of the first colonists to America; and how, in a few memorable instances, by a policy, alike skillful and Christian, they quenched the ferocity of their Indian neighbours, and pushed their trade into the interior safe and unmolested. Some of you here, who indulge in the luxury of fiction, will call to mind how, with a graphic and a winning style, COOPER, in his "Leather Stocking Tales," shows us how by advanced posts and small forts the first settlers of New York carried their fur trade to the very borders of the Canadas.

I must not, however, recall to your remembrance such a picture as this without presenting to your notice its possible disastrous contrast. For, if you do not soon undertake the more general improvement of your native population, the native men who have lived in your families, and been sharpened up by your civilized superiority, will give you, by and by, a visitation of sorest anguish. They will combine together, along the line of our interior border, in their several tribes, from Gallinas to Palmas; and then you will have here, in Africa, such a league of natives as the Indians once formed against the early colonists of Massachusetts; who will come down to the sea-board, in sanguinary ferocity and terrible array, to destroy every vestige of religion, every relic of civilization, and sweep us, if possible, into the sea!*

Now let me call your attention to the basis, which lies deep bedded in the native man's nature, for such a policy as I have endeavoured to point out. For the law of fitness must needs be regarded, or, otherwise, all your measures will prove fruitless. We must adjust our system to those conditions of society, and those idiosyncracies of the nature, which are likely to serve as a basis for general improvement.

Now, we have a basis for a policy such as I have been describing. There is, in the native man's moral constitution, a foundation for it, For, *first,* your petty tribes, to use a country phrase, would "kiss your feet," if you will give them protection from the raids of their more powerful, but lawless neighbours. The great felt need, and a great object of desire among our native population, is peace, order, and protection. Nothing do they crave more ardently than to be saved from the assaults and ravages of the mightier chiefs around them; and to be allowed constant facilities for trading. It was this great need, which, before the "Congo inundation," caused so many of the natives, fragments of larger tribes, the Deys, Veys, and Bassas, to leave their own localities, and settle on the lands of the St. Paul's farmers. They craved peace and security; and they felt that here, under our laws and magistracy it could be secured in larger measure than anywhere else, in our territory.

But a *second,* and a further basis for this policy is the trading propensity of the native. Greed is his master passion; as strong a characteristic as his superstition. See these native men, Pessas, Veys, Hurrahs, Ghibees, Mandingoes, bent and laden with palm oil, camwood, ivory, and rice on their backs; ending, perhaps, a twenty days' journey through the "bush," at the door of a "factory" or a traders' store. See therein that strong acquisitive principle, which is the impelling motive power of all this endurance and

---

*The prediction, contained in the above paragraph, had been scarcely uttered before the author was informed of its correctness and reality, as a *fact!* Immediately after the adjournment of the meeting, on the 1st of August, at Clay Ashland, Mr. S. Anderson, the commissioner to the Barline County, who had just returned from the interior, remarked to the Author, —"Well, you prophesied rightly to-day about native combinations against us. The interior tribes had effected a league, and were about commencing operations; but my expedition has broken the whole thing up. If the Government had not sent a commissioner to *Palaka,* and made the liberal offers she has to the Barline tribe, Liberia would soon have been most seriously assailed by hostile tribes on every side of us! 'Twas a great providence. We were only just in time to save ourselves from ruin!"

weariness; and recognize it as the germ, around which ultimately are to be gathered the accretions and the policy of as grand mercantile measures as the world has seen, in any of its quarters its palmiest days of commerce.

Let the government and people of Liberia seize upon and use this central principle of the native mind, as an instrument and facility for the promotion of its rule, general civilization, and the propagation of the Faith. And this is to be done by the measures and the plans which will open trade to the far interior. Regulate your own tribes; interest them in your government; give them peace and protection; afford them facilities for the gratification of their strong greed; tie them by the strong cords of amity, education, and respect to your government; and your fame will spread hundreds of miles in the interior; and powerful kings, remote from the sea, will soon be visiting your capitol, bringing their sons for training and culture; and seeking the acquaintance of your merchants, for the purpose of commercial intercourse.

And still a *third,* and further advantage will follow. Everybody knows the pride of the native man in speaking English. Now, just in proportion as we draw nigher to our country-folk by trading operations, so will native youth come and dwell with us, to learn our language and our customs; and thus the supply of labour will be fully met.

The bearing of this event upon population is important. During the last six or seven years the great demand of the nation has been for emigration—for an increase of civilized power in the land. And the usual tendency with us is to ascend the hill of Monrovia, and to look across the sea to sight, if possible, the emigrant vessel, crowded with passengers. I do not blame this tendency. I am glad to see new men coming into this country, and thus increasing the Christian and civilizing power of the land. I cannot tell you the joy and gratitude with which I would hail the providence which would give us, this very year, twenty thousand men, of the African race, as an accession to our scanty population; if they could be well sustained and established here.

For myself, I as cordially welcome Barbadians, Jamaicans, Sierra-Leonians, as well as Americans, to this common heritage of the Negro—as the Emigrant Commissioners, at New York, greet the Germans, Italians, Swedes, English, and Irish, who arrive at that port by hundreds of thousands; and thus, every year, swell the already vast population of the great Republic of America.

At the same time, we must not forget that we have a multitudinous immigrant population here at hand, indigenous to the soil; homogenous in race and blood; a people "to the manner born;" fitted to all the needs of this infant state; wanting only in the elements of civilization, and the training of the Christian life. It is our duty to supply this deficiency. We were sent here, in God's providence, to stimulate, by government rule, by law, by example, and by teaching, the dormant energies and the latent capacities of this uncivilized population, and, by gradual steps and processes, guide them up to the higher levels of improvement and civilization.

Of their capability of reaching to any of the heights of superiority, *we* have attained, no man here can doubt, who looks at the superior men, clergymen, doctors, merchants, councilors—native men—who have risen to a position at Sierra-Leone. We see every day, even in a state of simplicity, their manifest *physical* superiority; and all our intercourse with them, as chiefs or traders, discovers to us, an acuteness, penetration, and mental power, which assures us all of the presence here of an acumen, now rude, latent, and mostly hidden, but which needs only to be brought out and cultivated to evidence power and capacity.

An English Minister, not long since, declared that it was the interest of Great Britain to train the West African people "in the arts of civilization and government, until they shall grow into a nation capable of protecting themselves and of managing their own affairs."

Surely if Earl Grey, a man of a different race, felt this sense of obligation, what a shame will it not be to us, a people of Negro blood, if we come back here to the land of our ancestors, and seat ourselves here, amid a needy people, kindred in race and blood, and at once, in the pride of our accidental superiority, eschew obligation and responsibility. Such a course as this will surely be to sow the seeds of disaster and ruin, right amidst the most glowing prosperity; to wrap up the germs of retribution in the brilliant folds of a seeming successfulness.

No, fellow citizens, whether willing or unwilling, whether from necessity or at the urgent call of Christian duty, we *must* educate and elevate our native population. Here we are a "feeble folk," in the midst of their multitudes. If we neglect them, then they will surely drag us down to their rude condition and their deadly superstitions; and our children at some future day, will have cast aside the habiliments of civilized life, and lost the fine harmonies and the grand thoughts of the English tongue. We must undertake the moulding and fashioning of this fine material of native mind and character; and, by the arts of Christian training and civilized life, raise up on the soil a new population for the work of the nation—a virginal civilization ready to start, with elastic vigour, on the noble race for superiority, and to achieve the conquest of the continent for Christ and His Church.

Fellow Citizens—I have spoken to-day with the greatest freedom, in setting forth the conviction of that new school of opinion which has arisen in Liberia, which cries out for justice and duty to Africa. I have taken it for granted that you were brave men and women enough to hear the plain truth, without offence or hesitancy. I deem it a duty that we should talk with all candour and simplicity concerning our national affairs; eschewing all flattery and "mutual admiration." For it is with a nation as with a child. If you cannot tell a youth his faults, without his flying into a passion, there is no hope for him. So, likewise, if a people must always be petted and flattered, and made to believe they are the greatest nation in existence; and cannot bear a plain account of their weaknesses and deficiencies, their case is hopeless. England is one of the oldest and greatest of European nations; and yet there is no people on the earth who so continually find fault with themselves as the English. "They grumble," says an English prelate, "about everything. But then, when they grumble, they go to work to correct the thing they complain of." And this is the secret of their great power, their constant improvement, their marvelous growth.

And it is this, their constant dissatisfaction with an imperfect state and their aim after an ideal perfection, which gives them that quality which *we* are yet to attain, namely *prescience*—the disposition to work for the future. We have but little of it in Liberia, in church or state. Everything is for the present. But this is the reverse of both the noble and the natural; opposed to the divine instinct of our being.

> "Man's heart the Almighty to the *future* set
> By secret and inviolable springs."

And we must strive to rise to the higher measurement of our being and our duty.

Fellow Citizens—there are grand epochs in the history of races and of men, full of the sublimest import. Such, I verily believe, is the period in which we are living. The great activities of commerce and of trade; the doubts and questionings of science, geography, and adventurous travel; the intensities of generous hope; the brotherly yearnings of Christian desire, seem all converging, in this our day, towards the continent of Africa. We are approaching, if, indeed, we are not now well-nigh, the latter days of the world, and the work of the Lord has still one grand complement to the fullness of its mission—that is, the regeneration of Africa. To a large participation in this work, we, the citizens of this republic, are most surely called; and the arduousness and burden of this calling, painful as indeed they are, are utterly insignificant, when compared with the grandeur of the duties involved, and the majesty of the consummation aimed at. It is our privilege to engage in this magnificent work, and to participate in the moral glories which will follow the redemption of a continent. The work will surely be done even if we neglect our duties. But sad and shameful will it be if we blindly miss one of the grandest opportunities human history has ever afforded for moral achievement and the blessedness of man. Other races of men have had such opportunities and nobly met them. This is the time of the Negro!

And, as there are important periods in the history of man, so, likewise, are there fit men, who always start up in the nick of time, with that breadth of mind, that largeness of soul, and that heroic nobleness of purpose, which show that they are equal to their opportunities, and prepared to work with men, with angels, and with God, for the highest good of earth and for the Divine glory. Here, on this coast of Africa, is this grand opportunity, given of God, to men of the African race. May we have resolution, strength, and manliness enough so to bear ourselves that the future records of our day may bear witness to our high public spirit, or solemn sense of duty, our thrift, our energy, our love of race, our patriotism, and our fear of God.

For such high performance our faculties alone are incomplete. We need, for these grand ends, not only the genius of men, but the quickening influences and the grand suggestions of superior powers. And I invoke upon this Republic the succours and assistances of that awful but beneficent Being, who rules the destinies of nations, to give wisdom to our rulers; to dispose this people to the habits of industry, sobriety, and perseverance; to guide the nation in the ways of peace, prosperity, and abounding blessedness; to the glory of His own Name, and for the restoration of a Continent!

"The Destined Superiority
of the Negro"

A Thanksgiving Discourse, 1877

> For your shame ye shall have double, and for confusion
> they shall rejoice in their portion.—Isaiah 41:7

The promise contained in the text is a variation from the ordinary rule of
the divine government. In that government, as declared in the Holy
Scriptures, shame signifies the hopeless confusion and the utter destruction of the wicked. But in this passage we see an extraordinary display of
God's forbearance and mercy. Shame, here, is less intense than in other
places. In this case it stands, indeed, for trial and punishment, but for
punishment and trial which may correct and purify character.

The allusion is supposed to refer to the Jews after their restoration, and
the passage is regarded as teaching that, for all their long-continued
servitude and suffering, God, in the end, would make them abundant
recompense. Great shame and reproach He had given them, through long
centuries; but now, when discipline and trial had corrected and purified
them, He promises them double honor and reward.

As thus explained, the text opens before us some interesting features of
God's dealing with nations; by the light of which we may, perchance,
somewhat determine the destiny of the race with which we are connected.
My purpose is to attempt, this morning, an investigation of God's disciplinary and retributive economy in races and nations; with the hope of
arriving at some clear conclusions concerning the destiny of the Negro
race.

1. Some peoples God does not merely correct; He destroys them. He

---

From Alexander Crummell, *The Greatness of Christ and Other Sermons* (New York:
Thomas Whittaker, 1882), Sermon 20, pp. 332–52.

visits them with deep and abiding shame. He brings upon them utter confusion. This is a painful but a certain fact of Providence. The history of the world is, in one view, a history of national destructions. The wrecks of nations lie everywhere upon the shores of time. Real aboriginal life is rarely found. People after people, in rapid succession, have come into constructive being, and as rapidly gone down; lost forever from sight beneath the waves of a relentless destiny. We read in our histories of the great empires of the old world; but when the traveller goes abroad, and looks for Nineveh and Babylon, for Pompeii and Herculaneum, he finds nought but the outstretched graveyards which occupy the sites of departed nations. On the American continent, tribe after tribe have passed from existence; yea, there are Bibles in Indian tongues which no living man is now able to read. Their peoples have all perished!

When I am called upon to account for all this loss of national and tribal life, I say that God destroyed them. And the declaration is made on the strength of a principle attested by numerous facts in sacred and profane history; that when the sins of a people reach a state of hateful maturity, then God sends upon them sudden destruction.

Depravity prepares some races of men for destruction. Every element of good has gone out of them. Even the most primitive virtues seem to have departed. A putrescent virus has entered into and vitiated their whole nature. They stand up columnar ruins! Such a people is doomed. It cannot live. Like the tree "whose root is rottenness," it stands awaiting the inevitable fall. That fall is its property. No fierce thunder-bolt is needed, no complicated apparatus of ethereal artillery. Let the angry breath of an Archangel but feebly strike it, and, tottering, it sinks into death and oblivion!

Such was the condition of the American Indian at the time of the discovery of America by Columbus. The historical fact abides, that when the white man first reached the shores of this continent he met the tradition of a decaying population.

The New Zealand population of our own day presents a parallel case. By a universal disregard of the social and sanitary conditions which pertain to health and longevity, their physical constitution has fallen into absolute decay; and ere long it must become extinct.

Indeed, the gross paganism of these two peoples was both moral and physical stagnation; was domestic and family ruin; and has resulted in national suicide! It came to them as the effect, the direct consequence of great penal laws established by the Almighty, in which are wrapped the punishment of sin. Hence, if you reject the idea of direct interference in the affairs of peoples, and take up the idea of law and penalty, or that of cause and effect, it amounts to the same thing. Whether through God's fixed law, or directly, by His personal, direful visitation, the admission is the same. The punishment and the ruin come from the throne of God!

The most striking instances of the working of this principle of ruin are set before us in the word of God. The case of Egypt is a signal one. For centuries this nation was addicted to the vilest sins and the grossest corruption. There was no lack of genius among them, no imbecility of intellect. It was a case of wanton, high-headed moral rebellion. As generations followed each other, they heaped up abominations upon the impurities of their ancestors, until they well-nigh reached the heavens. Then the heavens became darkened with direful wrath! The earth quaked and trembled with God's fearful anger; and judgment upon judgment swept, like lava, over that doomed people, assuring them of the awful destruction which always waits upon sin. And the death of the first-born at the Passover, and the catastrophe of the Red Sea, showed that the crisis of their fate had come.

In precisely the same manner God dealt with the wicked people of Assyria, Babylon, Tyre, and Persia. Read the prophecies concerning these nations, and it seems as though you could see an august judge sitting upon the judgment-seat, and, of a sudden, putting on his black cap, and, with solemn gesture and a choked utterance, pronouncing the sentence of death upon the doomed criminals before him!

2. Turn now to the more gracious aspects of God's economy. As there are peoples whom He destroys, so on the other hand there are those whom, while indeed He chastises, yet at the same time He preserves. He gives them shame, but not perpetual shame. He disciplines; but when discipline has worked its remedial benefits, he recompenses them for their former ignominy, and gives them honor and prosperity.

The merciful aspect of God's economy shines out in human history as clearly as His justice and judgment. The Almighty seizes upon superior nations and, by mingled chastisements and blessings, gradually leads them on to greatness. That this discipline of nations is carried on in the world is evident. Probation, that is, as designed to teach self-restraint, and to carry on improvement, is imposed upon them, as well as upon individuals. It is part of the history of all nations and all races; only some will not take it; seem to have no moral discernment to use it; and they, just like wilful men, are broken to pieces. Some, again, fit themselves to it, and gain all its advantages. What was the servile sojourn of the children of Israel, four hundred years, in Egypt, but a process of painful preparation for a coming national and ecclesiastical responsibility? What, at a later period, the Babylonish captivity, but a corrective ordeal, to eliminate from them every element of idolatry? What was the feudality of Europe, but a system of training for a high and grand civilization?

Now it seems to me that these several experiments were not simply judicial and retributive. For vengeance crushes and annihilates; but chastisement, however severe, saves, and at the same time corrects and restores. We may infer, therefore, that these several providences were a mode of divine schooling, carried on by the Almighty for great ends which He wished to show in human history.

But how? in what way does God carry on His system of restorative discipline? The universal principle which regulates this feature of the Divine system is set forth very clearly in the Eighteenth Psalm: "With the merciful thou wilt shew thyself merciful; with an upright man thou wilt shew thyself upright; with the pure thou wilt shew thyself pure; and with the froward thou wilt shew thyself froward." These words show the principles by which God carries on His government. And they apply as well to the organic society as to single persons.

We have already seen that with the froward God showed Himself froward; that is, those who resist Him, God resists, to their utter shame and confusion. Their miseries were not corrective or disciplinary. They were the blows of avenging justice; the thunder-bolts of final and retributive wrath! In their case, moreover, there was a constitutional fitness to destruction, brought upon them by their own immoral perverseness. So, too, on the other hand, we may see qualities which God favors, albeit He does put the peoples manifesting them to trial and endurance. He sees in them cultivated elements of character, which, when brought out and trained, are capable of raising them to superiority. He does not see merit; and it is not because of desert that He bestows His blessings. But when the Almighty sees in a nation or people latent germs of virtues, he seizes upon and schools them by trial and discipline; so that by the processes of divers correctives, these virtues may bud and blossom into beautiful and healthful maturity.

Now, when the Psalmist speaks of the merciful, the upright, and the pure, he does not use these terms in an absolute sense, for in that sense no such persons exist. He speaks of men comparatively pure, upright, and merciful. Some of the nations, as I have already pointed out, were at the lowest grade of moral turpitude. On the other hand, there are and ever have been heathen peoples less gross and barbarous than others: peoples with great hardihood of soul; peoples retaining the high principle of right and justice; peoples with rude but strong virtues, clinging to the simple ideas of truth and honor; peoples who guarded jealously the purity of their wives and the chastity of their daughters; peoples who, even with a false worship, showed reluctance to part with the gleams which came, though but dimly, from the face of the one true God of heaven!

Now the providence of God intervenes for the training and preservation of such peoples. Thus we read in Genesis that, because of man's universal wickedness, "it repented the Lord that he made man"; but immediately it says that he approved "just Noah, and entered into covenant with him." So, after the deluge, God saw, amid universal degeneracy, the conspicuous piety of one man; for obedience and faith were, without doubt, original though simple elements of Abraham's character. To these germinal roots God brought the discipline of trial; and by them, through this one man, educated up a people who, despite their faults, shed forth the clearest religious light of all antiquity, and to whom were committed the oracles of God.

The ancient Greeks and Romans were rude and sanguinary Pagans; and so, too, the Germans and the Scandinavian tribes. Yet they had great, sterling virtues. The Greeks were a people severely just; the Spartans, especially, rigidly simple and religious. The Romans were unequalled for reverence for law and subjection to legitimate authority. Tacitus, himself a heathen, extols the noble and beneficent traits of German character, and celebrates their hospitality and politeness. The Saxons, even in a state of rudeness, were brave, though fierce; truthful; with strong family virtues, and great love of liberty.

Added to these peculiarities we find the following characteristics common to each and all these people—common, indeed, to all strong races; wanting in the low and degraded. The masterful nations are all, more or less, distinguished for vitality, plasticity, receptivity, imitation, family feeling, veracity, and the sentiment of devotion. These qualities may have been crude and unbalanced. They existed perchance right beside most decided and repulsive vices; but they were deeply imbedded in the constitution of these people; and served as a basis on which could be built up a character fitted to great ends.

Archbishop Trench, in his comment upon the words of the "Parable of the Sower," —that is, that "they on the good ground are they who, in an honest and good heart, having heard the word, keep it" —says, "that no heart can be said to be absolutely good; but there are conditions of heart in which the truth finds readier entrance than in others." So we maintain that there are conditions of character and of society, to which the divine purposes of grace and civilization are more especially fitted, and adapt themselves. Such, it is evident, is the explanation of the providential spread of early civilization. It passed by the more inane peoples, and fastened itself to the strong and masculine. Such, too, was the spontaneous flow of early Christianity from Jerusalem. It sought, as by a law of affinity, the strong colonies of Asia Minor, and the powerful states along the Mediterranean; and so spread abroad through the then civilized Europe.

Does God then despise the weak? Nay, but the weak and miserable peoples of the earth have misused their prerogatives, and so unfitted themselves to feel after God.

And because they have thus perverted the gifts of God, and brought imbecility upon their being, they perish. The iniquity of the Amorites in Joshua's day was full—as you many see in Leviticus xviii—full of lust and incest and cruelty and other unspeakable abominations; and they were swept from the face of the earth! They perished by the sword; but the sword is not an absolute necessity to the annihilation of any corrupt and ruined people. Their sins, of themselves, eat out their life. With a touch they go. It was because of the deep and utter demoralization of Bois Gilbert that he fell before the feeble lance of Ivanhoe; for, in the world of morals, weakness and death are ofttimes correlative of baseness and infamy.

On the other hand the simplest seeds of goodness are pleasing to the Almighty, and He sends down the sunshine of His favor and the dews of His conserving care into the darkest rubbish, to nourish and vivify such seeds, and to "give them body as it pleaseth Him; and to every seed his own body." And the greatness of the grand nations has always sprung from the seeds of simple virtues which God has graciously preserved in them; which virtues have been cultured by gracious providences or expanded by Divine grace, into true holiness.

3. Let us now apply the train of thought thus presented to the history and condition of the Negro; to ascertain, if possible, whether we can draw therefrom expectation of a future for this race.

At once the question arises: Is this a race doomed to destruction? or is it one possessed of those qualities, and so morally disciplined by trial, as to augur a vital destiny, and high moral uses, in the future?

To the first of these questions I reply that there is not a fact, pertinent to this subject, that does not give a most decisive negative. The Negro race, nowhere on the globe, is a doomed race!

It is now nigh five hundred years since the breath of the civilized world touched, powerfully, for the first time, the mighty masses of the Pagan world in America, Africa, and the isles of the sea. And we see, almost everywhere, that the weak, heathen tribes of the earth have gone down before the civilized European. Nation after nation has departed before his presence, tribe after tribe! In America the catalogue of these disastrous eclipses overruns, not only dozens, but even scores of cases. Gone, never again to take rank among the tribes of men, are the Iroquois and the Mohegans, the Pequods and the Manhattans, the Algonquins and the brave Mohawks, the gentle Caribs, and the once refined Aztecs!

In the Pacific seas, islands are scattered abroad like stars in the heavens; but the sad fact remains that from many of them their population has departed, like the morning mist. In other cases, as in the Sandwich Islands, they have long since begun their

> Funeral marches to the grave!

Just the reverse with the Negro! Wave after wave of a destructive tempest has swept over his head, without impairing in the least his peculiar vitality. Indeed, the Negro, in certain localities, is a superior man, to-day, to what he was three hundred years ago. With an elasticity rarely paralleled, he has risen superior to the dread inflictions of a prolonged servitude, and stands, to-day, in all the lands of his thraldom, taller, more erect, more intelligent, and more aspiring than any of his ancestors for more than two thousand years of a previous era. And while in other lands, as in cultivated India, the native has been subjected to a foreign yoke, the negro races of Africa still retain, for the most part, their original birthright. The soil has not passed into the possession of foreign people. Many of the native kingdoms stand this day, upon the same basis of power which they held long centuries ago. The adventurous traveler, as he passes farther and farther into the interior, sends us reports of populous cities, superior people, and vast kingdoms; given to enterprise, and engaged in manufactures, agriculture, and commerce.

Even this falls short of the full reality. For civilization, at numerous places, as well in the interior as on the coast, has displaced ancestral heathenism; and the standard of the Cross, uplifted on the banks of its great rivers, at large and important cities, and in the great seats of commercial activity, shows that the Heralds of the Cross have begun the conquest of the continent for their glorious King. Vital power, then, is a property of the Negro family.

But has this race any of those other qualities, and such a number of them, as warrants the expectation of superiority? Are plasticity, receptivity, and assimilation among his constitutional elements of character?

So far as the first of these is concerned there can be no doubt. The flexibility of the negro character is not only universally admitted; it is often formulated into a slur. The race is possessed of a nature more easily moulded than any other class of men. Unlike the stolid Indian, the Negro yields to circumstances, and flows with the current of events. Hence the most terrible afflictions have failed to crush him. His facile nature wards them off, or else, through the inspiration of hope, neutralises their influence. Hence, likewise, the pliancy with which, and without losing his distinctiveness, he runs into the character of other people; and thus bends adverse circumstances to his own convenience; thus, also, in a measurable degree, linking the fortunes of his superiors to his own fate and destiny.

These peculiarities imply another prime quality, anticipating future superiority; I mean imitation. This is also universally conceded, with, however, a contemptuous fling, as though it were an evidence of inferiority. But Burke tells us that "imitation is the second passion belonging to society; and this passion," he says, "arises from much the same cause as sympathy." This forms our manners, our opinions, our lives. It is one of the strongest links of society. Indeed, all civilization is carried down from generation to generation, or handed over from the superior to the inferior, by the means of this principle. A people devoid of imitation are incapable of improvement, and must go down; for stagnation of necessity brings with it decay and ruin.

On the other hand, the Negro, with a mobile and plastic nature, with a strong receptive faculty, seizes upon and makes over to himself, by imitation, the better qualities of others. First of all, observe that, by a strong assimilative tendency he reduplicates himself, by attaining both the likeness of and an affinity to the race with which he dwells; and then, while retaining his characteristic peculiarities, he glides more or less into the traits of his neighbors. Among Frenchmen, he becomes, somewhat, the lively Frenchman; among Americans, the keen, enterprising American; among Spaniards, the stately, solemn Spaniard; among Englishmen, the solid, phlegmatic Englishman.

This peculiarity of the Negro is often sneered at. It is decried as the simulation of a well-known and grotesque animal. But the traducers of the Negro forget that "the entire Grecian civilization is stratified with the elements of imitation; and that Roman culture is but a copy of a foreign and alien civilization." These great nations laid the whole world under contribution to gain superiority. They seized upon all the spoils of time. They became cosmopolitan thieves. They stole from every quarter. They pounced, with eagle eye, upon excellence wherever discovered, and seized upon it with rapacity. In the Negro character resides, though crudely, precisely the same eclectic quality which characterized those two great, classic nations; and he is thus found in the very best company. The ridicule which visits him goes back directly to them. The advantage, however, is his own. Give him time and opportunity, and in all imitative art he will rival them both.

This quality of imitation has been the grand preservative of the Negro in all the lands of his thraldom. Its bearing upon his future distinction in Art is not germain to this discussion; but one can clearly see that this quality of imitation, allied to the receptivity of the race, gives promise of great fitness for Christian training, and for the higher processes of civilization.

But observe, again, that the imitative disposition of the negro race leads to aspiration. Its tendency runs to the higher and the nobler qualities presented to observation. Placed in juxtaposition with both the Indian and the Caucasian, as in Brazil and in this land, the race turns away from the downward, unprogressive Indian, and reaches forth for all the acquisitions of the Caucasian or the Spaniard. And hence wherever the Negro family has been in a servile position, however severe may have been their condition, without one single exception their native capacity has always

—glinted forth
Amid the storm;

preserving the captives exiles of Africa from utter annihilation; stimulating them to enterprise and aspiration; and, in every case, producing men who have shown respectable talent as mechanics and artisans; as soldiers, in armies; as citizens of great commonwealths; not unfrequently as artists; not seldom as scholars; frequently as ministers of the Gospel; and at times as scientific men, and men of letters.

I referred, at the beginning, and as one of the conditions of a Divine and merciful preservation of a people—for future uses, to the probation of discipline and trial, for the cultivation of definite moral qualities. Is there any such large fact in the history of this race? What else, I ask, can be the significance of the African slave-trade? What is the meaning of our deep thraldom since 1620? Terrible as it has been, it has not been the deadly hurricane portending death. During its long periods, although great cruelty and wide-spread death have been large features in the history of the Negro, nevertheless they have been overshadowed by the merciful facts of great natural increase, much intellectual progress, the gravitation of an unexampled and world-wide philanthropy to the race, singular religious susceptibility and progress, and generous, wholesale emancipations, inclusive of millions of men, women, and children.

This history, then, does not signify retribution; does not forecast extinction. It is most plainly disciplinary and preparative. It is the education which comes from trial and endurance; for with it has been allied, more or less, the grand moral training of the religious tendencies of the race.

Here, then, are the several conditions, the characteristic marks which, in all history, have served to indicate the permanency and the progress of races. In all other cases they have been taken as forecasting greatness. Is there any reason for rejecting their teachings, and refusing their encouragements and inspirations, when discovered in the Negro?

I feel fortified, moreover, in the principles I have to-day set forth, by the opinions of great, scrutinizing thinkers. In his treatise on Emancipation, written in 1880, Dr. Channing says: "The Negro is one of the best races of the human family. He is among the mildest and gentlest of men. He is singularly susceptible of improvement."

Alexander Kinmont, in his "Lectures on Man," declares that "the sweet graces of the Christian religion appear almost too tropical and tender plants to grow in the soil of the Caucasian mind; they require a character of human nature of which you can see the rude lineaments in the Ethiopian, to be implanted in, and grow naturally and beautifully withal." Adamson, the traveller who visited Senegal, in 1754, said: "The Negroes are sociable, humane, obliging, and hospitable; and they have generally preserved an estimable simplicity of domestic manners. They are distinguished by their tenderness for their parents, and great respect for the aged—a patriarchal virtue which, in our day, is too little known." Dr. Raleigh, also, at a recent meeting in London, said: "There is in these people a hitherto undiscovered mine of love, the development of which will be for the amazing welfare of the world. . . . Greece gave us beauty; Rome gave us power; the Anglo-Saxon race unites and mingles these; but in the African people there is the great, gushing wealth of love which will develop wonders for the world."

1. We have seen, to-day, the great truth, that when God does not destroy a people, but, on the contrary, trains and disciplines it, it is an indication that He intends to make something of them, and to do something for them. It signifies that He is graciously interested in such a people. In a sense, not equal, indeed, to the case of the Jews, but parallel, in a lower degree, such a people are a "chosen people" of the Lord. There is, so to speak, a *covenant* relation which God has established between Himself and them; dim and partial, at first, in its manifestations; but which is sure to come to the sight of men and angels, clear, distinct, and luminous. You may take it as a sure and undoubted fact that God presides, with sovereign care, over such a people; and will surely preserve, educate, and build them up.

2. The discussion of this morning teaches us that the Negro race, of which we are a part, and which, as yet, in great simplicity and with vast difficulties, is struggling for place and position in this land, discovers, most exactly, in its history, the principle I have stated. And we have in this fact the assurance that the Almighty is interested in all the great problems of civilization and of grace carrying on among us. All this is God's work. He has brought this race through a wilderness of disasters; and at last put them in the large, open place of liberty; but not, you may be assured, for eventual decline and final ruin. You need not entertain the shadow of a doubt that the work which God has begun and is now carrying on, is for the elevation and success of the Negro. This is the significance and the worth of all effort and all achievement, of every signal providence, in this cause; or, otherwise, all the labors of men and all the mightiness of God is vanity! Nothing, believe me, on earth; nothing brought from perdition, can keep back this destined advance of the Negro race. No conspiracies of men nor of devils! The slave trade could not crush them out. Slavery, dread, direful, and malignant, could only stay it for a time. But now it is coming, coming, I grant, through dark and trying events, but surely coming. The Negro—black curly-headed, despised, repulsed, sneered at—is, nevertheless, a vital being, and irrepressible. Everywhere on earth has been given him, by the Almighty, assurance, self-assertion, and influence. The rise of two Negro States within a century, feeble though they be, has a bearing upon this subject. The numerous emancipations, which now leave not more than a chain or two to be unfastened, have, likewise, a deep, moral significance. Thus, too, the rise in the world of illustrious Negroes, as Touissant L'Ouverture, Henry Christophe, Benjamin Banneker, Eustace the Philanthropist, Stephen Allan Benson, and Bishop Crowther.

With all these providential indications in our favor, let us bless God and take courage. Casting aside everything trifling and frivolous, let us lay hold of every element of power, in the brain; in literature, art, and science; in industrial pursuits; in the soil; in cooperative association; in mechanical ingenuity; and above all, in the religion of our God; and so march on in the pathway of progress to that superiority and eminence which is our rightful heritage, and which is evidently the promise of our God!

"Industrial Education: How to Apply the Unclaimed Bounty"

Argument of Rev. Alexander Crummell of this City before the House Committee of Education and Labor, January 29th [1880].

MR. CHAIRMAN:—The very first thing to be noticed in the consideration of the subject before us is the vast, intricate problem of Negro life in this country. The main feature of it is the divorce of the black race from all the great activities of the land. It is a state of divorcement from the mercantile life of the country; from the scientific life of the land; from its literary life; and from its social life. The principle of caste pervades the entire status of black life throughout this entire country.

But fixed, positive, persistent, yea, malignant as at times this feeling of repugnance shows itself, it is impossible to keep the black man in a position of caste. No matter what may be the purpose of the power-holding class in this nation; no matter what may be the design or determination of the white race; no particular class can be put in a designated position and kept there. For there are tendencies in the institutions of this land, in its fundamental principles, in its active spirit, to break down such a determination.

In the first place this is a democratic country; and you can take no particular class of people in this country and shut them out from the influences of the democratic principle; from the idea of equality which seems to be the governing principle of the country.

It is impossible, in the next place, to expatriate the black race from this land. They are here forever. They and their descendants are to remain here to the last period of time. The folly of this idea is evident. The black race increases in this country at the rate of 60,000 a year; and instead of

From *The People's Advocate,* 14 February 1880.

sending off the increase of one month, say 5,000 persons, there are not 100 black men exported from this country in a year. At this rate, in order to expatriate the black race from this land, you would have to wait for many thousand millenniums. They are to remain here permanently in the land; and they cannot be kept down by the caste principle in a fixed and unalterable position.

How is this problem of caste, which tends to degrade the black race to be solved? The race is separated from all the grand activities of a nation's life. It seems to be the set purpose of the white race that they shall be nothing else but servants. The seeming purpose of the people of this country is that they shall hold the status of serfs, and fill places of servitude alone.

It is very evident that in order to break this up, the bestowment of suffrage is insufficient. The black race has been enfranchised. Enfranchisement has not changed their status or condition. It is evident that education and learning, simply and alone, cannot do it.

They may have that to a very large degree. Learned men may be raised up among them, —brilliant scholars may be produced, great geniuses spring up from the midst of them—and yet the masses may remain in a state of degradation.

There is no absolute connection between learning and character; between mental culture and social prosperity. A people may have learning and yet be poor, degraded and vicious.

Anyone who has gone through the U[nited] States, and more especially in the large cities, must have noticed the condition of the black race, and learned these general facts. They are servants; and the only employment they can get is that of service. They are shut out from trades. There are no facilities for their entering the great industries of the land. Combinations exist in every state, in every city and in every village, which prevent them from getting a knowledge of trades and business.

In the large cities of the Atlantic seaboard one sees every where tendencies to pauperism.

Look right here in the city of Washington, the Capital of the Nation, and see the penury which exists among the black race. And why? Simply from lack of employment. Because they are confined to one single groove of activity—the position of servants. It is not only so here at Washington, it is the same in Boston, New York, Philadelphia, Baltimore, Richmond, Charleston, Savannah, and New Orleans. Everywhere in this country the white men seem bound to keep the black race in the same state of servitude.

The general sentiment of the country seems fixed, that black youth shall not reach the higher activities of life; and the result is pauperism on every side and of every character.

Schools have been established since the emancipation. Common-school education has been embraced by them in almost the entire extent of the country. High-schools have been established. Colleges and Universities have opened their doors, and in all of these, colored young men have received the higher culture of the land. And yes, when they have come out of these Colleges, well furnished, and instinct with bright talents and high geniuses, in many cases it has been impossible for them to get employment, and they have sunk down in numbers of cases, to the waiter's position, or been forced into the status of servants on steamboats and in hotels.

I went, in 1872, in the city of New York, into the kitchen of the Union League Club, and there I saw a young man with a copy of Euripides and Tacitus, in the originals, sitting there with his apron upon him awaiting his turn, as a servant, to stand as a waiter behind the table. I have seen young men who have graduated from college as lawyers and doctors, who have been forced at last to gain a livelihood as servants.

It is evident then that the great problem of industrial life of the black race in this country is yet to be solved in some new way that has not yet been reached. It is to be solved by raising the whole plane of their life to a higher elevation. It is to be solved by touching all the springs of life and activity. It is to be solved by stimulating the mechanical and industrial capacities of the race in this land.

Some plan must be fallen upon by which the rising generation among us can be learned in handicraft. Some scheme must be projected by which our youth can, with success, be equipped for the trades. And here, in the good providence of God, is a good opportunity, in the use of this fund, in order to effect this end. We are utterly opposed to the appropriation of it to the use of colleges and universities. The higher education must take care of itself. When colored men throughout the nation by their industry and activity secure wealth, then let them send their sons to Yale or Harvard, and indulge in the luxury of classical learning; but just now that is not the great, the absolute need of the black race in general in this land. Moreover, the largest facilities are already offered for the higher learning of colored men.

The colleges of the East, with rare exceptions, are open to black youth. The colleges of the West are opened unto them. Special colleges for the race have been established in the South. There is no great difficulty then, about securing college education for the colored youth of this country. This is not our great need.

The great, eminent, universal need of the black race in this country is training in skilled labor, in mechanical knowledge and handicraft. Now, here is a grand opportunity to carry out these purposes. What we ask the government is to found scholarships for this object. We want the whole of this fund to be appropriated for just this simple purpose. We do not want a farthing of it appropriated for any other purposes. There is no need that it should be appropriated for any other purpose. I know, indeed, that several colleges are applying here for a portion of this fund for their own sustentation. But we object to the use of this fund for these ends. Let these colleges take care of themselves, and support their own professors.

Gentlemen, I am anxious to say nothing that may seem disagreeable to anyone present to-day; especially to the reverend gentlemen here, representatives of colleges. One thing however seems very apparent in the history of this country. The general sentiment of this nation seems always to have been that the black man is fit for use.

When he was first brought from Africa, 200 years ago, a slave, it was because he was fit for use. For generations he has been employed on board plantations, amassing wealth for the great proprietors in the South— because he was fit for use.

He has recently been emancipated, and still the idea is current in this country that he is still fit for use. He is thought fit for use by both political parties in the country. They wish to employ them for their own purposes; and all the time while using the black man, no idea has been entertained of his right to use himself; his own power and resources for his own benefit.

Here, gentlemen, you have a magnificent sum of money, the result, largely, of the services of the black race, and in the distribution of it the feeling still seems predominant that the black man is fit for use. Now I say let these colleges take care of themselves. Generous men and women are constantly dying and relieving their needs by large sums of money. Why then, should this fund be appropriated for the support of colleges and professors? It looks to me as if there is to be a repetition of this use of the black man for the good of others.

We claim that this fund should be used *directly* for the benefit of the black man in this land. I myself, and my friends are opposed to its distributions to the various colleges and the support of professors. Let there be a commission appointed in this city, under the government, as trustees of this fund, and let the money go directly for the support of colored youth. Say, for instance, in the State of Mississippi there is a black boy of genius and talent; another in Texas; another in Virginia or Maryland, and they have got genius and talent which fit them for mechanism, agriculture, or to become engineers or workers in metal; —let them appropriate a special fund for their support in some agricultural school or some institution where they can learn scientific agriculture or engineering. And then the servitude into which the whole race seems gravitating at this time will soon pass away; and we, as the white in this country will have mechanics, engineers, workers in metal and handicraftsmen. This will raise the whole tone of our living throughout the country and of the race throughout the entire land.

We beg to thank the Committee for the kind hearing which it has given us this day.

"The Black Woman of the South: Her Neglects and Her Needs"

Address before the "Freedman's Aid Society." [Meth. Epis. Church] Ocean Grove, N.J., Aug. 15th, 1883.

It is an age clamorous everywhere for the dignities, the grand prerogatives, and the glory of woman. There is not a country in Europe where she has not risen somewhat above the degradation of centuries, and pleaded successfully for a new position and a higher vocation. As the result of this new reformation we see her, in our day, seated in the lecture-rooms of ancient universities, rivaling her brothers in the fields of literature, the grand creators of ethereal art, the participants in noble civil franchises, the moving spirit in grand reformations, and the guide, agent, or assistant in all the noblest movements for the civilization and regeneration of man.

In these several lines of progress the American woman has run on in advance of her sisters in every other quarter of the globe. The advantage she has received, the rights and prerogatives she has secured for herself, are unequaled by any other class of women in the world. It will not be thought amiss, then, that I come here to-day to present to your consideration the one grand exception to this general superiority of women, viz., "THE BLACK WOMAN OF THE SOUTH."

In speaking to-day of the "black woman," I must needs make a very clear distinction. The African race in this country is divided into two classes, that is—the *colored people* and the *negro population*. In the census returns of 1860 this whole population was set down at 4,500,000. Of these, the *colored* numbered 500,000; the *black* or *negro* population at 4,000,000. But notice these other broad lines of demarkation between

From Alex Crummell, *Africa and America: Addresses and Discourses* (Springfield, Mass.: Willey and Co., 1891), pp. 59–82.

them. The colored people, while indeed but *one-eighth* of the number of the blacks, counted more men and women who could read and write than the whole 4,000,000 of their brethren in bondage. A like disparity showed itself in regard to their *material* condition. The 500,000 colored people were absolutely richer in lands and houses than the many millions of their degraded kinsmen.

The causes of these differences are easily discovered. The colored population received, in numerous cases, the kindness and generosity of their white kindred—white fathers and relatives. Forbidden by law to marry the negro woman, very many slave-holders took her as the wife, despite the law; and when children were begotten every possible recognition was given those children, and they were often cared for, educated, and made possessors of property. Sometimes they were sent to Northern schools, sometimes to France or England. Not unfrequently whole families, nay, at times, whole colonies, were settled in Western or Northern towns and largely endowed with property. The colored population, moreover, was, as compared with the negro, the *urban* population. They were brought in large numbers to the cities, and thus partook of the civilization and refinement of the whites. They were generally the domestic servants of their masters, and thus, brought in contact with their superiors, they gained a sort of education which never came to the field hands, living in rude huts on the plantations. All this, however casual it may seem, was a merciful providence, by which some gleams of light and knowledge came, indirectly, to the race in this land.

The rural or plantation population of the South was made up almost entirely of people of pure negro blood. And this brings out also the other disastrous fact, namely, that this large black population has been living from the time of their introduction into America, a period of more than two hundred years, in a state of unlettered rudeness. The Negro all this time has been an intellectual starvling. This has been more especially the condition of the black woman of the South. Now and then a black man has risen above the debased condition of his people. Various causes would contribute to the advantage of the *men:* the relation of servants to superior masters; attendance at courts with them; their presence at political meetings; listening to table-talk behind their chairs; traveling as valets; the privilege of books and reading in great houses, and with indulgent masters—all these served to lift up a black *man* here and there to something like superiority. But no such fortune fell to the lot of the plantation woman. The black woman of the South was left perpetually in a state of hereditary darkness and rudeness. Since the day of Phillis Wheatly no Negress in this land (that is, in the South) has been raised above the level of her sex. The lot of the black *man* on the plantation has been sad and desolate enough; but the fate of the black woman has been awful! Her entire existence from the day she first landed, a naked victim of the slave-trade, has been degradation in its extremest forms.

In her girlhood all the delicate tenderness of her sex has been rudely outraged. In the field, in the rude cabin, in the press-room, in the factory, she was thrown into the companionship of coarse and ignorant men. No chance was given her for delicate reserve or tender modesty. From her childhood [she] was the doomed victim of the grossest passions. All the virtues of her sex were utterly ignored. If the instinct of chastity asserted itself, then she had to fight like a tigress for the ownership and possession of her own person; and, ofttimes, had to suffer pains and lacerations for her virtuous self-assertion. When she reached maturity all the tender instincts of her womanhood were ruthlessly violated. At the age of marriage—always prematurely anticipated under slavery—she was mated, as the stock of the plantation were mated, *not* to be the companion of a loved and chosen husband, but to be the breeder of human cattle, for the field or the auction block. With that mate she went out, morning after morning to toil, as a common field-hand. As it was *his,* so likewise was it her lot to wield the heavy hoe, or to follow the plow, or to gather in the crops. She was a "hewer of wood and a drawer of water." She was a common field-hand. She had to keep her place in the gang from morn till eve, under the burden of a heavy task, or under the stimulus or the fear of a cruel lash. She was a picker of cotton. She labored at the sugar mill and in the tobacco factory. When, through weariness or sickness, she has fallen behind her allotted task then came, as punishment, the fearful stripes upon her shrinking, lacerated flesh.

Her home life was of the most degrading nature. She lived in the rudest huts, and partook of the coarsest food, and dressed in the scantiest garb, and slept, in multitudinous cabins, upon the hardest boards!

Thus she continued a beast of burden down to the period of those maternal anxieties which, in ordinary civilized life, give repose, quiet, and care to expectant mothers. But, under the slave system, few such relaxations were allowed. And so it came to pass that little children were ushered into this world under conditions which many cattle raisers would not suffer for their flocks or herds. Thus she became the mother of children. But even then there was for her no suretyship of motherhood, or training, or control. Her own offspring were *not* her own. She and husband and children were all the property of others. All these sacred ties were constantly snapped and cruelly sundered. *This* year she had one husband; and next year, through some auction sale, she might be separated from him and mated to another. There was no sanctity of family, no binding tie of marriage, none of the fine felicities and the endearing affections of home. None of these things were the lot of Southern black women. Instead thereof a gross barbarism which tended to blunt the tender sensibilities, to obliterate feminine delicacy and womanly shame, came down as her heritage from generation to generation; and it seems a miracle of providence and grace that, notwithstanding these terrible circumstances, so much struggling virtue lingered amid these rude cabins, that so much womanly worth and sweetness abided in their bosoms, as slaveholders themselves have borne witness to.

But some of you will ask: "Why bring up these sad memories of the past? Why distress us with these dead and departed cruelties?" Alas, my friends, these are not dead things. Remember that

"The evil that men do lives after them."

The evil of gross and monstrous abominations, the evil of great organic institutions crop out long after the departure of the institutions themselves. If you go to Europe you will find not only the roots, but likewise many of the deadly fruits of the old Feudal system still surviving in several of its old states and kingdoms. So, too, with slavery. The eighteen years of freedom have not obliterated all its deadly marks from either the souls or bodies of the black woman. The conditions of life, indeed, have been modified since emancipation; but it still maintains that the black woman is the Pariah woman of this land! We have, indeed, degraded women, immigrants, from foreign lands. In their own countries some of them were so low in the social scale that they were yoked with the cattle to plow the fields. They were rude, unlettered, coarse, and benighted. But when they reach *this* land there comes an end to their degraded condition.

"They touch our country and their shackles fall."

As soon as they become grafted into the stock of American life they partake at once of all its large gifts and its noble resources.

Not so with the black woman of the South. Freed, legally she has been; but the act of emancipation had no talismanic influence to reach to and alter and transform her degrading social life.

When that proclamation was issued she might have heard the whispered words in her every hut, "Open Sesame;" but, so far as her humble domicile and her degraded person was concerned, there was no invisible but gracious Genii who, on the instant, could transmute the rudeness of her hut into instant elegance, and change the crude surroundings of her home into neatness, taste, and beauty.

The truth is, "Emancipation Day" found her a prostrate and degraded being; and, although it has brought numerous advantages to her sons, it has produced but the simplest changes in her social and domestic condition. She is still the crude, rude, ignorant mother. Remote from cities, the dweller still in the old plantation hut, neighboring to the sulky, disaffected master class, who still think her freedom was a personal robbery of themselves, none of the "fair humanities" have visited her humble home. The light of knowledge has not fallen upon her eyes. The fine domesticities which give the charm to family life, and which, by the refinement and delicacy of womanhood, preserve the civilization of nations, have not come to *her*. She has still the rude, coarse labor of men. With her rude husband she still shares the hard service of a field-hand. Her house, which shelters, perhaps, some six or eight children, embraces but two rooms. Her furniture is of the rudest kind. The clothing of the household is scant and of the coarsest material, has ofttimes the garniture of rags; and for herself and offspring is marked, not seldom, by the absence of both hats and shoes. She has rarely been taught to sew, and the field labor of slavery times has kept her ignorant of the habitudes of neatness, and the requirements of order. Indeed, coarse food, coarse clothes, coarse living, coarse manners, coarse companions, coarse surroundings, coarse neighbors, both black and white, yea, every thing coarse, down to the coarse, ignorant, senseless religion, which excites her sensibilities and starts her passions, go to make up the life of the masses of black women in the hamlets and villages of the rural South.

This is the state of black womanhood. Take the girlhood of this same region, and it presents the same aspect, save that in large districts the white man has not forgotten the olden times of slavery, and, with, indeed, the deepest sentimental abhorrence of "amalgamation," still thinks that the black girl is to be perpetually the victim of his lust! In the larger towns and in cities, our girls, in common schools and academies, are receiving superior culture. Of the fifteen thousand colored school teachers in the South, more than half are colored young women, educated since emancipation. But even these girls, as well as their more ignorant sisters in rude huts, are followed and tempted and insulted by the ruffianly element of Southern society, who think that black *men* have no rights which white men should regard, and black *women* no virtue which white men should respect!

And now look at the *vastness* of this degradation. If I had been speaking of the population of a city, or a town, or even a village, the tale would be a sad and melancholy one. But I have brought before you the condition of millions of women. According to the census of 1880 there were, in the Southern States, 3,327,678 females of all ages of the African race. Of these there were 674,365 girls between twelve and twenty, 1,522,696 between twenty and eighty. "These figures," remarks an observing friend of mine, "are startling!" And when you think that the masses of these women live in the rural districts; that they grow up in rudeness and ignorance; that their former masters are using few means to break up their hereditary degradation, you can easily take in the pitiful condition of this population, and forecast the inevitable future to multitudes of females, unless a mighty special effort is made for the improvement of the black womanhood of the South.

I know the practical nature of the American mind, I know how the question of values intrudes itself into even the domain of philanthropy; and, hence, I shall not be astonished if the query suggests itself, whether special interest in the black woman will bring any special advantage to the American nation.

Let me dwell for a few moments upon this phase of the subject. Possibly the view I am about suggesting has never before been presented to the American mind. But, Negro as I am, I shall make no apology for venturing the claim that the Negress is one of the most interesting of all the classes of women on the globe. I am speaking of her, not as a perverted and degraded creature, but in her natural state, with her native instincts and peculiarities.

Let me repeat just here the words of a wise, observing, tender-hearted philanthropist, whose name and worth and words have attained celebrity. It is fully forty years ago since the celebrated Dr. Channing said: "We are holding in bondage one of the best races of the human family. The Negro is among the mildest, gentlest of men. He is singularly susceptible of improvement from abroad. . . . His nature is affectionate, easily touched, and hence he is more open to religious improvement than the white man. . . . The African carries with him much more than *we* the genius of a meek, long-suffering, loving virtue."*

*"Emancipation." By Rev. W. E. Channing, D.D. *Works of W. E. Channing, D.D. A.U.A.Ed.* Pp. 820.

I should feel ashamed to allow these words to fall from my lips if it were not necessary to the lustration of the character of my black sisters of the South. I do not stand here to-day to plead for the black *man*. He is a man; and if he is weak he must go the wall. He is a man; he must fight his own way, and if he is strong in mind and body, he can take care of himself. But for the mothers, sisters, and daughters of my race I have a right to speak. And when I think of their sad condition down South, think, too, that since the day of emancipation hardly any one has lifted up a voice in their behalf, I feel it a duty and a privilege to set forth their praises and to extol their excellencies. For, humble and benighted as she is, the black woman of the South is one of the queens of womanhood. If there is any other woman on this earth who in native aboriginal qualities is her superior, I know not where she is to be found; for, I do say, that in tenderness of feeling, in genuine native modesty, in large disinterestedness, in sweetness of disposition and deep humility, in unselfish devotedness, and in warm, motherly assiduities, the Negro woman is unsurpassed by any other woman on this earth.

The testimony to this effect is almost universal—our enemies themselves being witnesses. You know how widely and how continuously, for generations, the Negro has been traduced, ridiculed, derided. Some of you may remember the journals and the hostile criticisms of Coleridge and Trollope and Burton, West Indian and African travelers. Very many of you may remember the philosophical disquisitions of the ethnological school of 1847, the contemptuous dissertations of Hunt and Gliddon. But it is worthy of notice in all these cases that the sneer, the contempt, the bitter gibe, have been invariably leveled against the black *man*—never against the black woman! On the contrary, *she* has almost everywhere been extolled and eulogized. The black man was called a stupid, thick-lipped, flat-nosed, long-heeled, empty-headed animal; the link between the baboon and the human being, only fit to be a slave! But everywhere, even in the domains of slavery, how tenderly has the Negress been spoken of! She has been the nurse of childhood. To her all the cares and heart-griefs of youth have been intrusted. Thousands and tens of thousands in the West Indies and in our Southern States have risen up and told the tale of her tenderness, of her gentleness, patience, and affection. No other woman in the world has ever had such tributes to a high moral nature, sweet, gentle love, and unchanged devotedness. And by the memory of my own mother and dearest sisters I can declare it to be true!

Hear the tribute of Michelet: "The Negress, of all others, is the most loving, the most generating; and this, not only because of her youthful blood, but we must also admit, for the richness of her heart. She is loving among the loving, good among the good (ask the travelers whom she has so often saved). Goodness is creative, it is fruitfulness, it is the very benediction of a holy act. The fact that woman is so fruitful I attribute to her treasures of tenderness, to that ocean of goodness which permeates her heart. . . . Africa is a woman. Her races are feminine. . . . In many of the black tribes of Central Africa the women rule, and they are as intelligent as they are amiable and kind."*

The reference in Michelet to the generosity of the African woman to travelers brings to mind the incident in Mungo Park's travels, where the African women fed, nourished, and saved him. The men had driven him away. They would not even allow him to feed with the cattle; and so, faint, weary, and despairing, he went to a remote hut and lay down on the earth to die. One woman, touched with compassion, came to him, brought him food and milk, and at once he revived. Then he tells us of the solace and the assiduities of these gentle creatures for his comfort. I give you his own words: "The rites of hospitality thus performed toward a stranger in distress, my worthy benefactress, pointing to the mat, and telling me that I might sleep there without apprehension, called to the female part of her family which had stood gazing on me all the while in fixed astonishment, to resume the task of spinning cotton, in which they continued to employ themselves a great part of the night. They lightened their labors by songs, one of which was composed extempore, for I was myself the subject of it. It was sung by one of the young women, the rest joining in a sort of chime. The air was sweet and plaintive, and the words, literally translated, were these: 'The winds roared and the rains fell; the poor white man, faint and weary, came and sat under our tree. He has no mother to bring him milk, no wife to grind his corn. Let us pity the white man, no mother has he,'" etc., etc.

Perhaps I may be pardoned the intrusion, just here, on my own personal experience. During a residence of nigh twenty years in West Africa, I saw the beauty and felt the charm of the native female character. I saw the native woman in her *heathen* state, and was delighted to see, in numerous tribes, that extraordinary sweetness, gentleness, docility, modesty, and especially those maternal solicitudes which make every African boy both gallant and defender of his mother.

---

*"Woman." From the French of M. J. Michelet, pp. 132. Rudd & Carleton, N.Y.

I saw her in her *civilized* state, in Sierra Leone; saw precisely the same characteristics, but heightened, dignified, refined, and sanctified by the training of the schools, the refinements of civilization, and the graces of Christian sentiment and feeling. Of all the memories of foreign travel there are none more delightful than those of the families and the female friends of Freetown.

A French traveler speaks with great admiration of the black ladies of Hayti. "In the towns," he says, "I met all the charms of civilized life. The graces of the ladies of Port-au-Prince will never be effaced from my recollections."*

It was, without doubt, the instant discernment of these fine and tender qualities which prompted the touching Sonnet of Wordsworth, written in 1802, on the occasion of the cruel exile of Negroes from France by the French Government:

> "Driven from the soil of France, a female came
>   From Calais with us, brilliant in array,
>   A Negro woman like a lady gay,
> Yet downcast as a woman fearing blame;
>   Meek, destitute, as seemed, of hope or aim
>   She sat, from notice turning not away,
> But on all proffered intercourse did lay
>   A weight of languid speech—or at the same
> Was silent, motionless in eyes and face.
>   Meanwhile those eyes retained their tropic fire,
>   Which burning independent of the mind,
> Joined with the luster of her rich attire
> To mock the outcast—O ye heavens be kind!
> And feel thou earth for this afflicted race!"†

But I must remember that I am to speak not only of the neglects of the black woman, but also of her needs. And the consideration of her needs suggests the remedy which should be used for the uplifting of this woman from a state of brutality and degradation.

I have two or three plans to offer which, I feel assured, if faithfully used, will introduce widespread and ameliorating influences amid this large population.

(a) The *first* of these is specially adapted to the adult female population of the South, and is designed for more immediate effect. I ask for the equipment and the mission of "sisterhoods" to the black women of the

*See "Jamaica in 1850." By John Bigelow.
†Wordsworth. Sonnets dedicated to Liberty.

South. I wish to see large numbers of practical Christian women, women of intelligence and piety; women well trained in domestic economy; women who combine delicate sensibility and refinement with industrial acquaintance—scores of such women to go South; to enter every Southern State; to visit "Uncle Tom's Cabin;" to sit down with "Aunt Chloe" and her daughters; to show and teach them the ways and habits of thrift, economy, neatness, and order; to gather them into "Mothers' Meetings" and sewing schools; and by both lectures and "talks" guide these women and their daughters into the modes and habits of clean and orderly housekeeping.

There is no other way, it seems to me, to bring about this domestic revolution. —We can not postpone this reformation to another generation. Postponement is the reproduction of the same evils in numberless daughters now coming up into life, imitators of the crude and untidy habits of their neglected mothers, and the perpetuation of plantation life to another generation. No, the effect must be made immediately, in *this* generation, with the rude, rough, neglected women of the times.

And it is to be done at their own homes, in their own huts. In this work all theories are useless. This is a practical need, and personal as practical. It is emphatically a personal work. It is to be done by example. The "Sister of Mercy," putting aside all fastidiousness, is to enter the humble and, perchance, repulsive cabin of her black sister, and gaining her confidence, is to lead her out of the crude, disordered, and miserable ways of her plantation life into neatness, cleanliness, thrift, and self-respect. In every community women could be found who would gladly welcome such gracious visitations and instructors, and seize with eagerness their lessons and teachings. Soon their neighbors would seek the visitations which had lifted up friends and kinsfolk from inferiority and wretchedness. And then, erelong, whole communities would crave the benediction of these inspiring sisterhoods, and thousands and tens of thousands would hail the advent of these missionaries in their humble cabins. And then the seed of a new and orderly life planted in a few huts and localities, it would soon spread abroad, through the principle of imitation, and erelong, like the Banyan-tree, the beneficent work would spread far and wide through large populations. Doubtless they would be received, first of all, with surprise, for neither they nor their mothers, for two hundred years, have known the solicitudes of the great and cultivated for their domestic comfort. But surprise would soon give way to joy and exultation. Mrs. Fanny Kemble Butler, in her work, "Journal of a Residence on a Georgian

Plantation in 1838–39," tells us of the amazement of the wretched slave woman on her husband's plantation when she went among them, and tried to improve their quarters and to raise them above squalor; and then of their immediate joy and gratitude.

There is nothing original in the suggestion I make for the "Sisters of Mercy." It is no idealistic and impractical scheme I am proposing, no new-fangled notion that I put before you. The Roman Catholic Church has, for centuries, been employing the agency of women in the propagation of her faith and as dispensers of charity. The Protestants of Germany are noted for the effective labors of holy women, not only in the Fatherland but in some of the most successful missions among the heathen in modern times. The Church of England, in that remarkable revival which has lifted her up as by a tidal wave, from the dead passivity of the last century, to an apostolic zeal and fervor never before known in her history, has shown, as one of her main characteristics, the wonderful power of "Sisterhoods," not only in the conversion of reprobates, but in the reformation of whole districts of abandoned men and women. This agency has been one of the most effective instrumentalities in the hands of that special school of devoted men called "Ritualists." Women of every class in that Church, many of humble birth, and as many more from the ranks of the noble, have left home and friends and the choicest circles of society, and given up their lives to the lowliest service of the poor and miserable. They have gone down into the very slums of her great cities, among thieves and murderers and harlots; amid filth and disease and pestilence; and for Christ's sake served and washed and nursed the most repulsive wretches; and then have willingly laid down and died, either exhausted by their labors or poisoned by infectious disease. Any one who will read the life of "Sister Dora" and of Charles Lowder, will see the glorious illustrations of my suggestion. Why can not this be done for the black women of the South?

(b) My *second* suggestion is as follows, and it reaches over to the future. I am anxious for a permanent and uplifting civilization to be engrafted on the Negro race in this land. And this can only be secured through the womanhood of a race. If you want the civilization of a people to reach the very best elements of their being, and then, having reached them, there to abide, as an indigenous principle, you must imbue the *womanhood* of that people with all its elements and qualities. Any movement which passes by the female sex is an ephemeral thing. Without them, no true nationality, patriotism, religion, cultivation, family life, or true social status is a possibility. In *this* matter it takes *two* to make one—mankind is a duality. The *male* may bring, as an exotic, a foreign graft, say of a civilization, to a new people. But what then? Can a graft live or thrive of itself? By no manner of means. It must get vitality from the *stock* into which it is put; and it is the women who give the sap to every human organization which thrives and flourishes on earth.

I plead, therefore, for the establishment of at least one large "INDUS-TRIAL SCHOOL" in every Southern State for the black girls of the South. I ask for the establishment of schools which may serve especially the *home* life of the rising womanhood of my race. I am not soliciting for these girls scholastic institutions, seminaries for the cultivation of elegance, conservatories of music, and schools of classical and artistic training. I want such schools and seminaries for the women of my race as much as any other race; and I am glad that there are such schools and colleges, and that scores of colored women are students within their walls.

But this higher style of culture is not what I am aiming after for *this* great need. I am seeking something humbler, more homelike and practical, in which the education of the land and the use of the body shall be the specialties, and where the intellectual training will be the incident.

Let me state just here definitely what I want for the black girls of the South:

1. I want boarding-schools for the *industrial training* of one hundred and fifty or two hundred of the poorest girls, of the ages of twelve to eighteen years.

2. I wish the *intellectual* training to be limited to reading, writing, arithmetic, and geography.

3. I would have these girls taught to do accurately all domestic work, such as sweeping floors, dusting rooms, scrubbing, bed making, washing and ironing, sewing, mending, and knitting.

4. I would have the trades of dressmaking, millinery, straw-platting, tailoring for men, and such like, taught them.

5. The art of cooking should be made a specialty, and every girl should be instructed in it.

6. In connection with these schools, garden plats should be cultivated, and every girl should be required, daily, to spend at least an hour in learning the cultivation of small fruits, vegetables, and flowers.

I am satisfied that the expense of establishing such schools would be insignificant. As to their maintenance, there can be no doubt that, rightly managed, they would in a brief time be self-supporting. Each school would soon become a hive of industry, and a source of income. But the *good* they would do is the main consideration. Suppose that the time of a girl's schooling be limited to *three,* or perchance to *two* years. It is hardly possible to exaggerate either the personal family or society influence which would flow from these schools. Every class, yea, every girl in an outgoing class, would be a missionary of thrift, industry, common sense, and practicality. They would go forth, year by year, a leavening power into the houses, towns, and villages of the Southern black population; girls fit to be thrifty wives of the honest peasantry of the South, the worthy matrons of their numerous households.

I am looking after the domestic training of the MASSES; for the raising up women meet to be the helpers of *poor* men the RANK AND FILE of black society, all through the rural districts of the South. The city people and the wealthy can seek more ambitious schools, and should pay for them.

Ladies and gentlemen, since the day of emancipation millions of dollars have been given by the generous Christian people of the North for the intellectual training of the black race in this land. Colleges and universities have been built in the South, and hundreds of youth have been gathered within their walls. The work of your own Church in this regard has been magnificent and unrivaled, and the results which have been attained have been grand and elevating to the entire Negro race in America. The complement to all this generous and ennobling effort is the elevation of the black woman. Up to this day and time your noble philanthropy has touched, for the most part, the male population of the South, given them superiority, and stimulated them to higher aspirations. But a true civilization can only then be attained when the life of woman is reached, her whole being permeated by noble ideas, her fine taste enriched by culture, her tendencies to the beautiful gratified and developed, her singular and delicate nature lifted up to its full capacity; and then, when all these qualities are fully matured, cultivated and sanctified, all their sacred influences shall circle around ten thousand firesides, and the cabins of the humblest freedmen shall become the homes of Christian refinement and of domestic elegance through the influence and the charm of the uplifted and cultivated black woman of the South!

"The Assassination of President Garfield"

Preached Sunday, July 10, 1881

> And one of them named Caiaphas, being the High
> Priest that same year, said unto them, Ye know nothing
> at all, nor consider that it is expedient that one man
> should die for the people, and that the whole nation
> perish not. John 11:49, 50

All through the week, my brethren, we, in common with the people of this land, have been passing through an ordeal of suspense, of agony, of almost despair; rarely parallelled in the history of this or any other country. Pain and suffering are the common lot of all men; but it is seldom that a whole nation is called to the intense, long-lingering anxiety which has been the lot of the many millions who make up this great nation. Day by day, nay, hour by hour, this entire republic has been on the rack, fearful of a report which would have brought anguish and bereavement to unnumbered hearts and households. For the entire people of this land have felt that the dreadful deed which brought our Chief Magistrate well nigh the shades of death was personal to themselves. When President Garfield was shot by a wild and reckless assassin, every citizen was shot at. His wounds were our wounds. His agonies were our agonies. It was not only that he, as President and Chief, stood officially before the people and the world the representative of the nation, and hence that to attack him was like an assault upon the flag of the country—an assault upon its every citizen; but, added to this, is the further fact, seen in various ways before this sad occurrence, that the genuine and intense personality of this man had

---

From Alexander Crummell, *The Greatness of Christ and Other Sermons* (New York: Thomas Whittaker, 1882), Sermon 19, pp. 312–31.

"bowed the heart" of its whole population, "as the heart of one man." Hence it is that a whole people have stood breathless, anxious, and appalled at his bedside; and strong men, when they heard of this calamity, fainted, and the tender hearts of women and children gave way to uncontrollable emotions, and the aged, in known instances, shocked at the awfulness of this assault, lay down and died!

Such interest, such sympathy, such fellowship in suffering with a suffering man has never before been witnessed. We know somewhat how great has been his anguish. But is it too great an exaggeration to say that thousands of people in this land, have suffered well nigh as much in *his* suffering as he himself has suffered? Is there any man here who can estimate the intense mental anguish, the harassing care of multitudes, as they have stood, day by day, trembling, almost despairing, for the life of this eminent man? Many years ago I read a poem, "The Death-Bed," by Thomas Hood. It is a most graphic representation of the aching anxiousness of the soul at the dreaded death of a sufferer; but never have I so felt them in my heart as, day by day, with an anxiousness beyond expression, I have sought the bulletins from the "White House."

> We watched her breathing through the night,
> Her breathing soft and low,
> As in her breast the wave of life
> Kept heaving to and fro.
>
> So silently we seemed to speak,
> So slowly moved about,
> As we had lent her half our powers
> To eke her living out.
>
> Our very hopes belied our fears,
> Our fears our hopes belied—
> We thought her dying when she slept,
> And sleeping when she died.

It is a terrible event, my brethren! The fruit of the distempered brain and the wild will of a reckless and bloody-minded man! But the Divine will runs right beside it, with beneficent intent, and corrective and saving ends. Just so it is in all the dark and dreadful occurrences of life. The Almighty maintains His omnipresent power amid dread disaster, as well as in benignant event.

Neither man nor devil can shut God out of the currents of history. And we see that He moves, that He *will* move, in all the shady, murky occurrences of life, ever

—from seeming evil
Still educing good.

It is this counteracting and governing will of Deity, seen everywhere, in the dark as well as in the bright histories of men, which we call *Providence*. We see it in this occurrence. There is a providence in this dreadful tragedy. President Garfield is not allowed, you may be sure, to suffer in vain. There are great moral uses discoverable in his sore trial. Albeit not intended by the Evil One, our great sufferer is manifestly a sacrifice for national good. And the flippant words of Caiaphas, which were, after all, an unconscious prophecy, set forth the great principle of expiation which runs through all the relations of life; but which reaches its highest point in the sufferings of the Crucified. Although it be one of its lower senses, we may see it exemplified in our suffering Chief Magistrate.

1. See, first of all, the sudden check this event has given to the gross secularization of the American mind. The race for wealth in this country, the eager, outstretched ambitions for mere earthly good, outstrip the rivalries of all other nations. They are so absorbing and so immense that they allow only the most slender intrusion of things sacred and divine. They make men earthly in all the purposes of life, and create that intense thirst for mere temporal gratification which is the special temptation of the young, and proves so widely the ruin of the old. The mind of the men of this land, beyond the general mind of other civilized nations, alien, for the most part, from art, unaddicted, save in the schools, to science and philosophy, runs with an eager, almost insane, craving after mere earthly good.

And yet, in an instant, as it were, this whole nation's secularity was brought to a stop. By one single flash of the telegraph, millions of men sickened of trade, and barter, and money-making. At a single whisper of national calamity, handicraft and farming, labor and service, are given up. The busy wheel of the factory ceases its whirl, and the song of the anvil is hushed. Wall street turns with disgust from its trade in stock, and mechanism puts aside the hammer and the plane.

In *this one* aspect undoubtedly that is a good which serves to arrest the blind rush after mere material ends. No one can measure the benediction, almost sacred in its nature, which lifts up a people, above earth and sense, into the domain of sentiment and feeling. It is a glorious incident in the life of any nation, when of itself pushes out of sight the gross and carnal, and advances spontaneously and in one mighty phalanx into the sphere of sensibility.

And next observe that with this sudden collapse of the temporal, uprises, as by a divine impulse, the grand outburst of a whole nation's intense and tearful sensibility. Not only women with their tender sympathies, and children with their warm and ardent feelings, but millions of men, with throbbing hearts, rushed, as it were, to this man's bedside, offering sympathy, devotedness, and gifts; nay, almost ready to tender their life-blood, to save the life of their loved and honored chief. See how this nation, for well nigh a week, has been given up to tears and indignation; alternate hope and fear; to prayer and supplications; and now, at the last, note the generous outpouring of riches, that the wife and children of this Chief Magistrate may not, in any event whatever, be left unprovided for and destitute!

My brethren, there is nothing fortuitous in these stirring occurrences. God's hand is manifestly visible, bright and beneficent, amid its darkest shades. Satan, indeed, and his dark-scarred instrument, "thought evil" in this bloody deed; but "God meant it unto good"; even the sudden wresting of a nation from gross, material purposes, and the uplifting them to the highest, noblest aims of life. And this I call a blessing. It is, indeed, almost a salvation, this sudden rising tidal wave of affection and sympathy in this nation's heart. Whether its gross materialism could have been disturbed in any ordinary way, is doubtful. Whether its dull lethargy could have been galvanized even into temporary life, by common occurrence, is a question. It seems as though some terrible thrill was needed; as though nothing but the threatened life of a grand victim could sweep away the film from the eyes of this nation, and enable it, of a sudden, to *see*.

I feel, as much as any man, the horror of this murderous act. But when I observe this grand demonstration of a nation's moral nature; when I see the *spiritual* bursting forth from the caverns of a people's cold, calculating secularity; I behold a providence that cannot be mistaken, and learn, besides, that it is sometimes expedient "that one man should die, that a whole nation perish not"!

2. But neither the keenness of our feelings nor the depth of our sensibilities should cause us to pass by great lessons which spring immediately from this sad event. People talk of it as a casualty. Some look at it as a mystery. But remember "that affliction cometh not forth of the dust, neither doth trouble spring out of the ground." There is nothing of chance or hap-hazard in this calamity. It requires no extraordinary insight to discover in it the principle of sequence. For, unless I make the greatest of mistakes, cause and effect are as plainly evident in this tragic occurrence as in any of the other incidents which go to make the history of the times.

Let me set before you some of the lessons which it seems to me that this nation is called upon, just now, to learn.

And (1) this attempted assassination brings vividly before us the intoxicating and demoralizing effects of our political system. It is a system calculated most directly to carry men beyond themselves, to taint the brains of thousands with incipient insanity, and to hurry them on to wild and irresponsible actions. We talk, in common parlance, of the wildness of money speculations and of the madness of unlawful lottery schemes. But these ventures are actual soberness compared with the intense and extravagant incitements which come out of our political agitations. We have, in our country, settled organisms and established modes in politics, which, in their operations, seem designed as certainly they do to produce widespread and convulsive upheavals. Why, the very caucusses of parties, and they are multitudinous, are flames. Our vast political assemblages, what are they but burning blasts? Our national conventions, but tempests? Our tumultuous and swarming canvasses, but paroxysms? Our grand elections, what but tremendous tornadoes? And then, when success has attended these almost frenzied partisan efforts, what can we call the uprising and the passionate pressure of the mighty army of anxious, greedy, determined office-seekers—what but blasting hurricanes?

There can be no doubt, as it strikes me, that this homicidal attack has sprung directly from this exciting system. This assassin's career goes to show that he possessed that temperament and that sort of brains, fitted, most precisely, to the counter-cries and the intemperate incitements of our recent political and partisan upheavals. His very letters, words, and utterances show that his mind for a long time had become stimulated to frenzy by agitations and strifes, of which you all know, but which may not be dwelt upon nor too plainly spoken of in this sacred place. The anxiousness for office was indeed an element in his conduct; and that is another feature of this deadly political inebriation. But the main characteristic of the assassin's motive and act, was partisan spleen and political dudgeon, chafed and inflamed to murderous purpose.

The clear-minded citizen of every name has seen somewhat, in the last ten days, the bane of this whole system. By blood, perchance—which God forbid—by death, a sudden revelation has been made of the organic but destructive system of fire, storm, and tempest which characterizes our national politics. This discovery, sad and humiliating as it may be, is somewhat compensatory for the prodigious evil which fathers it. And if this great lesson is thoroughly learned at this time, then, in the divine providence, it will be clearly seen how, at times, it is "expedient that one man should die, and that the whole nation perish not." For perish it will if reason, restraint, unselfishness, and sober duty are not made stronger and more conspicuous elements in our political strife.

3. Turn to another lesson suggested by this dark occurrence. We may see, just now, the ignoble fact that our people hold government and governmental rule as too cheap a thing in estimation. I have the impression that, outside of the thinking, cultured classes, the average American thinks that the governmental system of the land is simply his tool, the republic as only a thing for personal convenience. Allied to this notion is the other feeling, that neither nation, nor any officer thereof, must trench too much upon personal desire or individual purpose.

What is the common sentiment abroad in the land with regard to the Republic, as a nation? Do not men declare that it is a man-made thing? Do they not vociferate that civil government is merely human? That it is "of and by the people," with the narrow limitations of the assertion which they make? Nay, are there not large masses of people in the land who would resent as an insult and an outrage, the *denial* that any government, that is organic in its nature, was made "by the people"? And is it not owing to this that we look in vain on this soil for that filial, that reverential sentiment toward government which characterized even the higher pagan nations of antiquity?

It is this cheap idea of government, an idea as false as it is puerile, which has served to demoralize the American mind, and which has produced such wide unrestraint, not only in the civil, but in all the other relations of life. For if there is one special peculiarity of our national character, it is dislike of rule and authority. It comes out in civil affairs, in churches, in colleges, in common schools, and in families.

The notion of government most widely prevalent among us is that it is mostly a subjective thing. People feel that they must be left to govern themselves. External authority is a grievance and an irritation. And hence it arises that not only men and women, but children, in our day, and at a very early age, chafe under rule, reject authority, and spurn control.

One of the most alarming things in the life of the nation is the perversion that we discover in all the lines of life—the perversion of liberty into license. And when a people reach such a state that they lose sight of the magnitude of the very idea of government, and begin to eschew the principle of rule and authority, then they are rapidly verging toward anarchy, toward speedy and certain ruin.

One grand corrective to this error lies in the region of thought and principle. "People who have been entrapped by false opinions must be liberated by convincing truths." Hence, in these days, when the idea of obedience to constituted authority seems fading away, it is the duty of ministers of the Gospel to press upon the attention of the people the truth, that government is, *per se,* in itself, in idea, a grand and majestic thing. The fact must be set forth with prominence, that the nation is a creation and manifestation of God. For, my brethren, all civil power is from God Himself. When St. Paul, in one place, declares, "there is no power but of God," he asserts the magnitude of the very principle of government, and that in *all* relations. And when, in another, he commands, "Honor the king," he inculcates the duty of subjection to and reverence for constituted magisterial authority.

One of the deep undercurrents of American thought, in responsible circles, has been with regard to the drift of society to lawless freedom. Everywhere it has given thinking men the greatest concern and anxiety. It comes up, in this month of July, on the very eve of Independence Day, with a force and significance never felt before since 1776. It cannot be put down now until some true, solid basis is found, not only in opinion, but in practice and in law, for the security of that reverence and subjection to authority which is so much needed in civil, domestic, and, indeed, in all the other relations of life. And, in this respect, grieved and heart-sore as we all are at our President's sufferings, we may be brought to see "how expedient it is that one man should die for the people, and that the whole nation perish not."

3. Immediately connected with the point just considered is the common irreverence among us for rulers and persons in authority. Even (so-called) great men think that they show their superiority when they stand before multitudes and proclaim the dogma, that "civil officers are only the people's servants." And, certainly, if the notion of government just attacked, be true, then *this* notion concerning civil officers is certainly its legitimate inference. For, if government be the cheap thing men claim that it is, then its official representatives are cheap things too.

But, my friends, the notion is thoroughly false. The statement that officers are servants is only a half-truth; and half-truths are most generally whole lies. The President is indeed to serve the people. His office is, without doubt, an office of service; and this is no new discovery of this country, because it is a republic. Kings and emperors, in the oldest dynasties of the old world have, from time immemorial, acknowledged this obligation. One of the oldest royal houses of Europe has kept, as its perpetual family motto, the words, "*Ich dien,*" I serve. Even pagan rulers have been awfully impressed with the idea that "they acted in trust." But the notion that, because authority is a trust, and then, because it *is* a trust, that rulers are only the people's servants, shows blindness to the grander factor in the constitution of authority, viz., that "the powers that be are ordained of God," and that "they are the ministers of God attending continually upon this very thing," i.e., the exercise of civil authority.

Yes, there are two factors in all civil government, and in the exercise of all civil authority; and it is one of the gravest of all mistakes that it was not laid down thus, in the infancy of the nation, in the great charter of our freedom, the "Declaration of Independence." When Thomas Jefferson declared that "governments derive their just powers from the consent of the governed," and left his dogma crudely, at that point, he shut out a limitation which the pride and self-assertion of degenerate humanity is always too reluctant to yield, and too tardy to supply.

The theory of the Declaration is incomplete and misleading. Governments, my brethren, derive their just authority, *first* of all, from the will of God; and then *next,* from the consent of the governed. It is because of the exclusion of this prime factor in this axiom that the governments of the earth are all more or less sick and diseased. It is owing very considerably to national blindness to this truth that *we* have had so many sore evils in this land, and now, at last, a great, national disaster. The people of this country, in vast self-importance, have been accustomed to look down upon the chief magistracy of the land as a convenient instrumentality for personal ends. The office has been too much regarded as the facile agent of grand politicians, for party objects and partisan ambitions. But in this matter they have not been the only sinners. It has been the wont of the people, as well, to regard both the office and its functions as "good for use." This, in too many cases, has been one-half the meaning of the term "availability," applied to presidential candidates. The grand authority of a ruler, the reverence due to the Chief Magistrate, have been too generally forgotten. People in other lands do not look thus upon their kings and emperors and great chieftains. "Ah!" is the rebuke I hear coming up from the pews; "This is a Republic. Ours is a democratic country." "Well, what of that?" is my reply. Your President is as much a ruler, he is as truly a potentate as the Emperor of Russia or the Queen of Great Britain. He is your ruler and grand magistrate, and mine. And he sits in his chair of authority by the will of God, declared in governmental arrangements, as distinctly and positively as though he had been born to the office.

Alas! instead of thus regarding the dignities of the presidency as representing the *divine* sovereignty in human government; instead of honoring the President as incarnating the dread sovereignty of the nation; the habit has prevailed of regarding him as the biggest servant in the land. And intense canvasses have been carried on, the main stimulant to which has been the disposal, as through an elected instrument or machine, of thousands of offices. And then when an election has been carried, we have seen how cheap a thing people regarded their chief ruler, in the fact that the meanest men, greedy of office, could demand an audience at the "White House," and get it, too, with a facility which would be scouted by a manufacturer at Lowell, or a merchant in Boston. Nay, and worse than this—the cases have been numerous of men, when their applications have been rejected, who have turned, with "proud and haughty wrath," from the Chief Magistrate, taken his refusal as a personal insult, and assailed him with revenge and unforgiving malice.

Almighty God, in all the histories, has spoken "in divers manners" to various peoples. He has spoken by angels, by oracles and prophets, by dreams and revelations, and so made known His will to nations and to men. And He still speaks to them. He speaks to them at times by providences. Just now he has spoken to *this* nation, through the pistol-shot of an assassin. The miserable wretch, we know, is an execration to the Almighty, but He overrules his bloody deed to immediate good. In the flash of a murderer's pistol the whole nation sees suddenly and in glaring light the sin of its cheap estimate of the presidential office. And I venture to predict that, from this time, the office of Chief Magistrate will be withdrawn from the pressure of office-seekers; the White House will get the dignity, the reserve, the sanctity of national sovereignty; and the person of the chief ruler will henceforth be accessible only to persons of character, reputation, and personal responsibility.

And thus again, my friends, while our anguished hearts go out with tenderest sensibility and solicitude to our still endangered President, we learn "how expedient it is that one man should die for the people, and that the whole nation perish not!"

What I have spoken this day is nothing new. I make no pretence whatever to originality in the views I have expressed. The main truths I have brought before you have been not infrequently suggested by eminent persons; and I have been, and for a long time, so thoroughly convinced of their truth that they rush with unusual force upon my mind, at this juncture, and demand utterance. That great political prophet, Alexander Hamilton, predicted not a few of the evils I have pointed out, although he did not live to see them. In more recent times they have been seen and pointed out by a small body of men, called "Civil Service Reformers." And no body of men in the land has been more laughed at and ridiculed than they. Their publications have been numerous, and, I may add, in many cases as fruitless as numerous. But the lightning, the lightning of disaster, has done more for them than all their books and speeches and essays. It has shivered our civil service system, as now ordered, to pieces; and scattered the multitudinous swarms of office-seekers from the portals of the presidential mansion.

2. I have brought this subject before *this* congregation in particular, because although we colored men are not yet allowed either a large participation in politics, or governmental rule, or official patronage, I am, nevertheless, anxious that *my* people should be ranked among conservative men in this land, and stand among the firmest upholders of law and authority. The sudden rise to freedom, the newness of our participation in political prerogatives, above all the oscillation from extreme servitude to the right of suffrage—all naturally tend to land us in the extreme of wild and thoughtless democratic opinion, and expose us to the danger of mistaking license for liberty. Thank God, these dangers have been but little realized as yet. And may they never show themselves amid the black population of this country! As in the past, so in the future may it ever be, that the blood of this race may furnish no nursing-plot for treasons, seditions, and assassinations!

A people numbering more than six millions, with a rapidly-increasing birth-rate, growing on every side in knowledge and material power, must, from the very nature of things, become, ere long, a most formidable phalanx in the multitudinous population of the country. I pray Almighty God that *this* race may ever be found strong and determined for good, stable government, their influence weighty in the state for authority and order, the constant foes of revolutions, communism, and revolt;

> Zealous, yet modest, innocent, though free,
> Serene amidst alarms, inflexible in faith.

3. My words, this morning, have had respect, almost entirely, to the vicarious position of our Chief Magistrate. I have dwelt all along upon the

fact that this chief ruler has been called to suffering, perhaps to death, so that the nation may not die! I have preferred this line of thought, albeit the tender, sympathizing aspects of the case were far more inviting to every Christian heart. I know full well that

—Tears to human suffering are due.

And our deepest sympathies have thrilled at this awful tragedy, our hearts been faint and sickened many an hour, many a moment since its occurrence; and our prayer and cries constantly ascend to heaven for the recovery of the great sufferer. The other aspect of the case, however, seems to me no less tender and interesting. Certainly, if any man in this nation must needs be a victim, for mysterious, but definite national good, no nobler offering can be laid upon the altar of a nation's sacrifice than this man. If great good is to spring from this dreadful visitation, no more exalted victim could have been chosen than he. His personal virtues have been long conspicuous. His clear, unconcealed, yet unostentatious piety is everywhere known and acknowledged. The fine, unequalled qualities—a rare thing in our national history—which he has brought to the seat of national authority have excited both unusual surprise and unusual admiration. Statesmanlike in national politics, strong in intellectual capacity, pure in life and reputation, his character and abilities would give moral fitness to his sacrifice, if it should please God that he should succumb to the assassin's bullet!.

"The Negro as a Source of Conservative Power"

I was much interested the other day, nay, to tell the truth, I was much moved by a story, my wife read to me the other day of a crippled boy in the "Home of the Merciful Savior for Crippled Children" in this city. He was a cripple, I believe, from his birth. But he was crippled, not only in body, but still more in soul. He seemed given up to gross depravity. Stealing, lying, cursing and swearing seemed to be the habit of his nature; so that the children and servants of the house felt an abhorrence of him.

At a certain time, not long since, a Mrs. Gonzalez became his teacher. Under her influence and promptings the boy Eddie, began a struggle for reform. One by one he gave up his sinful habits: *first* stealing, *then* lying, and eventually swearing.

The case of the freedmen of the South is the case of "Eddie the Cripple," on a large scale. It is the same case in *two* respects: (1) Here we have an immense population who have been crippled, terribly crippled, alike in body and in soul; and (2) as cripples they need somewhat the same

I say they have been crippled.

(a) Look at it in the light of ancestry. For centuries, previous to the arrival of my race on this continent, they were a people broken and scattered crippled by the sway of ancestral paganism which like all heathenisms of the world, brings the [words lost] the question has arisen in my own mind, and I know it has disturbed the minds of others—where, under God, may this nation look for corrective influences, to stay the progress of the great social and political evils which are arising in the land? Whence shall come the conservative power of this nation? For, if ever a nation stood in need of a strong sturdy element to save it from destructive

Transcribed from MS.C. 315 "Address." The Schomburg Collection, New York Public Library, and printed with permission.

agencies working at its vitals, this nation does. That great disorganizing influences are at work leading to the dissolution of American society is most manifest. The very freedom of the land, the wide latitude of its liberties, the broad all-sweeping circumference of its suffrage, seem to have inebriated the crazed brains of latitudinarians in every quarter of the globe; and hither have they come, wild, frenzied, insensate, mad withal, on account of past restraint and hindrance; eager for license in the future; determined to make this soil the seed-bed of the most destructive political heresies.

And thus it comes to pass that *here* the elements of political confusion, are more prevalent, in the domain of thought, than in any other land in the world! Here we see the most deadly thrusts at organized society!

Let me point out just here the points in which American Society is menaced:—

1. The nation is endangered by a rising angry antagonism between the rich and the poor.
2. It has another peril from a growing indifference to law and civil order:—
3. The nation's existence is endangered by insane political excitements, allied to wide spread compt[illegible].

I have the conviction that in these several respects the black race, in the future of its elevation may serve as an element of safety; and that our trials and tribulations should be used as a mode of education for such a duty and such a noble service.

1. One of the most disturbing elements of American society is the angry antagonism which has sprung up between labour and capital; an antagonism as we have seen in multiplied instances which has endangered society, and which, ultimately, if not remedied is sure to bring on the most serious, if not bloody results. I am forced to say that I do not sympathize with the attitude of labour in its conflict with capital and: I feel desirous that the black race should keep clear of it. That there are evils, serious evils, connected with this subject, that capital here, as almost everywhere else in the world, is more or less selfish, grasping, cold-hearted, and that labour is frequently ill paid, neglected, despised, is evident from the very nature of things; for the "love of money is the root of all evils." But, that the white labour of this country is oppressed and down trodden, that capital is

grinding the faces of the poor, to such a degree too, as to cause and to warrant the revolution which is taking place in this country, is one of those stretches of the truth which in my opinion, approaches very nigh to the borders of fable and reaches the outer limits of fiction. How any large class of whites in America can take the position of the labor organizations, and affirm, as they do, the reality of tyranny they suffer is perfectly astounding. If it were the *black* labour of the South I could easily understand it; and I could at once proffer my warmest sympathies. But as it regards *white* labour all the facts are against the theory. Look for a moment at some of these facts:—Look at the marvellous advance in the wages of labourers during the last twenty-five years. Look at the prices returned for skilled labour in all the trades. Look at the multitudes of poor men who have become property-holders in return for their honest toil. Look at the vast numbers of men who being day labourers have risen to be wealthy farmers, manufacturers, and merchants. Look at the immense amount of monies stored away in Savings Banks, the hoarded treasure of the poor. Look at the universal suffrage of white men in all states of the country. Look at the vast political power of the masses, in this land. Look at the fact that the *wealthiest* men, —the grand millionaires of the land, numbered by thousands, are *not* the heirs of *inherited* property, not the scions of old aristocratic and wealthy families, but the sons of hardy toil, men who began life with literally nothing in their hands and who by skill, forecast, industry, and economy have become the monied princes of the U.S.!

These are the facts which cannot be denied. They are manifest on the surface of society. And in the light of them I maintain that there is no need of the threatening revolution of labour which seems so imminent. Abuses of capital there are: and they must be corrected; but the white labourer in this land is *not* a wage slave. He is the freest, best paid, most highly endowed politically than any other labourer in the world.

And this fact is a warning to the black race to keep away from entanglements of this labour-revolution which is raising its head in America. It is not based upon truth: and being false it is mischievous. Let us, as a people stand apart from its error and its mischief; not merely passively, as witnesses of a growing evil; but with the purpose, when the danger ripens of giving to the state the mighty influence of millions of thrifty, honest, clearheaded intelligent citizens; knowing our own rights, ready to uphold the prerogatives of enterprise, the rights of property, and the sway of Law.

2. The American nation is imperiled by a growing indifference to law and order. (I repeat what I said to you the other day, i.e.) that the ideas of

liberty in our American system have been so exaggerated that they have run into license. Civil Freedom has been carried to its farthest extreme on this soil; and now touches the point of lawlessness. It has reached the terminal point of reasonableness. If it goes over, anarchy can be the only result. *That* result is not as yet arrived at: but we are not very far from it. For it is manifest that in all sections unrestraint and misrule have the freest sway. Multitudes deliberately set aside authority and law. Political corruption has mastered all the great cities of the union, and the law-abiding classes, are subjected to the authority of lawless men. Not seldom are judges overawed by the popular will; and juries render verdicts right in the face of law and fact, to satisfy an unhealthy public sentiment. For some sections courts and justice are whimsical fictions, and *Lynch Law* has become the governing power of the land. The insanity of unrestraint which thus infects the public life of the country, finds its counterpart in the misrule and confusion of families; the ungoverned tempers of children, the lack of discipline in schools, the disorder of churches, and the mismanagement and corruption of corporations.

The pestilence of lawlessness you will thus see is ravaging the land and destroying its thousands of victims.

How desirable, under these circumstances that an element of sobriety, of order, and self-restraint should be ready at hand, as an antidote to the wide-spread evil of misrule which threatens this nation! What a blessed thing it would have been for misguided and frenzied France, if there had been such a latent element amid her confused peoples, at the time of the first French revolution? How much misery would have been saved that unhappy country! How much bloodshed stayed! What a multitude of lives saved! Why should not the coloured people of this land furnish just such an element? Why should not *we*, with our many millions, our increasing intelligence, and our strong religious susceptibilities furnish this needed contingent.

Under the severities of a mortifying Providence, we have learned the discipline of restraint that is the compensation the Almighty has given us for the wrongs and the cruel discipline of slavery. We have unlearned the savagery and the fanaticism of blatant American democracy. Of all classes of the American freemen, we have come to a clearer knowledge and appreciation of Law which guarantees freedom; of freedom, regulated by Law.

We are the *only* people in the land untainted as yet by infidelity. We are the only people free from the poison of treason. The virus of revolution has never yet entered our blood. The vagaries of socialism, have never yet circled our brains, nor the wild dreams of communism disturbed our imagination or our reason.

Simple and unlettered not enervated by a fastidious culture, nor disorganized by an enervating luxury; we have, as a people, the advantage of simplicity, of ingenuousness of plain common sense, and of the instincts [of] nature and genuine manhood.

If we can add on to these the habits of temperance and sobriety; the deep religious training of the churches and the schools; and the high morality which comes from the scriptures of God; we shall start up, when the day of our political freedom arrives, a mighty army of voters, governed by the law of righteousness, wielding civil prerogatives as a means for human blessedness; using the ballot at the dictate of conscience; and employing all the suffrages of citizenship as instruments as well to execute the will of God, as to promote the interests of men and the commonwealth.

But only on these conditions! If the profligacy of the whites is imitated by us; if Alcohol is allowed a masterful control; if Moral Purity is widely eschewed; if political ambition comes to have the widest deepest influence; if the greed of gain gets to be the craze of our circles; if luxurious living spreads as a pestilence in our communities; then we shall be but a host of dead men in the nation; although the census may declare our numbers as hundreds of millions and our population crowd both the states and the cities of the land.

3. One more peril to the American system calls for notice, and that is the wild insanity and the increasing corruption of our political life. For our political life and action are not seldom hurricanes i.e. in their fierceness, burning blasts in their heat and intensity. So extravagant are the incitements of partisanship, that they leave but little room for thought and sober reason. The masses of men, carried away by the tempestuousness of overwrought passion, seem for the time to put sense and judgement out of sight.

Interfused with the heat of political methods is the dissoluteness of venality and bribery, —so vast and so pervading that the great cities of the land seem lost in corruption and their large populations given up to the divination of "signs."

The strain, both of passion and corruption is too great for any system to endure for any great length of time. The history of the world shows that when communities lose their integrity, and reason loses its authority, and morality is set aside in public affairs as a superfluity; then nations begin their decline to ruin! A check can be given to that decline if, at an early period, some strong corrective, some saving influence can be brought to bear upon society, to save it from utter decay.

What this nation needs is an element in political life, —drawn from the churches of God and the great schools of thought, an element raised above petty ambitions; controlled by moral sentiment; zealous for public good; obligated to divine and sacred principles.

Is our political education preparing us to furnish this element? By the letter of the law the black race in this nation has been affranchised: by the will of the people the black race, in large sections of this union has been, right in the face of the law, —disfranchised! What are the special teachings which may come to us by this disastrous providence? Can we not get *some* advantages from this forced abstentation from the political life of the land?

In the *first* place we are made spectators of the madness of the white race in their political gladiatorship. We stand off and see, with our own eyes, the carelessness; the unscrupulousity, the bold, brazen dishonesty of lawyers, scholars, statesmen, clergymen, and hosts of professors of religion in their political processes, in well nigh half the union; endeavoring to keep the negro a subject race! And we see, as the consequence of this political dishonesty, the loss of honour, the lowering of the morality, the lack of virtue, the decline of true religion; in men, in families, in business transactions, in churches; the result of the political profligacy which so widely pervades American Society! Whole communities agonizing with all the subtlety of brain, with all the arts of intellect, with all the energy of will to crush the Negro and yet blindly and unconsciously, narrowing the orbit of that brain; shrivelling the capacity of their own intellect; dwarfing the moral nature and cutting their own throats!

All this is a schooling; a schooling—if we are *bad* men—stimulating *us* to run the race of politics; when *our* time comes, as come it will, with swift feet, for pelf, for reward, for corruption, just as the whites do: —and then for wreck in the very region of the Soul and for ruin. But, if we are wise witnesses of *their* follies and their guilt, if we are virtuous spectators of their political crimes; we are beholding the ghastly wounds of the nation. We are learning its deepest needs, we are being taught by the providences of the Almighty, our future duty and responsibility—to come up to the certain full and unfettered citizenship and authority which are certainly before us; *the* needed contingent in the great commonwealth of society;

true men, sober men, self-restrained men; determined that society shall not go to ruin and that government shall exert its own divine and rightful functions.

Conclusion: I know very well the answer which not unlikely may come from not a few in reply to what I have said to you this morning, i.e.—Why should *we* feel any concern for the safety of this nation. Have we not the deepest cause for alienation and dislike? Are *we* not the most despised of all the classes of the American people? Are not our souls filled with the scornful reproof of the wealthy and the despitefulness of the proud? Why then, should we be anxious to give this wicked nation strength and assurance? Why, in any way, concern ourselves about it?

Let me close the suggestions made this day with a few reasons.

1. And first of all let me say that we are citizens of this nation, and as such we must make some sort of a contribution to its life and character. We are American citizens. We have no other country; it is evidently one of the certainties of both our own and of [our] children's lives that we shall go on, in all the future of our blood lineage, bound up with all the interests of this country. As a people we are here to stay; and the possibility of our removal from this land is just about as great as the uprooting of the giant forests of California; and the transportation of them, roots, trunks, branches, all intact to the Sandwich Islands!

We are American citizens; and living and acting in the land we must for the necessity of life and action contribute somewhat to its life and character. We must be doing either good or evil. Such a thing as the neutral influence of men, in the state, is an impossibility. First of all *self love* challenges all the elements of saving and effective influences from our personal life. We can not live aright; we cannot get the upbuilding of superior men unless we give to the state the qualities of industry, thrift, enterprise, and progress. And thus every idea of personal advantage demands that *we* make some endeavors for the preservation and the strengthening of the nation.

But not only self-love, but *Christian duty* requires that we should do everything possible to serve the State. The State is that great organic institution, established by the Almighty for the continuance and the development of humanity through all the ages. Man cannot live without it; i.e. if he would rise to manly elevation and grand superiority. It is, next to Christianity, the one grand agent for the civilization of man; and hence it is the duty of the citizen everywhere, to build up the commonwealth.

Sustentation of the State is the building up of our own personal selves. A destructive purpose or policy is suicide! For the State is a part of ones own personal self; and we can't destroy it, without destroying ourselves. It is thus, in every way, our DUTY as a people to render our special contribution to the strengthening and compacting of the great American republic.

2. The contribution to the needs of the land of some saving and conservative influences seems to me a special function of our race. Lowly and depressed as we have been; rejected as we still are, we possess qualities and hold a position which trained and sanctified will enable us to guarantee this perilled nation the very element of safety that it needs. I know no people coming to this land which can confer the gifts the Negro has to offer to save this nation. The nation needs a quiet element added to its distracted moral forces. This is the nature of the Negro.

The nation needs a law abiding quality to rectify the swaggering self-assertive spirit which it has cultivated in all its history. Submission to authority is a native characteristic of the Negro. The nation needs a patient, plodding hard-handed and industrious population for its material interests. The Negro, for two-hundred years, has demonstrated this capacity. The nation needs a hopeful and aspiring element—a class of people looking forward to somewhat vast and great in the future, for unreached and noble destinies. The Negro is the newest contingent; with the largest demands and the strongest cravings, and unsatisfied longings, of any other class. The nation needs the saturation of a religious sentiment in every province of thought and activity. The Negro is characteristically a religious being; needing only the corrective of wider scriptural knowledge, and deeper spiritual insight, for the highest moral elevation, and for the purest spiritual influences!

Where else can the nation get these needed qualities? What other people amid its heterogeneous population can arise and help to neutralize the insanity of her political frenzy, and the wildness of her intemperate theorizing?

Not from the crazed Bohemian, with his criminal propensities and his animal instincts! Not from the German, with his godless speculations and his wild theories! Not from the superstitious Italian, ignorant of the simplest alphabet of freedom, and paralyzed, in every faculty by the stupidness of priestcraft! Not from the angry Irishman, with his "blind hysterics" and his "school boy heat!" Not even from the more sober Anglo-Saxon; who is always preaching submission to oppressed people;

yet himself ever shrieking "Liberty or death!" at a disagreeable tax, or an imaginary encroachment.

Satisfied that you have the qualities and the capacity fitted for a noble future career, I would exhort every man of the race to settle himself to the noblest endeavors for the upbuilding of character. Do not be discouraged at the lowliness of our position, or at the humiliations of our past career: Almighty God has often, in the history of man, taken just such humble, nay, obscure peoples as us as instruments for his noblest purposes. Yea God hath chosen the foolish things of the world to confound the wise . . . yea things which are despised hath God chosen, yes even things which are not, "nobodies" as the world calls them, "to bring to nought things that are."

For my own part I have the highest hopes and indulge in the largest expectations for this race of ours, on this American soil. The Almighty does not preserve, rescue and build up any lowly people merely for ignoble ends. He always has special purposes and designs, in every one of His special providences. Wonderfully has He raised us up from degradation! Marvellous have been the prerogatives of wealth and education and franchises to us. And although vast areas of training and moral culture are yet *before* us, yet we can look *behind* and see the vast tracts of improvement we have trod during the last twenty-five years of freedom. And hence I look *forward* with highest hope into the future. I look down the long alleys of coming times, and I see the multitudes of this new race, men women children, —all traces of their former servitude gone; their eyes brightened with intelligence and virtue; freedom and manliness in their posture; thrift and wide-spread industry, visible at their homesteads [words crossed out] rejoicing in the burdens of responsible citizenship, and bringing forward the noblest gifts and devotedness for its strength and perpetuity.

"I see them in their winding way"

—Millions of men in successive generations; the pillars of the state; conservators of order; the upholders of stable government; maintaining virtue; illustrating pure religion; the reliance of a great people, in every time of trial, and in every day of danger! And so, by the virtuous influence of the Negro, challenging the title of Saviours of the country which once enslaved them!

Such a noble heritage, such a grand fortune and futurity, I verily believe to be the privilege of this race on this soil. God never preserves, enlightens and exalts a lowly people for ignoble ends. All through the ages has He, over and over again, "exalted men of low degree." He hath "chosen the weak things of the world," least "things which are despised," for the amplest providences, for the most exalted destinies.

For this high destiny we need all the succor and assistances of culture and training; the strength which comes from industry and wealth; the regulation which the religion of Jesus brings to the hearts of men and to the bosoms of families! But it is only on these conditions that we shall answer this high calling; and if we fail in them, we too shall perish in the general destruction of the land!

We bless God for all the favours and the mercies of the year! for health, comfort, prosperity, the means of grace and for the hope of glory. We bless Him for even the tribulations of our lot in this land, which is, without doubt, a schooling for future greatness. We bless Him for the promise, discovered to sight by signal providences, of usefulness and exalted service, for Him, in this nation, in coming times. And we beseech Him, for the Redeemer's sake to make us faithful men and women, in our families, with our children, in the church. In the entire Race; for the glory of His great name, for the succor and safety of the nation and for the good of man.

"The Discipline of Freedom"

Quit you like men, be strong. 1 Corinthians 16:13

There is a very large liberty allowed clergymen, on Thanksgiving-day, in the choice of topics for the pulpit; and I shall use that liberty today in the train of thought which I am about to present to your consideration. I am to speak to you concerning our sad condition, as a people, at the present; and to suggest what seems to me their most pressing duties.

If I were to submit myself to the sway of impulse or emotion, I should dwell entirely upon the outrages in the South which, during the last nine months, have swept, like an avalanche; over the devoted heads of our race. But I am satisfied that a crisis in the history of a people, is not the time for impulse; but rather for thought and judgement. It should always be remembered that while there is a place in all the affairs of men for feeling, and the expression of feeling, experience goes to show that the indulgence in this sentiment, is to a large extent, a useless expenditure of force; and, especially, from the further fact that mere sentiment leads but seldom to any practical results or useful ends.

I shall not then give way to my feelings, albeit, I feel strongly concerning these dreadful wrongs and outrages.

I think, however, that these occurrences, dark and dire as they are, may serve as counsellors of God, which may help to point out the duty of a distressed people. The immediate suggestions which I think arise from them, are such as these viz—"What can be done for the elevation of the Negro Race in this land?" Is this elevation to come from within, or, from without? Will feeling and emotion subserve the interests of the race? Or, on the other hand, are strong and vigorous remedies our special need and demand?

Transcribed from MS.C. 16. "The Discipline of Freedom." Schomburg Collection, New York Public Library, and printed with permission.

I have the deep conviction that we are, under God, to look to a large extent, to *ourselves* for relief; that we must work from within to outer circles of influence and power, in order to get the might and success we need. On this line I shall speak this morning.

I begin with the statement of what is to me an appalling fact! Nothing has struck me so forcibly amid the outrages of the South, as the deep conviction of the black man's weakness. There is no new thought to any of us. Our entire history as a Race, on this continent, has been a perpetual entailment of weakness. But never before has it been brought so vividly to my mind! And with this conviction save at the same time the words of Milton, that.

"To be weak is to be miserable!"

But whence arises the weakness of our Race? Alas! for us, all along through this reign of terror, our afflicted people have been at sea! We have had no coherence of race, we have had no unity of policy! We have shewn no resistance to outrage! We have had no organized maintenance of our rights! We have had no concerted appeal to authority and law! We have had no wise leadership to self-defense! Everywhere, even amid crowded populations, ours has been a relaxed and nerveless hand! Our feeble forces, like a rope of sand! Like the leaves of the forest our poor people, in divers sections, were scattered abroad at the fierce breath of their enemies! In all this tempest of rage and murder, weakness was the general [condition].

This spectacle contrasts very strongly with our condition in a state of servitude. *Then,* all our powers were marshalled to definite ends. The Race was one great machine, every member in his place; working with severest regularity, and producing vast and valuable results. Within a range of both narrow and material interests, but alas, with a constant muzzling of our personal wills, the whole world saw the physical value of the Negro Race. Every man was made to stand in his own place; every man to do his own work; every man to yield a distinct and telling product! Out of this came labour; industrial order; servile systematized energy and activity; great increases of Negro population; vast crops of Corn, Rice, Tobacco, and Cotton; enormous revenues to individuals, and to the national treasury.

And all this, my brethren sprang from the *discipline* of slavery! But alas, what a terrible system it was!

The act of Emancipation lifted in a sudden, our million masses into a state of freedom. I cannot pause to speak of the unspeakable blessings which have come to us from the gift of freedom! I can only indulge in a mere passing glimpse at these blessings: —personal freedom; the right of will; the exercise of the acquisitive principle; suffrage; property-holding; schooling and education; aspiration; family rights; freedom of conscience and religion!

All this was gain to us; incalculable gain and advantage which ages of slavery could never have brought us.

But while there was gain, there was also loss. We had, in our previous condition, the discipline of slavery. But it is manifest that we had not yet reached forth and acquired the DISCIPLINE OF FREEDOM!

Understand me, my brethren, I do not fault the Race, because of this lack of discipline. It is not an extemporaneous acquisition on the part of any people. It always takes centuries of training to gain it. The French are a clear illustration of this fact.

For centuries this people were despoiled by a heartless Hierarchy and a senseless and dissolute nobility. At last, in a paroxysm of rage and fury, they swept away, with a bloody hand, the dominancy of both church and state; and spread desolation abroad through every province of the nation, by the most destructive revolution of modern [times]. In a moment, as it were, the discipline of tyranny was gone! and civil liberty was secured. But though more than a hundred years have elapsed, the French have not, even to the present, learned the discipline of freedom.

For 400 years the Greeks grovelled beneath the iron heel of the Turk, and sank into unspeakable degradation. In [1821–32], driven to desperation, they fought their way, through blood and fire, to nationality and freedom. But the weakness of servility still lingers in the Hellenic blood. The ancient fires of freedom are not yet fully kindled in their veins; and the world will likely have to wait a while to see the spirit and behold the noble manhood which showed itself on the plains of Marathon, and at the pass of Thermopylae.

You see thus that it is not in human nature to make the sudden transitions from abasement to superiority. It takes time for any people to recover themselves. It demands a system of severest training for human nature to reach the strength of manliness.

Not less, however, is it the duty of a people to know their defects and weaknesses, and to seek the remedy for them.

I see, I think, the deadly trials and the formidable hindrances which are our heritage in this land. At the same time I have the strong conviction that our future success and triumph are to come from our own inward resources, from the force of the CHARACTER which we may attain through discipline.

Our misfortunes spring so largely from our weakness that, so far as I as a Teacher, am concerned, I feel, constantly impelled to urge the acquisition of strength. In the battle of life the weak go to the wall. They may scream and screech, never so violently; but down they go! The strong stand; —They stand even in the face of formidable opposition. The simple demonstration of inward resources; evidences character, and assures respect and consideration.

But whence comes strength to a race or people? Not from mere outward circumstances.

> We may not hope from outward things to win
> The passion and the life, whose fountains are within.

Environment, without doubt tells powerfully upon both the character and the destiny of men. But it is not an absolute and independent force. The successful struggles against it, in innumerable cases, serve to show that it is, in itself, an auxiliary agent in moulding and fashioning men. The source of all this virile power in a people is the soul.

A people may have wealth; they may have letters; they may have political power; they may have grand armies and formidable navies; But after all, these are but visible things. Oftentimes in the history of man they have melted suddenly away; like the snow-drift beneath the scorching rays of the sun. But, on the other hand, if a people are preserved with a spirit of self-control, they have, without doubt a strong staff of accomplishment.

Let me point out, just here, some of the chief points in which we need the discipline of freedom. I look, first of all, at the weakness and the ruin which spring from our political follies!

Year by year, our people, under the leadership of astute men, are stimulated into wild excitement upon political affairs. During a canvass thousands neglect their business; and, what with the inflammatory harangues of interested men, and the freest use of whisky, the blood and brains of the people are wildly excited and at times numbers of men are shot down in vain and profitless encounters!

And what is it all for? If the political greatness of our race were put forth for the vindication of some grand political principle, nothing but admiration would be due the actors in them. For, at times, *political* martyrdom is as much a duty as religious. But alas no such qualities are discoverable. The politics of our people in the South are mainly for office. The *people* are more or less anxious to maintain their franchises. But the leaders, to a very large extent, are men crazy for position! It is the rarest thing, in any populous district, to find these men, Teachers in Sunday Schools; zealous promoters of common schools; Temperance Reformers: prominent in the churches; upholders of Industries and Reform. So far as *moral* elevation is concerned, your coloured Politician is a cypher! Nay if you come down to a lower plane than even this, you will find him wanting. There are great political questions pregnant with deep moral significance powerfully appealing to the American mind. Here, for instance, is the great topic of the "Saloon plague"; the pestilence of Divorce; the great topic of "Civil service Reform," on which depends, as I believe, the possibility of the Nation's life. Whoever sees the faintest allusion to these, or any kindred topics of high principle, on the part of these leaders? So far as I can see, the range of their economic science, the circle of their political philosophy is—OFFICE!

For myself I confess shame and confusion at the spectacle which presents itself *here,* at this seat of government! I see scores of men, well dressed, and of fair intelligence; but no way distinguished for temperance habits; and by no means deeply imbued with piety; hanging around the Departments, clamoring for office! The idea never seems to come to them that the government of a country is not an agency to supply men with a living! That an administration is not an "employment agency!" Nevertheless our coloured politicians seem to think that to furnish *them* with an office is the highest function of the government, and the best USE to put the race to! And when, after painful labours, they fail in their applications it is ludicrous to see the gnashing of their teeth; but solemn enough to hear their bitter curses!

But what, at the best, does all this effort amount to? Why it serves simply to put a few political hacks into office! And when they get their places, of what value are these men to the black race? Why you all know as well as I, that in nine cases out of ten these creatures turn their backs upon the Negro and repudiate their race!

No other people in this land would allow such leaders to use them in this manner! If an Irish or a German politician should treat *his* people, as many of our so-called leaders treat us, they would soon bring him in oblivion.

Now, I say that all this is nothing more nor less than trading on politics! And it is a losing game on the part of our race. They work, they strive, they get excited, they spend their money; they waste their time; they debauch themselves with whiskey; and ofttimes they arouse the ire of white ruffians and get shot down! And all—*for what?* To put a handful of selfish men in a few petty offices.

Now I call this a useless expenditure of force, and it ought to be stopped! The exercise of our civil prerogatives is a duty. We are not worthy the rights of freemen if we fail to use every opportunity to maintain our civil rights. But this trading in politics is the most pitiful and humiliating of all things! It is everywhere a waste of powers. The time, talent, energy, the money, zeal and excitement spent upon skillful, but useless politicians, if garnered up, and used for useful purposes, would found Savings Banks, would start worthy mechanics and tradesmen in lucrative businesses; would set agoing springs of action in divers departments of noble activity.

If I had the voice which could reach the cabins and the huts of the South, I would say to the millions of my brethren in the rural districts and the cities—"Stand up like men for your suffrage, but get rid of your self-seeking Leaders! Have nothing to do with the Traders in Politics! Shun the leadership of crazy office-seekers, who care nothing for your race, nor for your selves. Leaders you must have. But don't put up with any but righteous and race-devoted men! If you can't find such now, have patience! Scores of devoted youth, full of the instinct of race are coming forth from the schools; and the day is almost at hand when a host of real black patriots will arise in this land, —men, not always screeching and scrambling after office, but full of anxious solicitudes to build up their people!

2. I turn to a second point wherein we need the most rigid discipline. I refer to the weakness which comes from our educational hallucinations. One of the results of Emancipation was the wide outburst [blank space] The outcome of this passion has been the gathering of multitudes of youth into schools, academies, and colleges. Nothing, in our time, has been comparable with the zeal, the self sacrifice, the lavish expenditure of parents, in order to give their freed children the enlightenment and the superiority which come from letters.

I am sorry to say that this movement, grand and noble in its main characteristics, has been widely coloured by injudiciousness and folly. In the *first* place, our people are schooling at fourteen and fifteen years of age, hundreds of boys and girls who ought to be in the workshop or the field learning how to make a living. The pride of their childrens' scholarship leads thousands of parents to over indulgence of their offspring, and the fostering of habits of unthrift and indolence. Multitudes of our youth, — youth who have no love of learning, who can never make scholars; are kept at school, for years, when they ought to be learning the art of securing a livelihood. The result of this is that we are turning out, yearly, upon society, a host of youth with a mere smattering of learning; who turn their backs on labour, who despise the simple employments of their parents, who like soft places, and who are determined to live—whether honestly or otherwise—in the easiest manner possible and with the least possible toil. Never was there a generation of colored youth so anxious, as now, for soft places, delicate hands, fashionable dress, and unlaborious days!

In the higher fields of learning we are making an equally gross mistake. Not a few young men and women get the higher culture of academies and colleges. But of what advantage, i.e. to large numbers, is it to them, to their parents, or, to society, it is difficult to say. They graduate, loaded perchance with Latin and Greek and Science. But alas, in frequent cases, they have not a thimble full of manhood behind it!

The fallacy in all this lies in the forgetfulness of the true end of letters and learning. That end is manhood. If Latin and Greek don't serve to make a youth a man, all the outlay of money, all the expenditure of sacrifice upon him is like "pouring out water upon the ground." The value of a family is the manhood and womanhood it can give the world. To produce this result in sons and daughters, we use the training of the household and the [illegible] the schools; we employ, according to our ability, the instrumentalities of teaching; the agency of books; the appliances of science, Art, and culture.

But for *what*? For anything in themselves? Why the object we have in view is the education of the youth, i.e. the development of hidden powers, the cultivation of unseen and latent qualities. Who wants to put culture upon a nin-compoop? If there is nothing in the fellow, if nothing can be got out of him; why all the learning you bestow upon him will be like a ✓ "Jewel of gold in a swine's mouth."

It is just in this point we are making the wildest expenditures of force; it is the expenditure of large gifts of learning upon mediocrities and dullards!

Parents are the guardians of their children. Theirs is the obligation to decide the fortunes and, to some extent, their destiny in life. In this decision it should always be remembered that duty is always higher than literature or culture. The *one* is a principle: the other is a facility or instrument. Fitness for duty in life is immeasurably more important than all the culture of the schools, than all the lore of academies.

The great need of our people is practical duty in the family, and in the community in which we live. That is the best education which fits men for the relations of human life. The schooling of children, however elegant it may be, if it don't enable them to do their duty, to answer the obligations, and to meet the necessities of life, is both vain and idle. Just here is the demand for judgement and forecast.

If a man is going to be the captain of a ship, he need not go to a cooking school. If he is going to be a cook, he need not study navigation. The knowledge of cooking may be of service to the captain; an acquaintance with navigation may at some time be a blessing to the cook. But remember two things: (1) That in the book of life we don't go by chances; and (2) That no one man can sweep the entire circle of responsibility. The law of fitness rules everywhere with the wise and prudent; and fitness is that true idea which should rule and guide in the preparation for the business and burdens of human life. Senator Stamforth is constantly appealed to, by men laden with Greek and Latin, for employment; and he sends numbers of them to drive the street cars in California! If they had been properly trained for life, these men would have been brought up in the callings, and trained to the thrift which would have acquainted them with the industries of life.

Society *needs* scholars: *our* rising colored society needs scholars—but they are not needed
[blank spaces]
Things are terribly out of place when the youth who are only fitted for the most the ordinary duties of life are allowed to waste time and the money of their parents in the halls of colleges instead of
[blank spaces]
Just this is one great mistake we as a people are making in this land; and here is the place for instant immediate prudence and discretion. The needs of our race are, to a large extent, material. We are oppressed everywhere by terrible poverty, and menial occupation. Let us address ourselves to the special necessities of our case, and discipline ourselves to common sense and practical wisdom in the affairs of life. The future is sure to take care of itself. In time we shall, without doubt, rise to the higher levels of emolument, and reach the nobler positions of acquisition and station.

(3) One more point of weakness deserves attention. I refer here to the social follies which are consuming us. Extravagance in dress; extravagance

in entertainment; extravagance in pleasure-seeking; extravagance in feast-ing; extravagance in house-adornment; are universal evils of the race in this land.

My conviction is that, in these respects, we exceed every other people in America. The German, the Irishmen, the Italian is an economist com-pared with the Negro. We complain, and rightly too, of our exclusion from the trades and business occupations of the country. But, if I mistake not, in the line of our employments, we earn as much as any other people. But alas the waste in ostentation, feasting, in pic-nics and excursions.

The prodigality of these excesses is sad enough of itself; but the dread disaster is on the train of evils which spring therefrom. Think of the ruin it brings to children, the vice it introduces into families and society! See the young men it hurries to profligacy! Mark the ravages it makes in female purity! And reflect upon the loss of property which it causes and entails.

It is in the circles of the large cities of the land one sees the glowing calamities this extravagance has brought upon our communities! Families once in seeming affluence brought down to sudden absolute penury!

"The Social Principle among a People, and Its Bearing on Their Progress and Development"

Thanksgiving Day, 1875

> They helped every one his neighbor, and every one said
> to his brother, Be of good courage. So the carpenter
> encouraged the goldsmith, and he that smootheth with
> the hammer him that smote the anvil, saying, It is ready
> for the soldering; and he fastened it with nails that it
> should not be moved. Isaiah 41:6, 7

More than a month has passed away since we received the proclamation of our Chief Magistrate appointing the 25th of November a day of public thanksgiving to Almighty God.

And, in accordance with this pious custom, we, in common with millions of our fellow-citizens, have met together this morning to offer up our tribute of praise and thankfulness to our common Parent in heaven, for all the gifts, favors, blessings, and benefactions, civil, domestic, religious, and educational, which have been bestowed upon us during the year; for the blessings of heaven above; for the precious fruits brought forth by the sun; for the precious things of earth and the fulness thereof; for the golden harvests of peace, unstained by blood, and unbroken by strife; for the constant stream of health which has flowed through our veins and households, untainted by plague or pestilence; for the babes whom the Lord has laid upon your arms and given to your hearts; for the plentiful supply of food which has been granted us from the fields, and

---

From Alexander Crummell, *The Greatness of Christ and Other Sermons* (New York: Thomas Whittaker, 1882), Sermon 18, pp. 285–311.

which has laden our boards; for the goodly instruction which trains the mind and corrects the hearts of our children, and prepares them for responsibility, for duty, and eternity; for the civil privileges and the national freedom, in which we are permitted to participate; for the measure of success which God has given His Gospel, and for the hope that is ours that the Cross shall yet conquer everywhere beneath the sun, and that JESUS shall rule and reign through all the world. For these and all other gifts and blessings we render our tribute of praise and gratitude to the Lord, our Maker, Preserver, and Benefactor, through JESUS CHRIST our Lord!

Grateful as is this theme of gratitude, and inviting as it is for thought and further expression, it is not my purpose to pursue it to-day. I feel that we should turn the occasion into an opportunity for improvement and progress.

Especially is this the duty of a people situated as we are in this country; cut loose, blessed be GOD, for evermore, from the dark moorings of servitude and oppression; but not fully arrived at—only drifting towards, the deep, quiet waters of fullest freedom and equality. Few, comparatively, in numbers; limited in resources; the inheritors of prodigious disasters; the heirs of ancestral woes and sorrows; burdened with most manifest duties and destinies; anxious for our children; thoughtful for our race; culpability and guilt of the deepest dye will be ours, if we do not most seriously consider the means and instruments by which we shall be enabled to go forward, and to rise upward. It is peculiarly a duty at this time when there is evidently an ebb-tide of indifference in the country, with regard to our race; and when the anxiety for union neutralizes the interest in the black man.

The agencies to the high ends I have referred to are various; but the text I have chosen suggests a train of thought, in a distinct and peculiar line. It shews us that spirit of unity which the world exhibits, when it would fain accomplish its great, commanding ends.

The prophet shews us here the notable sight, that is, that GOD comes down from heaven to put an end to the devices of the wicked. Whatever discord and strife may have before existed among them, at once it comes to an end. A common danger awaits them; a common peril menaces. At once they join hands; immediately their hearts are united. "They helped every one his neighbor, and every one said to his neighbor, be of good courage."

The lesson is one which we shall do well to learn with diligence; that it comes from the wicked, does not detract from its value. The world acts on many a principle which Christians would do well to lay to heart. Our Saviour tells us that "the children of this world are wiser in their generation than the children of light." So here, this principle of united effort, and of generous concord, is worthy of the imitation of the colored people of this country, if they would fain rise to superiority of both character and achievement. I shall speak, therefore, of the "*Social principle among a people; and its bearing on their progress and development.*"

What I mean by the social principle, is the disposition which leads men to associate and join together for specific purposes; the principle which makes families and societies, and which binds men in unity and brotherhood, in races and churches and nations.

For man, you will observe, is a social being. In his mental and moral constitution God has planted certain sympathies and affections, from which spring the desire for companionship. It is with reference to these principles that God declared of the single and solitary Adam, "It is not good for the man to live alone." It was no newly-discovered affinity of the Maker, no afterthought of the Almighty. He had *formed* His creature with a fitness and proclivity for association. He had made him with a nature that demanded society. And from this principle flows, as from a fountain, the loves, friendships, families, and combinations which tie men together, in union and concord. A wider and more imposing result of this principle is the welding of men in races and nationalities. All the fruit and flower of these organisms come from the coalescence of divers faculties and powers, tending to specific ends. For no one man can effect anything important alone. There never was a great building, a magnificent city, a noble temple, a grand cathedral, a stately senate-house which was the work of one single individual. We know of no important event in history, no imposing scheme, no great and notable occurrence which stands as an epoch in the annals of the race, which was accomplished by a single, isolated individual. Whether it is the upbuilding of Imperial Rome; or the retreat of the Ten Thousand; or the discovery of America; or Cook's or Anson's voyages around the globe; or the conquest of India; or the battle of Waterloo; everywhere we find that the great things of history have been accomplished by the combination of men.

Not less is this the case in those more humane and genial endeavors which have been for the moral good of men, and wherein the individuality of eminent leaders has been more conspicuous. We read of the evangelization of Europe, from the confines of Asia to Britain; and, in more modern times, we have the abolition of the Slave Trade and Slavery, the grand efforts for the relief of prisoners, the Temperance Reformation, the Sunday-school system. These were noble schemes, which originated in the fruitful brains and sprung from the generous hearts of single individuals, and which, in their gracious results, have made the names of Howard and Wilberforce, of Clarkson and Robert Raikes, bright and conspicuous. But yet we know that even they of themselves did not achieve the victories which are associated with their names. Thousands, nay, tens of thousands of the good and pious were aroused by their passionate appeals to stirring energy; and only when the masses of the godly were marshalled to earnest warfare, were those evils doomed; and they fell, never to rise again!

The application of this truth to the interests and the destiny of the colored race of America is manifest. We are living in this country, a part of its population, and yet, in divers respects, we are as foreign to its inhabitants as though we were living in the Sandwich Islands. It is this our actual separation from the real life of the nation, which constitutes us "a nation within a nation:" thrown very considerably upon ourselves for many of the largest interests of life, and for nearly all our social and religious advantages. As a consequence on this state of things, all the stimulants of ambition and self-love should lead this people to united effort for personal superiority and the uplifting of the race; but, instead thereof, overshadowed by a more powerful race of people; wanting in the cohesion which comes from racial enthusiasm; lacking in the confidence which is the root of a people's stability; disintegration, doubt, and distrust almost universally prevail, and distract all their business and policies.

Among a people, as in a nation, we find farmers, mechanics, sailors, servants, business men, trades. For life, energy, and progress in a people, it is necessary that all these various departments of activity should be carried on with spirit, skill, and unity. It is the cooperative principle, working in trades, business, and manufacturing, which is the great lever that is lifting up the million masses in great nations, and giving those nations themselves a more masterly superiority than they have ever known, in all their past histories. No people can discard this principle, and achieve greatness. Already I have shown that it cannot be done in the confined sphere of individual, personal effort. The social principle prevails in the uprearing of a nation, as in the establishing of a family. Men must associate and combine energies in order to produce large results. In the same way that a family becomes strong, influential, and wealthy by uniting the energies of parents and children, so a people go on to honor and glory, in the proportion and extent that they combine their powers to definite and productive ends.

Two principles are implied in the remarks I have made, that is, the *one* of mutuality, and the *other* of dependence.

By *mutuality* I mean the reciprocal tendencies and desires which interact between large bodies of men, aiming at single and definite ends. I mean the several sentiments of sympathy, cheer, encouragement, and combination, among any special body of people; which are needed and required in distinct departments of labor. Solitude, in any matter, is alien to the human heart. We need, we call for the aid of our fellow-creatures. The beating heart of man waits for the answering heart of his brother.

It is the courageous voice of the venturesome soldier that leads on a whole column to the heart of the fray. It is the cheering song of the hardy sailor as he hangs upon the shrouds, amid the fierceness of the tempest, that lifts up the heart of his timid messmates, and stimulates to boldness and noble daring. On the broad fields of labor, where the scythe, the plough, and the spade work out those wondrous transformations which change the wild face of nature to order and beauty, and in the end, bring forth those mighty cargoes of grain which gladden the hearts and sustain the frames of millions; there the anthems of toil invigorate the brawny arms of labor; while the sun pours down its fiery rays, and the midday heat allures in vain to the shade and to rest. Deep down in the dark caves of earth, where the light of the sun never enters, tens of thousands of men and children delve away in the coal beds, or iron mines, buried in the bowels of the earth; cheered on in their toilsome labor by the joyous voices and the gladdening songs of their companions. What is it, in these several cases, that serves at once to lighten toil, and to stimulate to hardier effort? Several principles indeed concur; but it is evident that what I call mutuality, i.e., sympathy and unison of feeling, act upon the hearts of soldiers, sailors, laborers, and miners, and spur them on to duty and endurance.

So, likewise, we may not pass by the other motive, i.e., the feeling of *dependence*. We need the skill, the energy, the achievement of our fellow-creatures. No man stands up entirely alone, self-sufficient in the entire circle of human needs. Even in a state of barbarism the rude native man feels the need of the right arm of his brother. How much more with those who are civilized and enlightened! If you or I determine upon absolute independencey of life and action, rejecting the arm and the aid of all other men, into how many departments of labor should we not at once have to multiply ourselves?

It is the recognition of this principle of association, which has made Great Britain, France, the United States, Holland, and Belgium the greatest nations of the earth. There are more partnerships, combinations, trades-unions, banking-houses, and insurance companies in those countries than in all the rest of the world together. The mere handful of men in these nations, numbering but one hundred millions, sway and dominate all the other nine hundred millions of men on the globe. Or just look at one single instance in our own day: here are England and France—fifty-eight millions of men—who, united, only a few years ago, humbled the vast empire of China, with its three hundred millions of semi-civilized inhabitants.

The principles of growth and mastery in a race, a nation, or people, are the same all over the globe. The same great agencies which are needed to make a people in one quarter of the globe and in one period of time are needed here, at this time, in this American nationality. We children of Africa in this land are no way different from any other people in these respects. Many of the differences of races are slight and incidental, and ofttimes become obliterated by circumstances, position, and religion. I can take you back to a period in the history of England when its rude inhabitants lived in caves and huts, when they fed on bark and roots, when their dress was the skins of animals. When you next look at some eminent Englishman, the personification, perchance, of everything cultivated, graceful, and refined, you may remember that his distant ancestors were wild and bloody savages, and that it has taken ten centuries to change him from the rudeness of his brutalized forefathers into an enlightened and civilized human being.

The great general laws of growth and superiority are unchangeable. The Almighty neither relaxes nor alters them for the convenience of any people. Conformity, then, to this demand for combination of forces is a necessity which we, as a people, cannot resist without loss and ruin. We cannot pay heed to it too soon; for if there has been anything for which the colored people of this country have been and now are noted, it is for disseverance, the segregation of their forces, the lack of the co-operative spirit. Neither in farming operations, nor trades, nor business, nor in mechanical employment, nor marketing, nor in attempts at grocery-keeping, do we find attempts at combination of their forces. No one hears anywhere of a company of fifty men to start a farm, to manufacture bricks, to begin a great trading business, to run a mill, or to ply a set of vessels in the coasting trade. No one sees a spontaneous movement of thirty or forty families to take possession of a tract of land for a specific monetary venture. Nowhere do we see a united movement in any State for general moral and educational improvement, whereby the masses may be delivered from inferiority and degradation.* The people, as a body, seem delivered over to the same humble, servile occupations of life in which their fathers trod, because, from a lack of co-operation they are unable to step into the higher callings of business; and hence penury, poverty, inferiority, dependence, and even servility is their one general characteristic throughout the country, along with a dreadful state of mortality.

And the cause of this inferiority of purpose and of action is two-fold, and both the fault, to some extent, of unwise and unphilosophic leaders. For, since, especially emancipation, *two* special heresies have influenced and governed the minds of colored men in this nation: (1.) The one is the dogma which I have heard frequently from the lips of leaders, personal and dear, but mistaken, friends, *that the colored people of this country should forget, as soon as possible, that they* ARE *colored people:* —a fact, in the first place, which is an impossibility. Forget it, forsooth, when you enter a saloon and are repulsed on account of your color! Forget it when you enter a car, South or West, and are denied a decent seat! Forget it when you enter the Church of God, and are driven to a hole in the gallery! Forget it when every child of yours would be driven ignominiously from four-fifths of the common schools of the country! Forget it, when thousands of mechanics in the large cities would make a "strike" rather than work at the same bench, in the same yard, with a black carpenter or brick-maker! Forget it, when the boyhood of our race is almost universally deprived of the opportunity of learning trades, through prejudice! Forget it, when, in one single State, twenty thousand men dare not go to the polls on election-day, through the tyranny of caste! Forget it, when one great commonwealth offers a new constitution for adoption, by which a man like *Dumas* the younger, if he were a North Carolinian, could be indicted for marrying the foulest white woman in that State, and merely because she was white! Forget that you are colored, in these United States! Turn madman, and go into a lunatic asylum, and then, perchance, you may forget it! But, if you have any sense or sensibility, how is it possible for you, or me, or any other colored man, to live oblivious of a fact of so much significance in a land like this! The only place I know of in this land where you can "forget you are colored" is the grave!

---

*I am advised by an intelligent friend, that the above allegations need modification; that some few such organizations have been made in two or three of the Southern States and in the City of Baltimore. The "COLORED EDUCATIONAL CONVENTION" of Virginia deserves distinguished consideration and great commendation.

But not only is this dogma folly, it is disintegrating and socially destructive. For shut out, for instance, as I am and you are from the cultivated social life of the superior classes of this country, if I forget that I am a black man, if you ignore the fact of race, and we both, ostrich-like, stick our heads in the sand, or stalk along, high-headed, oblivious of the actual distinctions which *do* exist in American society, what are you or I to do for our social nature? What will become of the measure of social life among ourselves which we now possess? Where are we to find our friends? Where find the circles for society and cheerful intercourse?

Why, my friends, the only way you, and I, and thousands of our people get domestic relations, marry wives and husbands, secure social relations, form good neighborhood and companionship, is by the very remembrance which we are told to scout and forswear.

2. The other dogma is the demand *that colored men should give up all distinctive effort, as colored men, in schools, churches, associations, and friendly societies.* But this, you will observe, is equivalent to a demand to the race to give up all civilization in this land and to submit to barbarism. The cry is: "Give up your special organization." "Mix in with your white fellow-citizens."

Now I waive, for the present, all discussion of abstract questions of rights and prerogatives. I direct my attention to the simple point of practicality; and I beg to say, that this is a thing which cannot be forced. Grieved, wearied and worried as humanity has been with the absurd, factitious arrangements of society in every quarter of the globe, yet men everywhere have had to wait. You can batter down oppression and tyranny with forceful implements; not so social disabilities and the exclusiveness of caste. The Saxon could not force it upon the Norman. Upon this point, if everything is not voluntary, generous, gracious, and spontaneous, the repulsive will is as icy, and as obstinate too, as Mt. Blanc. I wonder that the men who talk in the style I have referred to, forget that nine-tenths of the American people have become so poisoned and stimulated by the noxious influence of caste, that, in the present day, they would resist to the utmost before they would allow the affiliations, however remote, that implied the social or domestic principle.

Nay, more than this: not only would they reject your advances, but, after they had repelled you, they would leave you to reap the fruits of your own folly in breaking up your own distinctive and productive organisms, under the flighty stimulants of imaginative conceit.

And the disaster, undoubtedly, would be deserved; not, indeed, morally, for the inflictions of caste are unjust and cruel; but because of your unwisdom; for it is the office of common sense to see, as well the exact situation, to comprehend the real condition of things as they exist in this nation; as well as to take cognizance of the pernicious and atrocious virulence of caste!

Few things in policy are more calamitous in result than mere conceit. An unbalanced and blind imagination is one of the most destructive, most disastrous of all guides. Such I believe to be the nature of the suggestions which I reprobate. But remember, I do not condemn the men who hold them. Oppression and caste are responsible for many worse things than unwisdom, or blind speculation. How intolerable are the distinctions which hedge up our ardent, ambitious minds, on every side, I thoroughly apprehend! How the excited mind turns passionately to every fancied and plausible mode of escape, I can easily understand! But remember that the pilotage of a whole people, of an entire race, through the quicksands and the breakers of civil and social degradation, up to the plane of manly freedom and equality, while it is, by its very hazards, calculated to heighten the pulse, and to quicken the activity of the brain, is, nevertheless, just that sort of work which calls for the coolest head, and the hardest, most downright reasonableness. When you are pleading for natural rights, when men are endeavoring to throw off the yoke of oppression, you may indeed

> —imitate the action of the tiger,
> Stiffen the sinews, summon up the blood.

But a war against a gross public sentiment, a contest with prejudices and repulsions, is a thing of a different kind, and calls for a warfare of an opposite character. You cannot destroy caste with a ten pounder! You cannot sweep away a prejudice with a park of artillery!

I know, to use the words of another, "how difficult it is to silence imagination enough to make the voice of Reason even distinctly heard in this case; as we are accustomed from our youth up to indulge that forward and delusive faculty ever obtruding beyond its sphere; of some assistance indeed to apprehension, but the author of all error; as we plainly lose ourselves in gross and crude conception of things, taking for granted that we are acquainted with what indeed we are wholly ignorant of";* so it seems to me the gravest of all duties to get rid of all delusions upon this subject; and to learn to look at it in the light of hard, serious, long-

*Bishop Butler.

continued, painful, plodding work. It is *work,* you will observe, not abnormal disturbances, not excitement; but a mighty effort of moral and mental reconstruction, reaching over to a majestic end. And then when that is reached and secured, then all the hindrances of caste will be forever broken down!

Nothing is more idle than to talk of the invincibility of prejudice. The Gospel is sure to work out all the issues and results of brotherhood, everywhere under the sun, and in this land; but, until that day arrives, we are a nation, set apart, in this country. As such, we have got to strive—not to get rid of ourselves; not to agonize over our distinctive peculiarities; but to accept the situation as Providence allows it, and to quit "ourselves as men," in, if you say so, painful and embarrassing circumstances; determined to shift the groove of circumstance, and to reverse it.

The special duty before us is to strive for footing and for superiority in this land, *on the line of race,* as a temporary but needed expedient, for the ultimate extinction of caste, and all race distinctions. For if *we* do not look after our own interests, as a people, and strive for advantage, no other people will. It is folly for mere idealists to content themselves with the notion that "we are American citizens"; that, "as American citizens, ours is the common heritage and destiny of the nation"; that "special solicitude for the colored people is a superfluity"; that "there is but one tide in this land; and we shall flow with all others on it."

On the contrary, I assert, we are just now a "peculiar people" in this land; looked at, repulsed, kept apart, legislated for, criticised in journals, magazines, and scientific societies, at an insulting and intolerable distance, *as* a peculiar people; with the doubt against us whether or not we can hold on to vital power on this soil; or whether we have capacity to rise to manhood and superiority.

And hence I maintain that there is the greatest need for us all to hold on to the remembrance that we are "colored men," and not to forget it!

While one remnant of disadvantage abides in this land, stand by one another! While proscription in any quarter exists, maintain intact all your phalanxes! While antagonism confronts your foremost men, hold on to all the instincts of race for the support of your leaders, and the elevation of your people! While the imputation of inferiority, justly or unjustly, is cast upon you, combine for all the elements of culture, wealth, and power! While any sensitiveness or repulsion discovers itself at your approach or presence, hold on to your own self-respect, keep up, *and be satisfied with,* your own distinctive circles!

And then the "poor, forsaken ones," in the lanes and alleys and cellars of the great cities; in remote villages and hamlets; on old plantations which their fathers' blood has moistened from generation to generation; ignorant, unkempt, dirty, animal-like, repulsive, and half heathen—brutal and degraded; in some States, tens and hundreds of thousands, not slaves, indeed, according to the letter of the law, but the tools and *serfs* of would-be oppressors: stand by THEM until the school-master and preacher reach them as well as us; and the noble Christian civilization of the land transforms their features and their forms, and changes their rude huts into homes of beauty; and lifts them up into such grand superiority, that no one in the land will associate the word "Negro" with inferiority and degradation; but the whole land, yea, the whole world shall look upon them by-and-by, multitudinous in their brooding, clustered masses, "redeemed, regenerated, disenthralled," and exclaim, "Black, but comely!" But, while they are low, degraded, miserable, almost beastly, don't forget that you are colored men, as well as they; "your brothers' keepers."

Do not blink at the charge of inferiority. It is not a race peculiarity; and whatever its measure or extent in this country, it has been forced upon you. Do not deny it, but neutralize and destroy it, not by shrieks, or agonies, or foolish pretense; but by culture, by probity, and industry.

I know the natural resource of some minds, under these painful circumstances, to cry out, "Agitate! agitate!" But *cui bono?* What advantage will agitation bring? Everything has a value, according to its relation to its own natural and specific end. But what is the bearing of agitation to a purpose which is almost entirely subjective in its nature. For, as I take it, the object we must needs have in view, in the face of the disabilities which confront our race in this land, is the attainment of such general superiority that prejudice *must* decline. But agitation has no such force, possesses no such value. Agitation is the expenditure of force: our end and aim is the husbandry of all our vital resources.

Character, my friends, is the grand, effective instrument which we are to use for the destruction of caste: Character, in its broad, wide, deep, and high significance; character, as evidenced in high moral and intellectual attainments; as significant of general probity, honor, honesty, and self-restraint; as inclusive of inward might and power; as comprehending the attainments of culture, refinement, and enlightenment; as comprising the substantial results of thrift, economy, and enterprise; and as involving the forces of combined energies and enlightened cooperation. Make this, *not* the exceptional, but the common, general reality, amid the diverse, wide-spread populations of the colored people in this country; and then all the theories of inferiority, all the assumptions of your native and invincible degradation will pass, with wonderful rapidity, into endless forgetfulness; and the people of the very *next,* nay, multitudes, in the decline of *this* generation, when they look upon us, will wonder at the degrading facts of a past and wretched history. Only secure high, commanding, and masterly Character, and then all the problems of caste, all the enigmas of prejudice, all unreasonable and all unreasoning repulsion, will be settled forever, though you were ten times blacker than midnight! Then all false ideas concerning your nature and your qualities, all absurd notions relative to your capacity, shall vanish! Then every contemptuous fling shall be hushed, every insulting epithet be forgotten! Then, also, all the remembrances of a servile heritage, of ancestral degradation, shall be obliterated! Then all repulsive feelings, all evil dislikes shall fly away! Then, too, all timid disconcert shall depart from us, and all cramped and hesitant manhood shall die!

Dear brethren and friends, let there be but the clear demonstration of manly power and grand capacity in our race, in general, in this country; let there only be the wide out-flashings of art and genius, from their brains; and caste will slink, at once, oblivious to the shades. But no mere self-assertion, no strong, vociferous claims and clamor, can ever secure recognition and equality, so long as inferiority and degradation, if even cruelly entailed, abide as a heritage and a cancer. And I maintain we must *organize,* to the end that we may attain such character. The whole of our future on this soil depends upon that single fact of magnitude—character. Race, color, and all the accidents thereof have but little to do with the matter; and men talk idly when they say "we must forget that we are colored men." What is needed is not that *we* should forget this fact, but that we should rise to such elevation that the *people of the land* be forced to forget all the facts and theories of race, when they behold our thorough equality with them, in all the lines of activity and attainment, of culture and moral grandeur. The great necessity in this land is that its *white* population should forget, be made to forget, that we are *colored* men! Hence there is a work ahead for us, for the overthrow of caste, which will consume the best part of a century. He, whoever he may be, commits the greatest blunder, who advises you to disband your forces, until that work is brought to its end. It was only *after* the battle of Waterloo that England and her allies broke up their armies, and scattered their huge battalions. Not until we, as a people, have fully vindicated our race; not until we have achieved to the full their rights and prerogatives; not until, by character, we challenge universal respect and consideration in the land, can we sing the song:

> —Come to the sunset tree,
> The day is past and gone,
> The woodman's axe lies free,
> And the reaper's work is done.

Until that time, far distant from to-day, should the cry be everywhere among us: "Combine and marshal, for all the highest achievements in industry, social progress, literature, and religion!"

I hasten to conclude with two brief remarks:

First, then, let me remind and warn you, my friends, that we, as colored men, have no superfluity of powers or faculties in the work which is before us, as a race, in this country. First of all, we all start with maimed and stunted powers. And next, the work before us is so distinct, definite, and, withal, so immense, that it tolerates no erratic wanderings to out-of-the-way and foreign fields.

And yet there are men who tell us that much of our work of the day is objective, that it lies among another people. But I beg to say that we have more than we are equal to in the needs of the six millions of our ignorant and benighted people, yet crippled and paralyzed by the lingering maladies of slavery. If we address ourselves strenuously and unitedly to *their* elevation and improvement we shall have our hands full for more than one generation, without flowing over with zeal and offices to a masterful people, laden with the enlightenment of centuries.

For one, I say very candidly that I do not feel it *my* special calling to wage war with and to extirpate caste. I am no way responsible for its existence. I abominate it as an enormity. *Theirs* is the responsibility who uphold it, and theirs is the obligation to destroy it. My work is special to my own people, and it is constructive. I beg leave to differ from that class of colored men who think that ours is a special mission, to leave our camp and to go over, as it were, among the Philistines, and to destroy their idols.

For my part, I am satisfied that my field of labor is with my own race in these times. I feel I have no exuberance of powers or ability to spend in any other field, or to bestow upon any other people. I say, as said the

Shunamite woman, "I DWELL AMONG MY OWN PEOPLE" (2 Kings: IV, 13); not, indeed, as mindless of the brotherhood of the entire species, not as forgetful of the sentiment of fellowship with disciples of every name and blood; but as urged by the feeling of kinship, to bind myself as "with hooks of steel" to the most degraded class in the land, my own "kinsmen according to the flesh." I have the most thorough and radical conviction that the very first duty of colored men, in this our day and generation, is in the large field of effort which requires the regeneration and enlightenment of the colored race in these United States.

And second, from this comes the legitimate inference suggested by the text, i.e., of union and co-operation through all our ranks for effective action and for the noblest ends. Everywhere throughout the Union wide and thorough organization of the people should be made, not for idle political logomachy, but for industrial effort, for securing trades for youth, for joint-stock companies, for manufacturing, for the production of the great staples of the land, and likewise for the higher purposes of life, i.e., for mental and moral improvement, and raising the plane of social and domestic life among us.

In every possible way these needs and duties should be pressed upon their attention, by sermons, by lectures, by organized societies, by state and national conventions; the *latter not* for political objects, but for social, industrial ends and attainments. I see nought in the future but that we shall be scattered like chaff before the wind before the organized labor of the land, the great power of capital, and the tremendous tide of emigration, unless, as a people, we fall back upon the might and mastery which come from the combination of forces and the principle of industrial co-operation. Most of your political agitation is but wind and vanity. *What this race needs in this country is* POWER—*the forces that may be felt.* And that comes from character, and character is the product of religion, intelligence, virtue, family order, superiority, wealth, and the show of industrial forces. THESE ARE FORCES WHICH WE DO NOT POSSESS. *We are the only class which, as a class,* IN THIS COUNTRY, IS WANTING IN THESE GRAND ELEMENTS. The very first effort of the colored people should be to lay hold of them; and then they will take such root in this American soil that only the convulsive upheaving of the judgment-day can throw them out! And therefore I close, as I began, with the admonitory tones of the text. God grant they may be heeded at least by YOU who form this congregation, in your sacred work *here,* and in all your other relations:

"They helped every one his neighbor, and every one said to his brother, Be of good courage. So the carpenter encouraged the goldsmith, and he that smootheth with the hammer him that smote the anvil, saying, It is ready for the soldering; and he fastened it with nails, that it SHOULD NOT BE MOVED!"

"Civilization as a Collateral and Indispensable Instrumentality in Planting the Christian Church in Africa"

In considering this subject, we have, at the very first, to rid ourselves of an idle fallacy which not seldom has possessed the minds of many good people. For the notion has been held that the special aim of missionary zeal is to fit the soul of a heathen man for heaven, and that this was the finality of a missionary service. The errors of such a notion may easily be seen.

Let us take just here the case of a single heathen man, and I am speaking now from personal experience.

The missionary enters a pagan village. He addresses himself to the salvation of the pagan people around him, and ere long he rejoices in the gain of a convert. The man is a naked pagan. He lives in a rude hut. His clothing is a quarter of a yard of coarse cotton. He eats out of a rude bowl. He clutches his food with his naked hand. He sleeps on a floor, the floor of beaten earth.

By the dint of painstaking effort and assiduity, by careful teaching and solicitude, the missionary has succeeded in lodging the clear idea of God, the principles of repentance and faith in the Redeemer; and the heathen man receiving the great salvation is prepared for heaven.

Now, the question arises, "Is this service of the missionary a finality of duty?" Who here would maintain such a notion? The man, albeit converted, is hardly a quarter of a man. The fact that he has received the

From *Addresses and Proceedings of the Congress on Africa Held under the Auspices of the Stewart Missionary Foundation for Africa* . . . (Atlanta, Ga.: Gammon Theological Seminary, 1896), pp. 119–24.

Gospel is evidence indeed that he has latent forces which may, under cultivation, raise him inwardly and outwardly to manhood; but as he stands before his teacher he is but a child! A crude, undeveloped and benighted child! A shadow of a man! Child, however, though he be, he is the head of a family. He is a husband. He is a father of children. He is a member of the community in which he lives. He is a laborer among his fellows.

What is to be done with this Christian man-child? Done, not, I mean, as to his inner spiritual condition. For the duty of the missionary in this particular is apparent. The missionary is to follow up the inculcation of divine truth and the flooding his soul with celestial light.

But what is to be done with this convert as to all the external circumstances of his life and being? Is he to be left in the rude, crude, half-animal conditions in which the missionary first found him? Surely not, for Christianity is, in all the ways of life, a new creation. This man-child is to be reconstructed. All the childishness of inheritance is gradually to be taken out of his brain, and all the barbarism of ages to be eliminated from his constitution.

Dropping for a moment the individual convert, let us take a wider view. The missionary ere long meets with other successes. Soon he gathers one or two score or a hundred converts; and a small church springs into existence. But, as in the case of the individual convert, so with this company. They are all nothing more than children, crude, raw, undeveloped, benighted children, nothing but the shadows of men. And in all temporal regards but a step beyond the lives of ancestral barbarism.

What is to be done with these rude, simple creatures? They are indeed to be fitted for heaven; but are they not to be fitted too for earth, for temporal elevation, for a resurrection from animalism? And has not the missionary been sent to them for this very purpose? They have received, it is true, the great salvation by repentance from sin and faith in the Lord Jesus Christ. They have been made, through grace, fit candidates for heaven. But are there now earthly duties and obligations which come home at once to them as members of Christ? Let us for a few moments rest this question just here while we attempt, in a very brief manner, an inquiry into the nature of the Christian system, and the aim and purpose of the Christian faith.

Let me interpose just here two or three principles which seem to me self-evident:

1st. Observe that Christianity is not simply and exclusively individualistic in its purposes.

2d. Christianity does not limit itself to celestial and external interests, but reaches out to temporal regards and achievements.

3d. Christianity in its full normal development implies the highest level of humanity amid all earthly relations.

If these are self-evident truths their bearing on the question would seem manifest. For the inference is quite direct that missionary effort reaches out beyond the conversion of the individual to the organisms of life.

By the organisms of life I refer to the family, to the school, to trades, to industries, to the State.

It seems then somewhat clear that, added on to the duty of personal salvation, comes the farther obligation of the reconstruction of society in its several forms.

For take either of these views of life, the individual or the social, in a heathen community it presents the same dark aspect. In either case it is humanity, maimed, crooked, low and degraded; falling short in every particular of that full development which is ever the aim of Christianity. The heathen convert, convert though he be, is a disorganized being, and needs reconstruction in every segment of his outer being and in every relation of his life. But while indeed the individual man is, in God's sight a large being, the family as an organism is a larger idea than he. And then, in its turn, albeit it is an important organism, yet society at large is greater and more important than the family. And then at a still further advance, the nation has a vastness of importance which is unequaled by either the individual, the family, or society.

The gospel of our Lord Jesus Christ is a grand and majestic economy, which, while taking in, indeed, the individual and his interests, stretches out, with divine and saving intents to the largest, widest circles of human interests below the skies.

But see how degradation dominates the features of these circles of interest in all heathen life!

The taint of heathenism has prostrated and degraded all family life in pagan lands; has debased all human industries to the level of animalism; has robbed the brain of man of every stimulus of noble thought; has shut out from the societies of circles of men the light of letters and the lamps of intelligence; and so, through long ages, ignorance, inferiority and superstition have had a universal and a degrading sway.

All these relations, however, are God's instruments, God's agencies for specific and noble ends on earth. But through ages of ignorance and superstition they have been debased to the level of bestiality! Hence, while the salvation of individual souls is the primal duty of the missionary, the obligation is manifest to lift up, as far and as fast as possible, the whole level of society into order, rectitude and excellence for the honor and glory of God and the progress of man.

It is manifest, however, that the rescue and conversion of individuals does not necessarily carry with it the uplifting and the renovation of the permanent organisms of social life. Godliness and culture, though somewhat related, are not natural correlatives. They have for centuries, in wide states and stages of advancement, stood far apart. Their union, in the progress of man, gives the assurance of reaching the highest planes of earthly superiority.

The aim of Christianity is to lift men up. It avails itself everywhere under right conditions of all providential appliances for this uplifting of degraded humanity.

Civilization is one of the grandest of God's gifts to man. And hence the adjunct of civilization is the needed factor to be added to the process of evangelization in a heathen community. It is only by this process that the grand transition can be made from the rudeness of barbarism.

The primary need, then, is spiritual existence. But then comes the immediate necessity—civilization. "What," it is asked, "do you mean by this word civilization?" I mean by it the clarity of the mind from the dominion of false heathen ideas. I mean by it the conscious impress of individualism and personal responsibility. I mean the recognition of the *body*, with its desires and appetites and passions as a sacred gift, and as under the law of divine obligation. I mean the honor and freedom of womanhood, allied with the duty of family development. I mean the sense of social progress in society. I mean the entrance of new impulses in the actions and policy of the tribe or nation. I mean an elevated use of material things and a higher range of common industrial activities. I mean the earliest possible introduction of letters, and books, and reading, and intelligence to the man, his family, and his social circles.

All this I maintain is the secondary obligation of missionary endeavor among heathen people. This obligation springs from the very nature of the Gospel. Look for a moment at the genius of the Christian faith. First of all observe how it puts upon every regenerate soul the obligation of progress and development. This progress is not simply progress in one section of the human being's nature, nor, on the other hand, is it individual in contrast with social progress. It is inclusive of both personal and organic progress. This progress is to take in the totality of his nature. It is to include the whole of his faculties and his powers. It is to sweep the entire circle of his relations. In his heathen state he lived almost a bestial life. In dress, in domicile, in eating and drinking, in the stint and narrowness of his needs, in the low range of his wants and his desires, and in the limitations of his activities, in the relations of household and wife, of parent and children, there is in heathen society the narrowest line of division from the brute creation, the strongest assimilation in the whole trend and tenor of life to the animal.

But with the incoming of the grace of God, comes at once the command for an immediate revolution in all the modes of existence, both within and without. The revolution is to touch all planes of the man's existence. It is to change all the features of his living. Up he is to rise from the animalism of his living and to struggle to manhood. He is to prepare indeed for heaven; but he is to strive to bring somewhat of the heavenly order and excellence into his earthly life; he is to fit himself for the relations and the duties of life. He is to put on the inner garment of salvation; but he is likewise to get, as soon as possible, for himself and wife and children and house and household all the seemly garniture of a new creation, both inward and outward. He is to glorify God in his body as well as in his spirit, which God has given him. This change, moreover, is to reach every section of his personal being. Christianity is a gift for the "sanctification of the whole body, mind and spirit of a man" to the best and noblest purposes. He is to rid himself of the cobwebs of gross, material and degrading ideas. He is to strive after new and elevated thought. He is to get it by the processes of reading, thinking, and intellectual effort; and he is to get the very best possible training, culture, and appointments for the bodily and temporal existence, both of himself and his family.

There is natural obligation to just this productive use of the talents given us, for in the very possession of talents there is always included a commission to use them. In man's natural state this sense of obligation comes tardily and reluctantly. But when the grace of God is given men, then there comes a fiery stimulus to human souls to make our talents, whether two, or five or ten, bring a larger value and a noble fruitage.

Dissatisfaction is thus the very first result of spiritual life in a heathen soul; dissatisfaction with the past slavery of sense, dissatisfaction with the limitations of activity, dissatisfaction with the low planes of subsistence and of life.

The heathen man has no right, in his convert life, to be content with a degraded status and an abject condition.

The primary duty, however, in this wide range of change and transition is the missionary's. He has no right to tolerate content with low conditions. He is under obligation to put judicious but positive discontent into his soul. His duty is, to pioneer his converts into all these new exercises and elevating ventures. But, simultaneously with the unrest which he generates, he must give the spur and stimulus and the revelations which lead to somewhat more human and cultivated in the life of man.

Progress, not passivity, is the law of all evangelization. Heathenism is always morbid and persistent stagnation. Christianity brings a vital, a progressive, and a regenerating spirit to the souls, the homes, and the civil life of all peoples.

This, too, is the genius of the Christian religion in its bearing upon all the organism of human life. It takes hold, indeed, of the single man, but it lays its powerful hand also, and as its rightful possession upon the family, the industries, the community, the tribe, the nation, and all the trades and occupations of life. All these belong to God.

Heathenism has brought them down to degradation and to rot, but the mission of the Gospel is to lift them up from the mire to cleanliness, to order, to spiritual life, to human blessedness. The delusion is ever to be scouted that if the soul be saved, then the Gospel has fulfilled its mission. It is nothing but a delusion. The Gospel never truly takes hold of a man until it has not only mastered the central domain of his being, his soul, but has likewise shaped and regulated the several outer conditions of his life.

It is this mastery of the external as well as the internal state of heathen life which is the ultimate, the final end of missionary endeavor: for Christianity implies the largest development of our faculties; Christianity signifies the uplifting of every craft and technique of industrial activity; Christianity is declaratory of the highest level of humanity.

This redemption, by the cross, of man's temporal condition as the accessory of his spiritual regeneration, is the testimony of history. The Lord Jesus has been everywhere in Christendom since the advent, the life of all souls, and the ransom of all pursuits. Everywhere where this faith of Christ has gone the barbarism of men has declined, and the cultivation of man has increased. Nowhere during these well nigh 2,000 years has the Gospel been divorced from the social and civil advancement of man. On the contrary in all the lands of its progress it has uplifted all the temporal incidents of human condition. It has breathed new life into the intellect of man; it has generated grand commercial activities; it has created most marvelous inventions; it has lifted nations out of the swamps of squalor and up to the highest planes of civility and refinement. It has now such a race of swift and agile glory that the peoples of all other religions of men have been left far behind in inglorious incapacity, so that now, in this year of grace, if you wish to find the imperial man he is the Christian man; if you wish to see the ideal nation, you must steer for the port of some great Christian nation. If you crave the influence and inspiration of some majestic and inspiring civilization, you must put yourself in immediate neighborhood to some grand people under the influence of Jesus Christ.

And all this is intrinsic. It is not casual. It is not the result of an accident. It is not historical coincidence. It is not miraculous intervention. It is that divine education of the great Redeemer which by the marvels of the Incarnation has touched and vitalized all the things of both the inner and the outer world, all the mysteries of the invisible spirits of men, and all the trades and businesses and material activities of human society, and so everywhere has "made all things new," to the glory of God.

Of course I mean nothing absolute in all this. This influence of Christianity has not yet reached its transcendent power in any land, and everywhere in Christendom one sees imperfection, and great limitations of Christian influence. What I mean is that, by comparison, Christianity is the most transforming agency upon the character of men, upon the order and the beauty of families, upon the glory and eminence of nations. The highest excellence in man, woman, races or nations, is Christian.

And this inherent and invariable characteristic of the faith is constantly manifesting itself to-day in all the fields of missions. In every fruitful and successful mission on earth civilization runs a parallel line with the processes of evangelization, and is one of its constant and immediate results.

The instances are many. I shall refer, however, to three well known cases. (1) When the American Board 60 years ago sent its missionaries to the Zulus, their physical and material condition was on the very lowest plane of rude barbarism. Common sense and an enlightened Christian judgment guided the missionaries in their evangelizing policy. The missionaries saw that God's kingdom among these people was to come here on earth, as well as hereafter, in heaven. They recognized the earthly uses of the faith of Jesus, as well as the heavenly and the eternal. And so while bending every spiritual effort for the conversion of the souls of these poor people, they addressed themselves at the same time to a revolution of their low temporal state, and to the production of practical ends in their physical condition. And what has been the result? Why, the whole plane of their mental, physical and governmental life has been changed, altered, elevated. Schools have been established among them. Tribal rule has been altered to strong national and legal government. Civilized industries have become widely introduced. Mines have been opened, and the entire people, in the increase of its population, in the thrift and cultivation of family life, in the growth of wealth, as well as in the spread of missions, is on the ascending scale of a ripe and flourishing civilization.

(2) Sierra Leone, in West Africa, with its youngest child, the Colony of Lagos, is another conspicuous instance. The West African missions of the Church of England and the English Wesleyans are the direct parents of the grand civilization which has sprung up on that benighted coast. It was the entrance of the word in that whole region, the word preached by missionaries, which has introduced and built up schools, colleges, trades, fine and orderly cities, and that vast trade which commands the rivalry of England, France, Germany and Italy; and which sends from those West African ports almost daily a heavily laden steamer.

(3) Nor must Japan be passed by in this enumeration of the civilizing agency of the Christian faith. For it is a well known fact that the fine capacities and the subtle genius of this great race lay slumbering for ages beneath the spell of narrow paganism. But the missionary came. The divine word from the lips of devoted men and from the page of sacred writ, was proclaimed; and at once a whole nation awoke to life, to animation, to fertile invention, to ingenious enterprise, to high martial valor. And now it looks as though a nation was born in a day.

"The Absolute Need of an Indigenous Missionary Agency for the Evangelization of Africa"

The planting of Christianity, by missions, is virtually the attempt to put an exotic element in a foreign and an alien field, and to make it indigenous therein. It is not exactly an act of grafting; for in that process the graft is the smaller agent, has the minor gift to make, and has to draw its major strength and vitality from the original stock.

Missionary work, on the other hand, is the endeavor to bring a high, noble and an eternal life into a region of stagnation and death. It is the attempt to introduce a divine and heavenly spirit into a province at once repellent and discordant. It is the endeavor to secure affinities between opposites of a most absolute nature. It is an undertaking to produce concord and harmony between elements of a most diverse and incongruous character. It is an aim after the adjustment of divine and human qualities, the one reaching upward to the heavens, and the other tending, with determined proclivities, to disaster and ruin.

The bare statement of the case discovers its prodigious difficulties. Consider the unnatural inherited ideas of heathen life; consider the master convictions which rule their being; consider the almost absolute animalism which has subjugated body, mind, and spirit; consider the crude springs of action which stimulate their general life; consider the dominant superstitions which master their spirit life; and consider the rude, uncouth language which is the vehicle of their narrow and stunted thought.

All this discloses somewhat the wide distance of the missionary from the heathen populace which surrounds him on his settlement in a pagan

From *Addresses and Proceedings of the Congress on Africa Held under the Auspices of the Stewart Missionary Foundation for Africa* . . . (Atlanta, Ga.: Gammon Theological Seminary, 1896), pp. 137–42.

land, for the work of the gospel. Here, then, we see the bridge which, at the very start, the missionary has to cross. He wishes to enter the domain of the heathen mind; but the entrance is closed, the door is locked. Moreover, the pagan has no sympathetic desires for the spiritual message of the missionary. There may be curiosity, there may be surprise; but in the proclamation of the truth of the gospel these special hindrances are sure to arise:

First, the bar of settled custom and the prejudice which follows; second, the formidable barrier of language; and, third, the natural repugnance to divine truth and the opposition it always breeds. How is this immense barrier to be crossed?

1. It seems evident to me that, from the very nature of the case, the native man, as far as possible, is to be used as the agency for conveying the new truths to his fellows:

So soon as the faith has become a deposit in the souls of converts, these converts, simple though they be, will without doubt have the easiest access to the minds of their own people. For it is not theology which is the first gift of missions to the heathen. No multitude of dogmas are needed for them to lay hold of the salvation of the cross, to live a holy life, or to get to heaven.

The message of salvation is the simplest, plainest, most apparent of all things; easily understood, when put in clear, plain, apt words, in the vernacular. The message of the gospel is "repent" and "believe in Christ." All men, the rudest of men, have sinned and regretted or sorrowed over their sins; and hence they can take in, at once, the call to repentance. So, too, all men have believed. The exercise of trust or credulity is universal in all human society. Hence all men apprehend at once the requirement of belief, when the proper object is convincingly set before them, when the demand is clearly made upon them.

Whatever hindrances then, whether of ignorance, or inaptitude, or mental disharmony, or racial incongruity, or, more especially, of lingual divergence, may exist on the part of the missionary, and which, as a consequence, prevents his effective delivery of the great message, these, to a large degree, are neutralized by the use of the native language, from the lips of intelligent native converts. For the native convert knows his people; knows their mind; knows their modes of thinking; knows their prejudices and passions; knows their rude primal faith; knows its abiding roots and its normal elements; knows the tiny rivulets by which it chimes in, in some minor ways, with the new religion; knows the primitive moralities of his own people, which need no effacement, but simply the breath of renovation from on high; knows the springs of action which move and stir and stimulate the lives of his kinsmen; knows all this as well as the regenerative process and power which have made him a new creature in Christ Jesus; and hence, with his minute acquaintance and his lingual facility, he is fitted at once to carry the message of salvation to the hearts and homes of his people.

In fine, it seems manifest that by knowledge, by sympathy, by kindness and sentiment, by his ready tongue and his evangelical spirit, the simplest native man, if pious, is by far the most facile agent for the propagation of the faith, and cannot too soon be brought into the service of the Master.

This necessarily may be regarded as an almost universal condition. The exceptions most likely, from the very nature of the case, will be exceedingly rare. For these two things are manifest: (1) that most men know the spirit of their own race better than strangers do, and (2) that most people know their native tongue better than foreigners.

2. But now, casting aside theory, we get both prestige and assurance for our position from the policy of the apostles, and the methods of the first propagators of the gospel. That policy is disclosed to us in the Acts, and incidentally in the Epistles.

And here, first of all, it is to be noticed that the apostles strove, from the very first, to make Christianity native and indigenous. They used every possible device to plant the church in the sentiment and spirit of the people they preached to. They strove to put the terms, the formularies, and the dogmas of the faith into the vernacular of the new people who were willing to receive the gospel. Jews themselves, they rose up to the altitude of a sanctified self-abnegation. They made everywhere the endeavor to divest the new faith of the old and worn-out garments of Judaism, and to give it as much as possible the forms, features and complexion of native life, in the several countries where they preached the gospel.

St. Paul is the foremost exponent of this grand Christian statesmanship: "And unto the Jews I became as a Jew, that I might gain the Jews; to them that are under the law, as under the law, that I might gain them that are under the law; to them that are without law, as without law (being not without law to God, but under the law to Christ), that I might gain them that are without law." I. Cor., 9:20–21.

Here we see the principle which guided the passage of the gospel from its Jewish environments into the Gentile world. The point of divergence was on the occurrence of the vision of St. Peter in the case of Cornelius. From that time the apostles went everywhere, preaching and founding churches; and in every instance where a group of disciples were converted, they took these crude, simple people, organized them into churches, and put all the several functions of the church into their hands.

They were but seldom people of the cultivated circles. Christianity ran its first course, and for a long period, among the outcast, the despised, the unnoticed people. It gathered its recruits chiefly from the common people. Turn to I. Cor., 1:26–28, and see the description of the first disciples given by St. Paul:

"For you see your calling, brethren, how that not many wise men after the flesh, not many mighty, not many noble, are called; but God hath chosen the foolish things of the world to confound the wise; and God hath chosen the weak things of the world to confound the things which are mighty; and base things of the world, and things which are despised, hath God chosen, yea, and things which are not, to bring to nought things that are."

Up from such bodies of simple men sprung the first preachers of the gospel. On the very first persecution of the Christians, on the martyrdom of Stephen, these simple disciples became scattered abroad. They traveled abroad as far as Phenice and Cyprus and Cyrene and Antioch, preaching the word, at the first to Jews only. But we are told that when they reached Antioch they spoke unto the Grecians. But it will be noticed that immediately, on the organization of the churches, they took the simple material and "ordained them" elders in every church; and with prayer and fasting commended them on the Lord on whom they believed. There was, as is evident, no time for formal, systematic, theological training. The organization of churches, the setting up of a ministry, were both extemporaneous, informal, conformable to immediate necessities.

The same fact shows itself most clearly in the charge of St. Paul to Titus: "For this cause left I thee in Crete, that thou shouldst set in order the things that are waiting, and ordain elders in every city."

This principle of availability is visible almost everywhere in the Epistles. The apostles, under the direction of the Spirit, seized upon every useful power discoverable among their converts. This may be seen in the variety of offices and functions in the different churches.

In Ephesians 4:7 St. Paul declares: "But unto every one of us is given grace according to the measure of the gift of Christ." And to this he adds, in the 11th and 12th verses: "And he gave some, apostles; and some, prophets; and some, evangelists; and some pastors and teachers, for the perfecting of the saints, for the work of the ministry, for the edifying of the body of Christ."

Now turn to the First Epistle of St. Paul to Timothy, the third and fifth chapters, and also his Epistle to Titus, and you will see at a glance every indication of the fact that the elders, teachers, helpers of the apostolic church were men and women of the humblest position and of the greatest simplicity alike of culture and of manners and learning.

And from all this the inference is the clearest that, just the reverse of our modern system of missions, the ranks of the ministry were filled up from native sources. Instead of long-continued supplies of new missionaries to the field, men were made to spring up from the bosom of the new Christian community; to assume ministerial duties, and then to carry the gospel to outer heathen provinces, and so spread the great salvation to benighted peoples.

The history of modern missions gives us facts of the most confirmatory nature in evidence of the position here taken. These facts are both negative, on the one hand, and positive on the other.

(1) We will take the negative first, and we shall find them full of light and instruction.

(a) Turn to the Roman missions in the Kingdom of Congo. The Portuguese entered that country in the 14th century. They baptized thousands of their converts. They built churches and cathedrals and monasteries. They secured the allegiance and submission of successive kings and princes and the great nobles of the land. They got complete control of all the interests of the country, both secular and religious.

They suffered no interference of other religionists. They had the clearest field conceivable for the working of their system.

What has been the fruit of Roman effort and Roman mastery? Nothing but utter and disastrous failure. The Kingdom of Congo is as much pagan to-day as it was 200 years and more ago! Their multitudinous baptisms have proven fruitless and empty effusions. Their numerous churches and cathedrals have either crumbled to dust, or become the abodes of bats and owls, of serpents and lizards. And the children of their seeming converts, from generation to generation, down to the present, have remained naked pagans, devotees of fetichism, and the abject victims of degraded greegreism.

And the cause of this utter collapse of effort, this useless expenditure of force, is manifest. The Roman church has failed for the simple reason that she has been willing to remain an exotic in the land of the Congo! She has been satisfied with an alien life, amid a foreign population! She has been content to abide as an extraneous element in the rudest of heathen people. She has never had the wisdom to create a Congo church by entering into the thought, the sentiment of the Congo people; by raising up a native ministry, and lodging the Christian faith and the word of God in the native language of the people whom they had conquered.

What is true of the Church of Rome in Africa is true, though to a far less degree, of the Church of England in India.

The English church seated herself in the Indies at an early day, subsequent to the days of Clive and Hastings. No one can deny the grand eleemosynary and educational and civilizing work which, in conjunction with the state, that church and people have done in the abolition of suttee and Juggernaut; in the prevention of child-murder; in the deliverance of the Indian people from the terrible exactions of heathen kings, princes and rulers; in the enlargement of industrial activities; in the wide facilities for the education of children; in the introduction of colleges and learning and culture; in the creation of new and higher wants among the masses; in all these and several other respects, the church and people of England have uplifted the peoples of India to a plane of elevation never known before in all their histories.

All this is, without doubt, a glorious record. And yet, notwithstanding these large and pervasive benevolences, see on the other hand the sad limitations of the English church. For there stands the stark and naked fact that with the grandest opportunities, the Church of England has not succeeded in nationalizing the church of God amid the multitudinous populations. Missions abound, but they have no considerable native ministry; they organized no native church; they have not entered widely into the vernacular.

Work and service and sacrifice have been abundant, but the Christian faith has not reached the status and the strength of nationality, or the feelings of the people, in their sympathies. It is still the church of England; it has yet to become the church of India.

Now let us turn to a more pleasing aspect of this matter. Look, first of all, at the work of this same church of England in West Africa. It began this work but little more than a century ago, at Sierra Leone. The objects of its solicitude were the simple, naked re-captives from the holds of slave-trading vessels; but it began at once with the endeavor to reach the mind, the sentiment and inner spirit of these peoples by two simple processes, viz.: (1) The employment of native helpers, and (2) the translation of the

Scriptures and the formularies of the church into the native languages of these re-captive people.

A large native ministry has been raised up from among them—deacons, priests and bishops—the church in its completest form. But long before this native catechists and readers and lay assistants were sent forth to teach their people; and the assistance of this indigenous agency is employed down to the present.

And the fruits of this national and common-sense policy is the creation of a native church and a native ministry in the native languages of the West Coast and in the interior, at Sierra Leone, at Lagos, in the interland, at Abbeokuta, at Ibadan, and for hundreds of miles along the banks of the Niger, in divers tribes and kingdoms, reaching out gradually but surely to the vast millions in the central quarters of the continent.

The work of missions in Nastal, under the direction of the "American Board" of the congregational body, is equally suggestive and equally confirmatory.

Sixty years ago the Zulus were a savage people, dominated by idolatrous practices, living in miserable huts, roaming wild in the wilderness, low and degraded in personal and family habits, given to tribal feuds and sanguinary fights.

The missionary from New England came among them, and the native people in large numbers were converted. But the very first impulse of the missionary was to avail himself of the best resources and high capacities of his converts. And now, according to the reports furnished by the American Board for 1895, while there are but 32 foreign missionaries and teachers, male and female, no less than 408 teachers, pastors and helpers are engaged in spreading the gospel among these people.

The like practical wisdom is seen in the conduct of missions to Fijians. At an early day the native convert was made to assume the responsibility of a missionary and a teacher to his own people. Care was taken to lift these people out of a stipendiary relation to a foreign missionary society. Immediately on their conversion they were taught the privilege and the duty of service to Christ, the obligation to labor for the conversion of their kinsfolk.

And so it came to pass that native preachers, native teachers, are the main agency in the evangelization of those Islands. The foreign element is hardly known among them. Among the ministers only *one* is a foreigner. Six ordained ministers, aided by 310 local preachers, carry on God's work in the entire circuit of the Islands.

"Civilization, the Primal Need of the Race"

There is no need, I apprehend, that I should undertake to impress you with a sense either of the need or of the importance of our assemblage here to-day. The fact of your coming here is, of itself, the clearest evidence of your warm acquiescence in the summons to this meeting, and of your cordial interest in the objects which it purposes to consider.

Nothing has surprised and gratified me so much as the anxiousness of many minds for the movement which we are on the eve of beginning. In the letters which our Secretary, Mr. Cromwell, has received, and which will be read to us, we are struck by the fact that one cultured man here and another there, —several minds in different localities, —tell him that this is just the thing they have desired, and have been looking for.

I congratulate you, therefore, gentlemen, on the opportuneness of your assemblage here. I felicitate you on the superior and lofty aims which have drawn you together. And, in behalf of your compeers, resident here in the city of Washington, I welcome you to the city and to the important deliberations to which our organization invites you.

Just here, let me call your attention to the uniqueness and specialty of this conference. It is unlike any other which has ever taken place in the history of the Negro, on the American Continent. There have been, since the landing of the first black cargo of slaves at Jamestown, Va, in 1619, numerous conventions of men of our race. There have been Religious Assemblies, Political Conferences, suffrage meetings, educational conventions. But *our* meeting is for a purpose which, while inclusive, in some respects, of these various concerns, is for an object more distinct and positive than any of them.

From *American Negro Academy, Occasional Papers,* no. 3 (Washington, D.C.: The American Negro Academy, 1898), pp. 3–7.

What then, it may be asked, is the special undertaking we have before us, in this Academy? My answer is the civilization of the Negro race in the United States, by the scientific processes of literature, art, and philosophy, through the agency of the cultured men of this same Negro race. And here, let me say, that the special race problem of the Negro in the United States is his civilization.

I doubt if there is a man in this presence who has a higher conception of Negro capacity than your speaker; and this of itself, precludes the idea, on my part, of race disparagement. But, it seems manifest to me that, as a race in this land, we have no art; we have no science; we have no philosophy; we have no scholarship. Individuals we have in each of these lines; but mere individuality cannot be recognized as the aggregation of a family, a nation, or a race; or as the interpretation of any of them. And until we attain the role of civilization, we cannot stand up and hold our place in the world of culture and enlightenment. And the forfeiture of such a place means, despite, inferiority, repulsion, drudgery, poverty, and ultimate death! Now gentlemen, for the creation of a complete and rounded man, you need the impress and the moulding of the highest arts. But how much more so for the realizing of a true and lofty *race* of men. What is true of a man is deeply true of a people. The special need in such a case is the force and application of the highest arts; not mere mechanism; not mere machinery; not mere handicraft; not the mere grasp on material things; not mere temporal ambitions. These are but incidents; important indeed, but pertaining mainly to man's material needs, and to the feeding of the body. And the incidental in life is incapable of feeding the living soul. For "man cannot live by bread alone, but by every word that proceedeth out of the mouth of God." And civilization is the *secondary* word of God, given for the nourishment of humanity.

To make *men* you need civilization; and what I mean by civilization is the action of exalted forces, both of God and man. For manhood is the most majestic thing in God's creation; and hence the demand for the very highest art in the shaping and moulding of human souls.

What is the great difficulty with the black race, in this era, in this land? It is that both within their ranks, and external to themselves, by large schools of thought interested in them, material ideas in divers forms are made prominent, as the master-need of the race, and as the surest way to success. Men are constantly dogmatizing theories of sense and matter as the salvable hope of the race. Some of our leaders and teachers boldly declare, now, that *property* is the source of power; and then, that *money* is the thing which commands respect. At one time it is *official position* which is the masterful influence in the elevation of the race; at another, men are disposed to fall back upon *blood* and *lineage,* as the root (source) of power and progress.

Blind men! For they fail to see that neither property, nor money, nor station, nor office, nor lineage, are fixed factors, in so large a thing as the destiny of man; that they are not vitalizing qualities in the changeless hopes of humanity. The greatness of peoples springs from their ability to grasp the grand conceptions of being. It is the absorption of a people, of a nation, of a race, in large majestic and abiding things which lifts them up to the skies. These once apprehended, all the minor details of life follow in their proper places, and spread abroad in the details and the comfort of practicality. But until these gifts of a lofty civilization are secured, men are sure to remain low, debased and grovelling.

It was the apprehension of this great truth which led Melancthon, 400 years ago, to declare—"Unless we have the scientific mind we shall surely revert again to barbarism." He was a scholar and a classic, a theologian and a philosopher. With probably the exception of Erasmus, he was the most erudite man of his age. He was the greatest Grecian of his day. He was rich "with the spoils of time." And so running down the annals of the ages, he discovered the majestic fact, which Coleridge has put in two simple lines:—

"We may not hope from outward things to win
The passion and the life whose fountains are within;"

which Wordsworth, in grand style, has declared,

"By the soul only the nations shall be free."

But what is this other than the utterance of Melancthon, —"Without the scientific mind, barbarism." This is the teaching of history. For 2,000 years, Europe has been governed, in all its developments, by Socrates, and Aristotle, and Plato, and Euclid. These were the great idealists; and as such, they were the great progenitors of all modern civilization, the majestic agents of God for the civil upbuilding of men and nations. For civilization is, in its origins, ideal; and hence, in the loftiest men, it bursts forth, producing letters, literature, science, philosophy, poetry, sculpture, architecture, yea, all the arts; and brings them with all their gifts, and lays them in the lap of religion, as the essential condition of their vital permanance and their continuity.

But civilization never seeks permanent abidence upon the heights of Olympus. She is human, and seeks all human needs. And so she descends, re-creating new civilizations; uplifting the crudeness of laws, giving scientific precision to morals and religion, stimulating enterprise, extending commerce, creating manufactures, expanding mechanism and mechanical inventions; producing revolutions and reforms; humanizing labor; meeting the minutest human needs, even to the manufacturing needles for the industry of seamstresses and for the commonest uses of human fingers. All these are the fruits of civilization.

Who are to be the agents to lift up this people of ours to the grand plane of civilization? Who are to bring them up to the height of noble thought, grand civility, a chaste and elevating culture, refinement, and the impulses of irrepressible progress? It is to be done by the scholars and thinkers, who have secured the vision which penetrates the center of nature, and sweeps the circles of historic enlightenment; and who have got insight into the life of things, and learned the art by which men touch the springs of action.

For to transform and stimulate the souls of a race or a people is a work of intelligence. It is a work which demands the clear induction of world-wide facts, and the perception of their application to new circumstances. It is a work which will require the most skillful resources, and the use of the scientific spirit.

But every man in a race cannot be a philosopher: nay, but few men in any land, in any age, can grasp ideal truth. Scientific ideas however must be apprehended, else there can be no progress, no elevation.

Just here arises the need of the trained and scholarly men of a race to employ their knowledge and culture and teaching and to guide both the opinions and habits of the crude masses. The masses, nowhere are, or can be, learned or scientific. The scholar is exceptional, just the same as a great admiral like Nelson is, or a grand soldier like Caesar or Napoleon. But the leader, the creative and organizing mind, is the master-need in all the societies of man. But, if they are not inspired with the notion of leadership and duty, then with all their Latin and Greek and science they are but pedants, trimmers, opportunists. For all true and lofty scholarship is weighty with the burdens and responsibilities of life and humanity.

But these reformers must not be mere scholars. They must needs be both scholars and philanthropists. For this, indeed, has it been in all the history of men. In all the great revolutions, and in all great reforms which have transpired, scholars have been conspicuous; in the re-construction of society, in formulating laws, in producing great emancipations, in the revival of letters, in the advancement of science, in the renaissance of art, in the destruction of gross superstitions and in the restoration of true and enlightened religion.

And what is the spirit with which they are to come to this work? My answer is, that *disinterestedness* must animate their motives and their acts. Whatever rivalries and dissensions may divide man in the social or political world, let generosity govern *us*. Let us emulate one another in the prompt recognition of rare genius, or uncommon talent. Let there be no tardy acknowledgment of worth in *our* world of intellect. If we are fortunate enough, to see, of a sudden, a clever mathematician of our class, a brilliant poet, a youthful, but promising scientist or philosopher, let us rush forward, and hail his coming with no hesitant admiration, with no reluctant praise.

It is only thus, gentlemen, that we can bring forth, stimulate, and uplift all the latent genius, garnered up, in the by-places and sequestered corners of this neglected Race.

It is only thus we can nullify and break down the conspiracy which would fain limit and narrow the range of Negro talent in this caste-tainted country. It is only thus, we can secure that recognition of genius and scholarship in the republic of letters, which is the rightful prerogative of every race of men. It is only thus we can spread abroad and widely disseminate that culture and enlightment which shall permeate and leaven the entire social and domestic life of our people and so give that civilization which is the nearest ally of religion.

"The Attitude of the American Mind toward the Negro Intellect"

For the first time in the history of this nation the colored people of America have undertaken the difficult task, of stimulating and fostering the genius of their race as a distinct and definite purpose. Other and many gatherings have been made, during our own two and a half centuries' residence on this continent, for educational purposes; but ours is the first which endeavors to rise up to the plane of culture.

For my own part I have no misgivings either with respect to the legitimacy, the timeliness, or the prospective success of our venture. The race in the brief period of a generation, has been so fruitful in intellectual product, that the time has come for a coalescence of powers, and for reciprocity alike in effort and appreciation. I congratulate you, therefore, on this your first anniversary. To me it is, I confess, a matter of rejoicing that we have, as a people, reached a point where we have a class of men who will come together for purposes, so pure, so elevating, so beneficent, as the cultivation of mind, with the view of meeting the uses and the needs of our benighted people.

I feel that if this meeting were the end of this Academy; if I could see that it would die this very day, I would nevertheless, cry out—"All hail!" even if I had to join in with the salutation—"farewell forever!" For, first of all, you have done, during the year, that which was never done so completely before, —a work which has already told upon the American mind; and next you have awakened in the Race an ambition which, in some

From *American Negro Academy, Occasional Papers,* no. 3 (Washington, D.C.: The American Negro Academy, 1898), pp. 8–19.

form, is sure to reproduce both mental and artistic organization in the future.

The cultured classes of our country have never interested themselves to stimulate the desires or aspirations of the mind of our race. They have left us terribly alone. Such stimulation, must, therefore, in the very nature of things, come from ourselves.

Let us state here a simple, personal incident, which will well serve to illustrate a history.

I entered, sometime ago, the parlor of a distinguished southern clergyman. A kinsman was standing at his mantel, writing. The clergyman spoke to his relative—"Cousin, let me introduce to you the Rev. C., a clergyman of our Church." His cousin turned and looked down at me; but as soon as he saw my black face, he turned away with disgust, and paid no more attention to me than if I were a dog.

Now, this porcine gentleman, would have been perfectly courteous, if I had gone into his parlor as a cook, or a waiter, or a boot-black. But my profession, as a clergyman, suggested the idea of letters and cultivation; and the contemptible snob at once forgot his manners, and put aside the common decency of his class.

Now, in this, you can see the attitude of the American mind toward the Negro intellect. A reference to this attitude seems necessary, if we would take in, properly, the present condition of Negro culture.

It presents a most singular phenomenon. Here was a people laden with the spoils of the centuries, bringing with them into this new land the culture of great empires; and, withal, claiming the exalted name and grand heritage of Christians. By their own voluntary act they placed right beside them a large population of another race of people, seized as captives, and brought to their plantations from a distant continent. This other race was an unlettered, unenlightened, and a pagan people.

What was the attitude taken by this master race toward their benighted bondsmen? It was not simply that of indifference or neglect. There was nothing negative about it.

They began, at the first, a systematic ignoring of the fact of intellect in this abased people. They undertook the process of darkening their minds.

"Put out the light, and then, put out the light!" was their cry for centuries. Paganizing themselves, they sought a deeper paganizing of their serfs than the original paganism that these had brought from Africa. There was no legal artifice conceivable which was not resorted to, to blindfold their souls from the light of letters; and the church, in not a few cases, was the prime offender.*

Then the legislatures of the several states enacted laws and Statutes, closing the pages of every book printed to the eyes of Negroes; barring the doors of every school-room against them! And this was the systematized method of the intellect of the South, to stamp out the brains of the Negro!

It was done, too, with the knowledge that the Negro had brain power. There was *then,* no denial that the Negro had intellect. That denial was an after thought. Besides, legislatures never pass laws forbidding the education of pigs, dogs, and horses. They pass such laws against the intellect of *men.*

However, there was then, at the very beginning of the slave trade, everywhere, in Europe, the glintings forth of talent in great Negro geniuses, —in Spain, and Portugal, in France and Holland and England;† and Phillis Wheatley and Banneker and Chavis and Peters, were in evidence on American soil.

It is manifest, therefore, that the objective point in all this legislation was INTELLECT, —the intellect of the Negro! It was an effort to becloud and stamp out the intellect of the Negro!

The *first* phase of this attitude reached over from about 1700 to 1820:—

Baptism, for well nigh a century, was denied Negro slaves in the colonies, for fear it carried emancipation with it. Legislation on Education began at a subsequent date. In 1740 it was enacted in SOUTH CAROLINA: "Whereas, the having slaves taught to write or suffering them to be employed in writing, may be attended with great inconvenience. Be it enacted, That all and every person or persons whatsoever who shall hereafter teach or cause any slave or slaves to be taught to write, or shall use or employ any slave as a Scribe in any manner of writing, hereafter taught to write; every such person or persons shall forever, for every such offense, forfeit the sum of £100 current money."

The next step, in South Carolina, was aimed against mental instruction of *every kind,* in reading and writing.

A similar law was passed in Savannah, Georgia. In 1711, in the Colony of Maryland, a *special enactment* was passed to bar freedom by baptism and in 1715, in South Carolina! See "*Stroud's Slave Laws.*"

†At the time when France was on the eve of plunging deeply into the slave trade and of ruining her colonies by the curse of Slavery, the ABBE GREGOIRE stept forth in vindication of the Negro, and published his celebrated work—"The Literature of Negroes." In this work he gives the names and narrates the achievements of the distinguished Negroes, writers, scholars, painters, philosophers, priests and Roman prelates, in Spain, Portugal, France, England, Holland, Italy and Turkey who had risen to eminence in the 15th century.

Not long after BLUMENBACH declared that "entire and large provinces of Europe might be named, in which it would be difficult to meet with such good writers, poets, philosophers, and correspondents of the French Academy; and that moreover there is no savage people, who have distinguished themselves by such examples of perfectibility and capacity for scientific cultivation; and consequently that none can approach more nearly to the polished nations of the globe than the Negro."

and as the result, almost Egyptian darkness fell upon the mind of the race, throughout the whole land.

Following came a more infamous policy. It was the denial of intellectuality in the Negro; the assertion that he was not a human being, that he did not belong to the human race. This covered the period from 1820 to 1835, when Gliddon and Nott and others, published their so-called physiological work, to prove that the Negro was of a different species from the white man.

A distinguished illustration of this ignoble sentiment can be given. In the year 1833 or 4 the speaker was an errand boy in the Anti-slavery office in New York City.

On a certain occasion he heard a conversation between the Secretary and two eminent lawyers from Boston, —Samuel E. Sewell and David Lee Child. They had been to Washington on some legal business. While at the Capitol they happened to dine in the company of the great John C. Calhoun, then senator from South Carolina. It was a period of great ferment upon the question of Slavery, States' Rights, and Nullification; and consequently the Negro was the topic of conversation at the table. One of the utterances of Mr. Calhoun was to this effect—"That if he could find a Negro who knew the Greek syntax, he would then believe that the Negro was a human being and should be treated as a man."

Just think of the crude asininity of even a great man! Mr. Calhoun went to "Yale" to study the Greek Syntax, and graduated there. His son went to Yale to study the Greek Syntax, and graduated there. His grandson, in recent years, went to Yale, to learn the Greek Syntax, and graduated there. Schools and Colleges were necessary for the Calhouns, and all other white men to learn the Greek syntax.

And yet this great man knew that there was not a school, nor a college in which a black boy could learn his A.B.C's. He knew that the law in all the Southern States forbade Negro instruction under the severest penalties. How then was the Negro to learn the Greek syntax? How then was he to evidence to Mr. Calhoun his human nature? Why, it is manifest that Mr. Calhoun expected the Greek syntax to grow in *Negro brains,* by spontaneous generation!

Mr. Calhoun was then, as much as any other American, an exponent of the nation's mind upon this point. Antagonistic as they were upon *other* subjects, upon the rejection of the Negro intellect they were a unit. And this, measurably, is the attitude of the American mind today: —measurably, I say, for thanks to the Almighty, it is not universally so.

There has always been a school of philanthropists in this land who have always recognized mind in the Negro; and while recognizing the limitations which *individual* capacity demanded, claimed that for the RACE, there was no such thing possible for its elevation save the widest, largest, highest, improvement. Such were our friends and patrons in New England, in New York, Pennsylvania, a few among the Scotch Presbyterians and the "Friends" in grand old North Carolina; a great company among the Congregationalists of the East, nobly represented down to the present, by the "American Missionary Society," which tolerates no stint for the Negro intellect in its grand solicitudes. But these were exceptional.

Down to the year 1825, I know of no Academy or College which would open its doors to a Negro.* In the South it was a matter of absolute legal disability. In the North, it was the ostracism of universal caste-sentiment. The theological schools of the land, and of all names, shut their doors against the black man. An eminent friend of mine, the noble, fervent, gentlemanly Rev. Theodore S. Wright, then a Presbyterian licentiate, was taking private lessons in theology, at Princeton; and for this offense was kicked out of one of its halls.

In the year 1832 Miss Prudence Crandall opened a private school for the education of colored girls; and it set the whole State of Connecticut in a flame. Miss Crandall was mobbed, and the school was broken up.

The year following, the trustees of Canaan Academy in New Hampshire opened its doors to Negro youths; and this act set the people of that state on fire. The farmers of the region assembled with 90 yoke of oxen, dragged the Academy into a swamp, and a few weeks afterward drove the black youths from the town.

These instances will suffice. They evidence the general statement, i.e., that the American mind has refused to foster and to cultivate the Negro intellect. Join to this a kindred fact, of which there is the fullest evidence. Impelled, at times, by pity, a modicum of schooling and training has been given the Negro; but even this, almost universally, with reluctance, with cold criticism, with microscopic scrutiny, with icy reservation, and at times, with ludicrous limitations.

Cheapness characterizes almost all the donations of the American people to the Negro: —Cheapness, in all the past, has been the regimen provided for the Negro in every line of his intellectual, as well as his lower life. And so, cheapness is to be the rule in the future, as well for his higher,

*"Oberlin College" in Ohio was the first, opening its doors to the Negro in 1836.

as for his lower life: —cheap wages and cheap food, cheap and rotten huts; cheap and dilapidated schools; cheap and stinted weeks of schooling; cheap meeting houses for worship; cheap and ignorant ministers; cheap theological training; and now, cheap learning, culture and civilization!

Noble exceptions are found in the grand literary circles in which Mr. Howells moves—manifest in his generous editing of our own Paul Dunbar's poems. But this generosity is not general, even in the world of American letters.

You can easily see this in the attempt, now-a-days, to side-track the Negro intellect, and to place it under limitations never laid upon any other class.

The elevation of the Negro has been a moot question for a generation past. But even to-day what do we find the general reliance of the American mind in determinating this question? Almost universally the resort is to material agencies! The ordinary, and sometimes the *extraordinary* American is unable to see that the struggle of a degraded people for elevation is, in its very nature, a warfare, and that its main weapon is the cultivated and scientific mind.

Ask the great men of the land how this Negro problem is to be solved, and then listen to the answers that come from divers classes of our white fellow-citizens. The merchants and traders of our great cities tell us— "The Negro must be taught to work;" and they will pour out their moneys by thousands to train him to toil. The clergy in large numbers, cry out—"Industrialism is the only hope of the Negro;" for this is the bed-rock, in their opinion, of Negro evangelization! "Send him to Manual Labor Schools," cries out another set of philanthropists. " 'Hic, haec, hoc,' is going to prove the ruin of the Negro" says the Rev. Steele, an erudite Southern Savan. "You must begin at the bottom with the Negro," says another eminent authority—as though the Negro had been living in the clouds, and had never reached the bottom. Says the Honorable George T. Barnes, of Georgia—"The kind of education the Negro should receive should not be very refined nor classical, but adapted to his present condition:" as though there is to be no future for the Negro.

And so you see that even now, late in the 19th century, in this land of learning and science, the creed is—"Thus far and no farther", i.e., for the American black man.

One would suppose from the universal demand for the mere industrialism for this race of ours, that the Negro had been going daily to dinner parties, eating terrapin and indulging in champagne; and returning home at night, sleeping on beds of eiderdown; breakfasting in the morning in his bed, and then having his valet to clothe him daily in purple and fine linen—all these 250 years of his sojourn in this land. And then, just now, the American people, tired of all this Negro luxury, was calling him, for the first time, to blister his hands with the hoe, and to learn to supply his needs by sweatful toil in the cotton fields.

Listen a moment, to the wisdom of a great theologian, and withal as great philanthropist, the Rev. Dr. Wayland, of Philadelphia. Speaking, not long since, of the "Higher Education" of the colored people of the South, he said "that this subject concerned about 8,000,000 of our fellow-citizens, among whom are probably 1,500,000 voters. The education suited to these people is that which should be suited to white people under the same circumstances. These people are bearing the impress which was left on them by two centuries of slavery and several centuries of barbarism. This education must begin at the bottom. It must first of all produce the power of self-support to assist them to better their condition. It should teach them good citizenship and should build them up morally. It should be, first, a good English education. They should be imbued with the knowledge of the Bible. They should have an industrial education. An industrial education leads to self-support and to the elevation of their condition. Industry is itself largely an education, intellectually and morally, and, above all, an education of character. Thus we should make these people self-dependent. This education will do away with pupils being taught Latin and Greek, while they do not know the rudiments of English."

Just notice the cautious, restrictive, limiting nature of this advice! Observe the lack of largeness, freedom and generosity in it. Dr. Wayland, I am sure, has never specialized just such a regimen for the poor Italians, Hungarians or Irish, who swarm, in lowly degradation, in immigrant ships to our shores. No! for them he wants, all Americans want, the widest, largest culture of the land; the instant opening, not simply of the common schools; and then an easy passage to the bar, the legislature, and even the judgeships of the nation. And they oft times get there.

But how different the policy with the Negro. *He* must have "an education which begins at the bottom." "He should have an industrial education," &c. His education must, first of all, produce the power of self-support, &c.

Now, all this thought of Dr. Wayland is all true. But, my friends, it is all false, too; and for the simple reason that it is only half truth. Dr. Wayland seems unable to rise above the plane of burden-bearing for the Negro. He seems unable to gauge the idea of the Negro becoming a thinker. He seems to forget that a race of thoughtless toilers are destined to be forever a race of senseless *boys;* for only beings who think are men.

How pitiable it is to see a great good man be-fuddled by a half truth. For to allege "Industrialism" to be the grand agency in the elevation of a race of already degraded labourers, is as much a mere platitude as to say, "they must eat and drink and sleep;" for man cannot live without these habits. But they never civilize man; and *civilization* is the objective point in the movement for Negro elevation. Labor, just like eating and drinking, is one of the inevitabilities of life; one of its positive necessities. And the Negro has had it for centuries; but it has never given him manhood. It does not *now,* in wide areas of population, lift him up to moral and social elevation. Hence the need of a new factor in his life. The Negro needs light: light thrown in upon all the circumstances of his life. The light of civilization.

Dr. Wayland fails to see two or three important things in this Negro problem:—

(a) That the Negro has no need to go to a manual labor school.* He has been for two hundred years and more, the greatest laborer in the land. He is a laborer *now;* and he must always be a laborer, or he must die. But:

(b) Unfortunately for the Negro, he has been so wretchedly ignorant that he has never known the value of his sweat and toil. He has been forced into being an unthinking labor-machine. And this he is, to a large degree, to-day under freedom.

(c) Now the great need of the Negro, in our day and time, is intelligent impatience at the exploitation of his labor, on the one hand; on the other hand courage to demand a larger share of the wealth which his toil creates for others.

---

*"I am not so old as some of my young friends may suspect, but I am too old to go into the business of 'carrying coals to Newcastle.' * * * * The colored citizen of the U.S. has already graduated with respectable standing from a course of 250 years in the University of the old-time type of Manual labor. The South of to-day is what we see it largely because the colored men and women at least during the past 250 years, have not been lazy 'cumberers of the ground,' but the grand army of laborers that has wrestled with nature and led these 16 States out of the woods thus far on the high road to material prosperity. It is not especially necessary that the 2,000,000 of our colored children and youth in the southern common schools should be warned against laziness, and what has always and everywhere come of that since the foundation of the world."

The Rev. A. D. Mayo, M.A., LL.D.
Address before State Teachers' Association (Colored)
Birmingham, Ala.

It is not a mere negative proposition that settles this question. It is not that the Negro does not need the hoe, the plane, the plough, and the anvil. It is the positive affirmation that the Negro needs the light of cultivation; needs it to be thrown in upon all his toil, upon his whole life and its environments.

What he needs is CIVILIZATION. He needs the increase of his higher wants, of his mental and spiritual needs. *This,* mere animal labor has never given him, and never can give him. But it will come to him, as an individual, and as a class, just in proportion as the higher culture comes to his leaders and teachers, and so gets into his schools, academies and colleges; and then enters his pulpits; and so filters down into his families and his homes; and the Negro learns that he is no longer to be a serf, but that he is to bare his strong brawny arm as a laborer; *not* to make the white man a Croesus, but to make himself a man. He is always to be a laborer; but now, in these days of freedom and the schools, he is to be a laborer with intelligence, enlightenment and manly ambitions.

But, when his culture fits him for something more than a field hand or a mechanic, he is to have an open door set wide before him! And that culture, according to his capacity, he must claim as his rightful heritage, as a man: —not stinted training, not a caste education, not a Negro curriculum.

The Negro Race in this land must repudiate this absurd notion which is stealing on the American mind. The Race must declare that it is not to be put into a single groove; and for the simple reason (1) that *man* was made by his Maker to traverse the whole circle of existence, above as well as below; and that universality is the kernel of all true civilization, of all race elevation. And (2) that the Negro mind, imprisoned for nigh three hundred years, needs breadth and freedom, largeness, altitude, and elasticity; not stint nor rigidity, nor contractedness.

But the "Gradgrinds" are in evidence on all sides, telling us that the colleges and scholarships given us since emancipation, are all a mistake; and that the whole system must be reversed. The conviction is widespread that the Negro has no business in the higher walks of scholarship; that, for instance, Prof. Scarborough has no right to labor in philology; Professor Kelly Miller in mathematics; Professor DuBois, in history; Dr. Bowen, in theology; Professor Turner, in science; nor Mr. Tanner in art. There is no repugnance to the Negro buffoon, and the Negro scullion; but so soon as the Negro stands forth as an intellectual being, this toad of American prejudice, as at the touch of Ithuriel's spear, starts up a devil!

It is this attitude, this repellant, this forbidding attitude of the American mind, which forces the Negro in this land, to both recognize and to foster the talent and capacity of his own race, and to strive to put that capacity and talent to use for the race. I have detailed the dark and dreadful attempt to stamp that intellect out of existence. It is not only a past, it is also, modified indeed, a present fact; and out of it springs the need of just such an organization as the Negro Academy.

Now, gentlemen and friends, seeing that the American mind in the general, revolts from Negro genius, the Negro himself is duty bound to see to the cultivation and the fostering of his own race-capacity. This is the chief purpose of this Academy. *Our* special mission is the encouragement of the genius and talent in our own race. Wherever we see great Negro ability it is our office to light upon it not tardily, not hesitatingly; but warmly, ungrudgingly, enthusiastically, for the honor of our race, and for the stimulating self-sacrifice in upbuilding the race. Fortunately for us, as a people, this year has given us more than ordinary opportunity for such recognition. Never before, in American history, has there been such a large discovery of talent and genius among us.

Early in the year there was published by one of our members, a volume of papers and addresses, of more than usual excellence. You know gentlemen, that, not seldom, we have books and pamphlets from the press which, like most of our newspapers, are beneath the dignity of criticism. In language, in style, in grammar and in thought they are often crude and ignorant and vulgar. Not so with "*Talks for the Times*" by Prof. Crogman, of Clark University. It is a book with largess of high and noble common sense; pure and classical in style; with a large fund of devoted racialism; and replete everywhere with elevated thoughts. Almost simultaneously with the publication of Professor Crogman's book, came the thoughtful and spicy narrative of Rev. Matthew Anderson of Philadelphia. The title of this volume is "*Presbyterianism; its relation to the Negro;*" but the title cannot serve as a revelation of the racy and spirited story of events in the career of its author. The book abounds with stirring incidents, strong remonstrance, clear and lucid argument, powerful reasonings, the keenest satire; while, withal, it sets forth the wide needs of the Race, and gives one of the strongest vindications of its character and its capacity.*

Soon after this came the first publication of our Academy. And you all

*I owe Mr. Anderson an apology for omitting this reference to his book on the delivery of this address. It was prepared while its author was in a foreign land; but had passed entirely from his memory in the preparation of this address.

know the deep interest excited by the two papers, the first issue of this Society. They have attracted interest and inquiry where the mere declamatory effusions, or, the so-called eloquent harangues of aimless talkers and political wire-pullers would fall like snowflakes upon the waters. The papers of Prof. Kelly Miller and Prof. Du Bois have reached the circles of scholars and thinkers in this country. So consummate was the handling of Hoffman's "Race Traits and Tendencies" by Prof. Miller, that we may say that it was the most scientific defense of the Negro ever made in this country by a man of our own blood: accurate, pointed, painstaking, and I claim conclusive.

The treatise of Prof. Du Bois upon the "Conservation of Race," separated itself, in tone and coloring, from the ordinary effusions of literary work in this land. It rose to the dignity of philosophical insight and deep historical inference. He gave us, in a most lucid and original method, and in a condensed form, the long settled conclusions of Ethnologists and Anthropologists upon the question of Race.

This treatise moreover, furnished but a limited measure of our indebtedness to his pen and brain. Only a brief time before our assembly last year, Prof. Du Bois had given a large contribution to the literature of the nation as well as to the genius of the race. At that time he had published a work which will, without doubt, stand permanently, as authority upon its special theme. *"The Suppression of the Slave Trade"* is, without doubt, the one unique and special authority upon that subject, in print. It is difficult to conceive the possible creation of a similar work, so accurate and painstaking, so full of research, so orderly in historical statement, so rational in its conclusions. It is the simple truth, and at the same time the highest praise, the statement of one Review, that "Prof. Du Bois has exhausted his subject." This work is a step forward in the literature of the Race, and a stimulant to studious and aspiring minds among us.

One further reference, that is, to the realm of Art.

The year '97 will henceforth be worthy of note in our history. As a race, we have, this year, reached a high point in intellectual growth and expression.

In poetry and painting, as well as in letters and thought, the Negro has made, this year, a character.

On my return home in October, I met an eminent scientific gentleman; and one of the first remarks he made to me was—"Well, Dr. Crummell, we Americans have been well taken down in Paris, this year. Why," he said, "the prize in painting was taken by a colored young man, a Mr.

Tanner from America. Do you know him?" The reference was to Mr. Tanner's "Raising of Lazarus," a painting purchased by the French Government, for the famous Luxembourg Gallery. This is an exceptional honor, rarely bestowed upon any American Artist. Well may we all be proud of this, and with this we may join the idea that Tanner, instead of having a hoe in his hand, or digging in a trench, as the faddists on industrialism would fain persuade us, has found his right place at the easel with artists.

Not less distinguished in the world of letters is the brilliant career of our poet-friend and co-laborer, Mr. Paul Dunbar. It was my great privilege last summer to witness his triumph, on more than one occasion, in that grand metropolis of Letters and Literature, the city of London; as well as to hear of the high value set upon his work, by some of the first scholars and literati of England. Mr. Dunbar has had his poems republished in London by Chapman & Co.; and now has as high a reputation abroad as he has here in America, where his luminous genius has broken down the bars, and with himself, raised the intellectual character of his race in the world's consideration.

These cheering occurrences, these demonstrations of capacity, give us the greatest encouragement in the large work which is before this Academy. Let us enter upon that work, this year, with high hopes, with large purposes, and with calm and earnest persistence. I trust that we shall bear in remembrance that the work we have undertaken is our special function; that it is a work which calls for cool thought, for laborious and tireless painstaking, and for clear discrimination; that it promises nowhere wide popularity, or, exuberant eclat; that very much of its ardent work is to be carried on in the shade; that none of its desired results will spring from spontaneity; that its most prominent features are the demands of duty to a needy people; and that its noblest rewards will be the satisfaction which will spring from having answered a great responsibility, and having met the higher needs of a benighted and struggling Race.

Index